THE UNCHANGING
AMERICAN VOTER

THE UNCHANGING AMERICAN VOTER

Eric R. A. N. Smith

University of California Press
Berkeley   Los Angeles   London

University of California Press
Berkeley and Los Angeles, California

University of California Press, Ltd.
London, England

© 1989 by
The Regents of the University of California

Library of Congress Cataloging-in-Publication Data
Smith, Eric R. A. N.
    The unchanging American voter / Eric R. A. N. Smith.
      p. cm.
    Bibliography: p.
    Includes index.
    ISBN 0-520-06526-3 (alk. paper)
      1. Voting—United States.   2. Public opinion—United
States.   3. Political participation—United States.   4. United
States—Politics and government—1945-   I. Title.
JK1967.S65   1989
324.973—dc19   88-30639
                                                      CIP

Printed in the United States of America
1   2   3   4   5   6   7   8   9

For Elizabeth

Contents

List of Tables

List of Figures

Acknowledgments

This book grew out of a seminar paper that I wrote when I was a student in one of Raymond E. Wolfinger's classes at the University of California, Berkeley. Under his guidance, I revised and eventually published this paper. I then put these ideas aside until I had finished my dissertation. I picked them up again when I was teaching at Columbia University. Again, Ray Wolfinger helped me with many patient suggestions and criticisms. For his help with this book, and for many other reasons, I am very grateful.

Other friends read portions of the manuscript or discussed the ideas with me. They gave me many useful suggestions and helped make this a much better book than it would have been without their assistance. Therefore, for their help and encouragement, I would like to thank Christopher Achen, Larry Bartels, Henry Brady, Dennis Chong, Jack Citrin, David Glass, Gary Jacobson, Kent Jennings, Ethel Klein, Richard McIntosh, Nelson Polsby, Dennis Quinn, Merrill Shanks, Peverill Squire, Robert Shapiro, Stephen Weatherford, John Woolley, John Zaller, and one anonymous reviewer for the University of California Press.

The Inter-University Consortium for Political and Social Research provided the data. While I was at Columbia University, Peter Kinberg and James McKnight assisted me with some of the data analysis. At Santa Barbara, Rick Herrera, Bill Hyder and Joan Murdoch helped me enormously with the computer work.

Columbia University's Council for Research and Faculty Development in the Humanities and Social Sciences and the Academic Senate of the University of California, Santa Barbara, provided me with funds for the research.

Finally, I want to thank Elizabeth for her love, support, and patience, Katie, who helped me type, and Stephanie, for inspiration.

Introduction

How much the American people know about politics has been a topic of a good deal of investigation and concern by political scientists over the years. Before the behavioral revolution in the 1940s, scholars and social commentators used to assume, without much evidence, that people know a great deal about politics. The image of rustic farmers sitting around the cracker barrel in the country store discussing politics is well fixed in American political mythology. The behavioral revolution rudely challenged that myth. In a series of studies of voting, behavioralists developed evidence showing that most voters do not know very much about politics (Berelson et al. 1954; Campbell and Kahn 1952; Campbell et al. 1954; Lazarsfeld et al. 1944). By the end of the 1950s, the situation had progressed to the point at which V. O. Key found it necessary to write a book defending the proposition that "voters are not fools" (Key with Cummings 1966, p. 7).

In recent American electoral behavior, how much voters know about politics and whether they should be considered "sophisticated" has continued to be the subject of debate.[1] That debate centers around the description of the American voter put forth by Angus Campbell, Philip Converse, Warren Miller, and Donald Stokes in their classic study, *The American Voter* (1960), and later fleshed out by Converse in "The Nature of Belief Systems in Mass Publics" (1964). The description they gave was not a particularly glowing one. The typical American voter, according to these investigators, knows little about politics, is not interested in

1. Kinder (1983) declared the matter settled, but as Luskin (1987) notes, debate and disagreement continue (Inglehart 1985; Jackson 1983; Peffley and Hurwitz 1985).

politics, does not participate in politics, does not organize his or her political attitudes in a coherent manner, and does not think in structured, ideological terms.

The latter two aspects of that description have come to be thought of as political sophistication. To be sophisticated, according to this view, people must have some sort of abstract principles with which they organize their beliefs and attitudes on the issues. For instance, one might believe in the principles of liberalism and hold a corresponding set of liberal opinions on the issues.

The findings of Philip Converse and *The American Voter* on this score were that remarkably few people were sophisticated. Only about half the people even recognized the terms "liberal" and "conservative," and only a few percent actually thought about politics in those terms. People's attitudes were also fairly mixed up—with most voters holding a seemingly incoherent mixture of liberal, moderate, and conservative positions. In short, few people seemed to have the sophistication necessary to follow politics at the level on which the nation's political leaders discussed it.

That description of the American public was, as it was later characterized, static. The voter Campbell and his colleagues described was not the voter of the late 1950s (the time at which they collected the data), but the unchanging American voter of all time. Although Campbell et al. thought that some changes were likely to occur—rising education would yield more informed and active voters, voting law changes would bring more people to the polls, and so forth—they thought they had identified the basic character of American voters and the factors that influenced them.

This picture of the unchanging American voter was challenged in a series of articles by political scientists who studied changes in the American electorate in the 1960s. The articles by Bennett (1973), Field and Anderson (1969), Nie and Andersen (1974), Pierce (1970, 1975), and Pomper (1972), as well as Nie, Verba, and Petrocik's *The Changing American Voter* (1976), argued that the electorate had made a great leap forward in political sophistication and ideological thinking between the 1960 and 1964 presidential elections. Their argument was that people change in response to the changing environment and that, in particular, the surge of protest and ideological rhetoric between 1960 and 1964 had resulted in a surge of sophistication. People learned to understand politics better, to relate the issues to the candidates more accurately, and to cast more intelligent, informed votes.

This sequence of events is the topic of this book. What happened in the

1960s? Did the "great leap forward" really happen? From a broader perspective, how much do people change in response to changes in their political environments? This is not merely a question of the political history
of the 1960s. This is a question about the political nature of the citizenry.
Can American society change so that people will learn more about politics, become more discerning in their selections of candidates, and grow
more sophisticated in the ways they think about politics?

My thesis is that the answer is largely no. To be sure, many changes
have occurred and will continue to occur. A complete review of the literature describing how the electorate has changed would fill many volumes.[2]
Yet for society as a whole, there is little to suggest that voters either did or
will become more or less sophisticated as time goes by.

Before the articles alleging that sophistication had grown in the 1960s,
The American Voter's static picture of people was generally accepted.
Those who argued that voters became more sophisticated between 1960
and 1964 relied on two sets of evidence—changes in the level of conceptualization index and changes in various indexes of attitude consistency.
Those indexes are methodologically flawed. The problem is that the indexes are time-bound. As I shall explain, the level of conceptualization
index simply cannot be compared across time under any circumstances.
Indexes of attitude consistency have problems when being compared
across time in general and, because of changes in question wording between 1960 and 1964, cannot be used at all to measure changes over
those specific years. The result is that the evidence upon which the great
leap forward argument hangs cannot be accepted. Without any evidence
in favor of the hypothesis that there was a surge in sophisticated thinking
in the 1960s, one must reject it and accept the null hypothesis—namely,
that Campbell, Converse, Miller, and Stokes were right.

To further the case against the surging sophistication hypothesis, we
will look at the other available measures of sophistication. Aside from
levels of conceptualization and attitude consistency, there are only a few
ways to measure sophistication over time. Although each measure has its
own problems, the problems are not as serious as those facing the levels
of conceptualization and attitude consistency indexes. The result of my
look at other measures supports *The American Voter*'s thesis. The other
measures show no change.

2. See, for instance, Abramson (1983), Burnham (1970), Crotty and Jacobson (1980), Hill and Luttbeg (1983), Ladd and Hadley (1978), Lipset and
Schneider (1983), Petrocik (1981), Sundquist (1983), Wattenberg (1984).

Finally, we will develop and test a model to explain political sophistication. Having built the model, I will use it to find out what changes in the independent variables might cause a significant growth in sophistication, that is, to see if I can predict any increases in sophistication on the basis of knowledge of its causes. For instance, I explore whether the trend of growing education might cause the public to develop a fuller understanding of politics. Once again, the results are not encouraging. The fact that none of the causes of sophistication identified in this study is likely to change enough to cause more than a trivial increase in political knowledge and understanding is further evidence that the American voter is, at least in this respect, unchanging.

On the Meaning of Political Sophistication

The term "political sophistication" is used in many ways. Often the precise meaning is not spelled out. The best starting point is Converse's (1964) description of belief systems. Converse proposed describing belief systems in terms of three characteristics: (1) range of opinions—the number of political issues upon which one holds opinions; (2) attitude consistency—the extent to which one has "consistent" attitudes, that is, attitudes in agreement with some generally accepted pattern such as all liberal or all conservative; and (3) level of conceptualization—the extent to which one uses abstractions such as "liberalism" and "conservatism" to organize one's beliefs and attitudes.[3] On the basis of Converse's set of characteristics, we can say that to be sophisticated, one must have a wide range of opinions and highly consistent attitudes that one must organize with broad capping abstractions. Although some people disagree with this description, it is fairly widely accepted (Luskin 1987).

Before accepting Converse's list of characteristics as the definition of sophistication, one should consider its source. Converse was describing characteristics of political belief systems, not of political sophistication. Although one may tend to treat the two as interchangeable (being highly sophisticated is the same as being an ideologue), it may not be such a good idea. To many scholars, the term "sophistication" implies something slightly different from ideological thinking.

The principal characteristic missing from this list is amount of factual

3. Converse (1964, p. 208) also discusses attitude centrality as an important characteristic of "idea-elements." Attitude centrality is certainly important, but it is not related to sophistication as the term is normally used.

information (Neuman 1986). Can one be sophisticated and yet still not know much about politics? Of course not. One may implicitly assume that those who are ideologues also have a great deal of information, but one should not make such casual assumptions in a definition. To accept the idea that "sophistication is a matter of how much and how a person thinks about politics, not what" (Luskin 1987, p. 881), one must be prepared to conclude that a person can be highly sophisticated yet ignorant of everyday politics. To take an extreme example, the inmates of mental institutions who think that they are Napoleon, Disraeli, and President Roosevelt and who spend great amounts of time thinking about the politics of "their" times would all have to be classified as highly sophisticated—despite the fact that they are out of touch with reality. The idea just does not work. Amount of factual information is an important aspect of what one thinks of as sophistication.

In sum, my initial working definition of sophistication is that it has four characteristics—range of opinions, attitude consistency, level of conceptualization, and amount of factual information. I say "initial" because I will have to modify this definition by the end of this study.

On Sophistication and Rationality

In the early voting behavior literature, sophistication and rationality were viewed as being closely related, if not identical. In particular, information was thought to be a "prerequisite of rationality" (Fiorina 1986, p. 6). To act rationally, one had to know a good deal about politics.

In the public choice literature, rationality means something quite different. It refers to the procedures people use to make decisions and seek goals (Ordeshook 1986). In many cases, if not most, it is rational not to seek information (Downs 1957; Enelow and Hinich 1984; Fiorina 1986).[4] That is, the costs of acquiring information usually exceed the benefits derived from having the information. Therefore it is rational to remain ignorant or to rely on "free" information.

To be sophisticated is to have a good deal of information. So for most people, it may be irrational to be sophisticated. The bottom line is that rationality and sophistication are different concepts (Fiorina 1986; Luskin 1987). Although early voting behavior work may have loosely used the

4. The principal exception to this is when people derive pleasure directly from having information. Here I want to focus on the use of information for achieving political goals.

term "rationality" and thus not distinguished the two, later work does clearly distinguish rationality and sophistication. In this study, I focus on sophistication alone. I am not concerned with rationality.

Why Sophistication Matters

Why do we care about sophistication? What difference does it make if voters are sophisticated? If we assume that people can influence government policy through voting and other forms of participation (e.g., letter writing, working in campaigns, etc.), then sophisticated voters should be better able than unsophisticated voters to get what they want from the government. Sophisticated voters can understand the policy choices that face them, evaluate those policies, and connect them to candidates better than the less sophisticated. Thus, whether people choose to vote for their own self-interests, those of society at large, or whatever, they are more likely to vote for candidates who will give them what they want; and they are more likely to understand what they are getting if they are sophisticated. In short, one of the assumptions underlying theories of democratic government is that people have some understanding of how their votes and other political actions influence the government. That understanding stems from sophistication.

Given that this is why sophistication is important, we can look back at our definition of sophistication and see that all the parts are important. Certainly attitude consistency and level of conceptualization are important because—as has often been mentioned—following serious political discussion in our country requires a good understanding of liberalism, conservatism, and how various issue positions are related to one another.

A point less often discussed in the literature is that political information is also very important because, without a base of political knowledge, one cannot follow the issues or connect them to the candidates. For instance, how can the 30 percent of the population who typically do not know which party controls the House of Representatives make intelligent decisions about whom to blame or reward for changes in the state of the economy? They cannot.

A great deal has been made of the rise in the levels of conceptualization index during the early 1960s. People, so it is said, have come to think in more ideological terms. Yet what difference would it make if people thought in ideological terms, but did not know which party controlled

Congress, what the differences between the parties were, or how the candidates stood on the issues? Not much. For a true increase in sophistication that would have some influence on politics and government, information must rise along with level of conceptualization. Indeed, the most important part of sophistication may well be level of information.

For these reasons, we will look not only at level of conceptualization and attitude consistency, as most investigators have done, but also at measures of political information. These information measures, as shown in Chapters 4 and 5 and "Concluding Comments," suggest a much different version of what happened in the 1960s than that suggested by the measures of ideological thinking. Earlier I stated that I would look at the information measures to corroborate what is learned by examining the level of conceptualization and attitude consistency indexes. I can now add that the information measures should be regarded as equally important measures of political sophistication. They certainly measure a different aspect of sophistication, one that has not received as much attention as the measures of ideological thinking, but which is no less important. Filling in the picture with these measures provides a better, fuller understanding of what happened in the 1960s.

Things to Come

Chapter 1 examines the reliability and stability of the levels of conceptualization index and shows that the index is stable, but unreliable. The candidate component of the levels index works particularly poorly.

Chapter 2 examines the validity of the levels index and argues that, although the index does measure sophistication, it does not measure the levels of conceptualization per se. Moreover, the levels index measures sophistication in such a way that it cannot be used to make comparisons over time.

Chapter 3 examines attitude consistency and issue voting, beginning with a review of the many studies on the change in question wording between 1960 and 1964 and the specific problems with comparisons across that time period. The chapter continues with a discussion of other problems facing those who would measure trends in consistency over time and argues that the apparent changes in attitude consistency during the 1960s cannot be taken at face value.

Chapter 4 examines other measures of sophistication—both information measures and other variables that are closely associated with political sophistication. The evidence indicates that sophistication did not grow in the 1960s—or for that matter, at any time from 1956 to 1976.

Chapter 5 builds and tests a model to explain political sophistication, then uses the model to simulate changes in sophistication. The goal is to find out what, if anything, might cause sophistication to change over time. The book concludes by arguing that there is no credible evidence for any but trivial changes in sophistication either in the 1960s or at any other time from the 1950s to the present. Moreover, there is little reason to expect any future changes in sophistication. The static description of *The American Voter* was the right description.

One

Reliability of the Levels of Conceptualization

The American Voter (Campbell et al. 1960) is probably the best known book on American voting behavior. One of its most important arguments is that most Americans know little about politics and think about politics in largely nonideological ways. That is, few people are very sophisticated about politics. As a consequence, elections cannot be interpreted as ideological mandates. In support of their argument, Campbell et al. presented data showing the public's lack of factual information about politics, its lack of opinions on major issues, and its failure to evaluate the two major parties and their presidential candidates in ideological terms according to the levels of conceptualization index. Their argument that the public is ill informed and nonideological quickly became the prevailing viewpoint among political scientists.

The paradigm that Campbell and his colleagues developed in *The American Voter* was far-reaching and powerful. A new way of looking at the American electorate existed. New possibilities for explaining public opinion and voting behavior were presented. New questions for research were raised. Many of those questions were addressed by investigators using the levels indexes or closely related measures (Field and Anderson 1969; Hagner and Pierce 1982, 1984; Inglehart 1979; Jacoby 1986; Klingemann 1973, 1979a, 1979b, 1979c; Luskin 1987; Miller 1987; Miller and Miller 1976; Neuman 1981, 1986; Nie and Andersen 1974; Nie et al. 1976; Pierce 1970, 1975; Pierce and Hagner 1980, 1982; Wassenberg et al. 1983). Indeed, in the twenty years following the publication of *The American Voter*, the level of conceptualization index became one of the most important measures of the public's political sophistication and ideological awareness.

In this time of rapid advancement in knowledge about the electorate, little thought was given to one of the fundamental requirements of science—the careful testing and validation of measures.

In the case of the levels of conceptualization, the failure to test the measures was a serious mistake. Although some of the conclusions based on the levels indexes were correct, others were badly in error. Had researchers examined the indexes earlier, they would have realized that although the indexes did measure one aspect of political sophistication, they did not measure the "levels of conceptualization" construct. Indeed, there is little evidence that any such beast exists. That is, the "levels" are a methodological artifact.

In this chapter, I begin examining the measures of the levels of conceptualization by looking at their reliability and stability. The stability of the levels is critical to arguments about the nature of sophistication. Campbell et al. assumed that one's level of conceptualization, and sophistication in general, are stable over time. Their critics argued that the levels can change substantially. In order to evaluate these arguments, one must find out how much the levels change. In order to do that, one must disentangle the reliability and stability of the measures.

I start with a brief review of the various versions of the levels indexes and the developments in the theory used to explain how to interpret them. Then I look at the cross-tabulations of the levels indexes over time and the associated test-retest correlations. Although these data are a good starting point, they cannot provide enough information to separate the reliabilities and stabilities unless one is willing to make some heroic assumptions. I go beyond the simple test-retest data to use more sophisticated methods in the last part of the chapter. With these methods, one can find out how reliable and stable the levels really are.

The Levels of Conceptualization Indexes

The original measure of the levels in Campbell et al. (1960) and Converse (1964) was based on a set of eight open-ended questions asking what the respondent liked and disliked about the two major parties and their presidential candidates. The questions were as follows:

Now I'd like to ask you what you think are the good and bad points about the two parties. Is there anything in particular that you like about the [Democratic/Republican] party? [Probe:] What is that? Anything else?

Is there anything in particular that you don't like about the [Democratic/ Republican] party? [Probe:] What is that? Anything else?

Now I'd like to ask you about the good and bad points of the two major candidates for president. Is there anything in particular about [candidate's name] that might make you want to vote for him? [Probe:] What is that? Anything else?

Is there anything in particular about [candidate's name] that might make you want to vote against him? [Probe:] What is that? Anything else?

Up to five responses to each question were recorded for each respondent, so the total number of responses to serve as a basis for coding each respondent ranged from zero to forty. Each respondent was classified on the basis of a reading of his or her interview transcript. The coders worked directly with the transcripts of the interviews so that they could best estimate the respondent's level of sophistication (i.e., the verbatim responses themselves were used in classifying the respondents; the responses were not reduced to codes as an intermediate step).

The theoretical key to the levels of conceptualization is the level of abstraction used by people when they think about politics. The authors of *The American Voter* believed that people would reveal their levels of abstraction in their answers to the questions regarding their likes and dislikes about the parties and candidates. They assumed that the language in which people responded to the questions would be stable over time. Thus if a person thought about politics at a certain level, he or she would consistently respond to questions in terms reflecting that level. For instance, an ideologue would use ideological labels fairly frequently; another person who thought in terms of group benefits would talk about little other than groups when evaluating the parties and candidates. One who thought in terms of groups would not, for instance, respond using the ideological labels of a recently viewed television advertisement.

The original index classified people into four levels or frames of reference—(1) ideology, (2) group benefits, (3) nature of the times, and (4) no issue content. Each level hypothetically corresponded to a level of "conceptual sophistication" at which voters thought when they evaluated the parties and candidates.[1] Campbell et al. (1960, p. 222) wrote that the highest level, ideological conceptualization, embraces "all respondents whose evaluations of the candidates and the parties have any suggestion of the abstract conception one would associate with ideology." This level

---

1. Throughout the remainder of this book, the terms "level of conceptualization" and "conceptual sophistication" are used interchangeably.

would include, for instance, those who said they like candidates because they are liberal or who explained their preferences in terms of broad principles such as government intervention in the marketplace.

The second level, comprising those who conceptualize politics in terms of group benefits, "was reserved for persons whose issue comment revolved around fairly concrete and short-term group interest, or what we have . . . described . . . as 'ideology by proxy'" (Campbell et al. 1960, p. 223). In other words, people who think in terms of group benefits include those who say they like candidates because of the candidates' pro-labor positions or because of their work in favor of Israel or some other group connection.

The third level, nature of the times thinking, contains "persons engrossed in simplistic associations between the 'goodness' and 'badness' of the times and the identity of the party in power, or who appeared to have exhausted their view of the situation with mention of some rather isolated and specific issue" (Campbell et al. 1960, p. 223). For instance, this includes people who say they dislike the incumbent because the inflation rate is so high or because crime is running rampant.

The fourth and lowest level, no issue content, "contains individuals who evaluated the political objects without recourse to issues that might fairly be related to debates over domestic public policy" (Campbell et al. 1960, p. 223). An example of this type would be people who explain why they like a candidate in terms of the candidate's good looks or speaking style or southern accent. The distribution of the public in 1956 over these four basic levels and the more detailed sublevels is shown in Table 1.[2]

The findings presented by Campbell et al. and later elaborated upon by Converse (1964) added a new dimension to the study of public opinion and quickly assumed great importance in the scholarly debate on the public's ideological awareness. Following the lead of *The American Voter*, a number of investigators developed measures of the levels of conceptualization. Pierce and Hagner and a few others replicated the original measure using the original method.[3] But because coding the individual

2. For a fuller description of the levels, including the sublevels, see Campbell et al. (1960, ch. 10).

3. The others are Klingemann (1973, 1979a, 1979b, 1979c) and Miller and Miller (1976). Pierce and Hagner's work is more important because they replicated the original measure for all years from 1956 to 1980, and they used their measure in a number of studies (Hagner and Pierce 1982, 1983, 1984; Hagner et al. 1983; Pierce 1970, 1975; Pierce and Hagner 1982; Wassenberg et al. 1983).

TABLE 1. The Distribution of the Levels of Conceptualization

	Proportion of Total Sample	*Proportion of Voters*
A. Ideology		
1. Ideology	2.5%	3.5%
2. Near-ideology	9	12
B. Group benefits		
1. Perception of conflict	14	16
single group interest	17	18
2. Shallow group benefit responses	11	11
C. Nature of the times	24	23
D. No issue content		
1. Party orientation	4	3.5
2. Candidate orientation	9	7
3. No content	5	3
4. Unclassified	4.5	4
	100%	100%

Source. Campbell et al. 1960, p. 249, t. 10-1.

interview transcripts one by one is time-consuming and expensive, most subsequent investigators have relied on the Party and Candidate Master Codes rather than on the original interview transcripts. The Master Codes are an elaborate set of codes prepared by Michigan's Center for Political Studies that describe the responses to the like/dislike questions.[4] Thus the "surrogate" indexes were constructed in a two-step coding process (using the Master Codes as an intermediate step) rather than in a single-step process (directly from the interview transcripts).

Because the surrogate indexes are based on the Master Codes, some of the subtlety of the original measure may have been lost. Although mentions of specific issues and ideological labels can be detected in the Master Codes, the more subtle qualities of "the degree of differentiation and the 'connectedness' of the ideas in which the critical issue perceptions were embedded" that Campbell and his colleagues (1960, p. 223) emphasized probably cannot be detected. The users of these newer indexes acknowledged these deficiencies but argued that their measures were sufficiently like the original to be substituted for it. However, no comparison

4. The Master Codes and the distribution of responses are repeated in the CPS American National Election Codebooks.

with the original indexes or other serious testing of the surrogate indexes was ever conducted. Thus although some claim that the surrogate measures are inferior to the original (e.g., Hagner and Pierce 1982; Luskin 1987), no evidence supports that claim.

The Field and Anderson (1969) surrogate index has three levels—explicit ideologue, implicit ideologue, and nonideologue. Describing their index, Field and Anderson (1969, p. 386) wrote, "We distinguish between two kinds of ideological statement, one which features explicit use of liberal-conservative terminology and another which stresses several implicitly ideological themes: the individual and the state, the role and power of government, welfare, free enterprise, and posture toward change." Field and Anderson's measure (hereafter called the F&A measure) is more lenient than *The American Voter* measure because a single remark, rather than a coherent pattern of comments, is sufficient to place a respondent in one of the ideological categories.

The measure that Nie, Verba, and Petrocik developed in *The Changing American Voter* (hereafter the CAV measure) is more complicated than the F&A measure because it delimits a full range of levels rather than simply distinguishing two types of ideologues from the rest of the population. Their index has seven levels—(1) ideologue, (2) near-ideologue, (3) group benefits and issues, (4) issue references, (5) group benefit responses, (6) party responses, and (7) apolitical or nature of the times responses (see Table 2).[5]

Although the categories in the CAV index differ from those of *The American Voter,* they were designed to reflect the same hierarchical distinctions in conceptual sophistication. The correlations between the original index and the CAV index demonstrate the similarity between the original index and the CAV index. The correlations, presented in Table 3, show that Nie and his colleagues did a fairly good job in copying the original index. With the exception of 1972,[6] the CAV combined index correlates fairly well (.58 to .77) with the original index. Although the correlations are hardly perfect (in fact, they cannot be because the origi-

---

5. For a complete description of the index, see Nie et al. (1976, pp. 18–23 and ap. 2C). Note that the verbal description of the levels in the appendix is correct, but the precise numeric codes are not. For the coding scheme, contact the authors.

6. The original index for 1972 behaves unlike the original index in any other year or any other index. It is an anomaly that I discuss later.

TABLE 2.   *The Changing American Voter*'s Levels
of Conceptualization

Apolitical or nature-of-the-times responses:	These respondents consistently gave non-political responses ("I like Eisenhower," "My husband is a Democrat") or nature of the times responses. Those unable to answer the question were also coded here.
Party responses:	Any vague reference to party moves a respondent out of the apolitical nature of the times category. A party response might be "I've always been a Democrat," "The Republicans are the better party," or "Ike's a Republican."
Group benefit responses:	A respondent is moved into this category if he or she mentions the benefits a particular group will be given or is denied, that is, "Democrats do more for the working man like me."
Issue references:	A respondent is placed in this category if one or more responses pertain to a particular issue.
Group benefits and issues:	A respondent is moved into this category if his or her evaluation of the parties or candidates involves references to both group benefits and issues.
Near-ideologues:	Respondents are placed in this category if they offer at least one explicit or implicit ideological mention but fail to give any issue responses or group benefit responses.
Ideologues:	Respondents are put into this category only if they make at least one implicit or explicit ideological mention and also make some reference to issues and group benefits.

Source. Nie et al. 1976, ap. 2C, p. 375.

nal index has four categories, and the CAV index has seven), they justify the Nie et al. claim that their index measures the levels. (In Chapter 2, when I discuss validity, I present further evidence on this point.)

Both F&A and CAV measures differ from *The American Voter* measure in that they have separate party and candidate components, based on the separate indexing of the responses to the party and candidate questions.

TABLE 3.   Intercorrelations of Original Levels
with CAV Levels

	Nie et al. Levels		
	---	---	---
	Overall Level	Party Component	Candidate Component
1956	.65	.65	.35
1960	.66	.70	.29
1964	.69	.65	.48
1968	.58	.57	.37
1972	.31	.27	.24
1976	.77	.72	.44

Source. Data are from the 1956–1976 CPS American National Election Studies. The data for the original index are from Pierce and Hagner.

Note: Cell entries are Pearson's r's.

The party and candidate components are combined into the overall measures by assigning respondents to the highest levels they achieve on either component—a separation that turns out to be useful for my inquiry.

Reliability

The first characteristic of any measure to consider is its reliability. In statistical theory, the term "reliability" refers to the squared correlation between the "true" score and the observed score of a measure (Carmines and Zeller 1979; Lord and Novick 1968). In other words, reliability is the strength of the relationship between the essence of the measure (without any error) and what one actually measures (which includes measurement error). Thus the smaller the amount of error in the measure, the greater the correlation between the true score and the observed score.

The problem with estimating the reliability of a measure is that neither the true score nor the error in measurement is observable. Because of this, scholars have devised a number of indirect methods of estimating reliability, the most common being to use it repeatedly over time and take the correlation over time as the estimate of the reliability.[7] This "test-

7. In some less rigorous methodological writing, reliability is actually defined as the correlation of a measure with itself over time. This definition generally

retest" correlation is equal to the correlation of the true and observed scores if two assumptions are met: (1) The error is randomly distributed; thus the errors are uncorrelated over time. (2) There has been no change in the true scores over time.

The assumption of no real change is a critical one. In dealing with the levels of conceptualization, one is looking at the two- and four-year time spans of the CPS National Election Studies. There may be a substantial amount of change over such a time period. Therefore, in assessing test-retest correlations, one must attempt to find out how much of the change is random and how much is real. In statistical terms, one must attempt to separate the reliability of the index (i.e., the correlation of observed score with true score) from the stability of the index (i.e., the correlation of the true scores at different times).

The classical test theory model assumes that the random component in observed measures is measurement error. If one were measuring a fixed characteristic, say the length of a room, this assumption would obviously be true. However, when one measures characteristics of people, the assumption is debatable. Converse (1964), for instance, assumed that the seemingly random change exhibited in response to attitude items indicates that many survey respondents have "non-attitudes." When asked about issues, people who did not have opinions supposedly gave random answers. Thus he blamed the respondents, not the questions, for producing the random error. Achen (1975), on the other hand, argued that the random responses are caused partly by the inherently ambiguous nature of the survey questions. That is, Achen maintained that the questions are at least partly to blame for the randomness. The point is that if both measurement instruments and the ways in which people generate their responses have random components, distinguishing the two sources can be difficult, if not impossible.

By "stability," I mean individual level stability, not aggregate stability. Individual stability is defined as the correlation between individuals' true scores over time. The levels of conceptualization, for instance, would be highly stable if few people changed how they thought about politics over time. Aggregate stability, which has been the focus of most of the litera-

---

works for most purposes, but it is statistically inadequate because it ignores the possibility of real change (i.e., the possibility that real change, rather than random measurement error, occurs between the test and the retest). In order to deal with that problem, one must turn to the classical test theory model with its concepts of true score and error score.

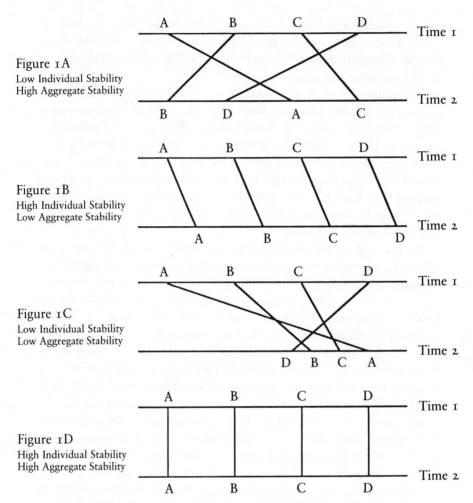

Figure 1A
Low Individual Stability
High Aggregate Stability

Figure 1B
High Individual Stability
Low Aggregate Stability

Figure 1C
Low Individual Stability
Low Aggregate Stability

Figure 1D
High Individual Stability
High Aggregate Stability

Figure 1. Hypothetical Combinations of Individual and Aggregate Stability

Note: The horizontal lines in each figure represent indexes at two time points. Four individuals—A, B, C, and D—are represented at each time point. The vertical or slanted lines show how the individuals change over time. The patterns of change yield the combinations of individual and aggregate stability.

ture on the levels, refers to changes in marginal distibutions over time. Combinations of either low individual stability with high aggregate stability or high individual stability with low aggregate stability are possible (as shown in Figure 1). The former could occur if there were a great deal of individual change but the changes offset one another so that the result was no change in the overall distribution. For instance, if all the people in the top level were to drop to the bottom level, while an equal number of people in the bottom level were to rise to the top, there would be a great deal of individual change, but no aggregate change (e.g., Figure 1A). The combination of high individual stability with low aggregate stability could occur, for instance, if everyone were to move up one level (e.g., Figure 1B). There would be a great deal of aggregate change over time because the distribution would move up, but there would also be high individual stability because everyone maintained the same position relative to everyone else. The key here is that correlations measure *relative*, not absolute, position. If respondents' relative positions remain the same over time, the correlation is high irrespective of whether those positions have moved up or down. Data presented below demonstrate that the levels have only moderate aggregate stability, but they have high individual stability. This combination has important implications for our understanding of what the levels indexes are measuring.

Hagner and Pierce (1982, pp. 789, 799, 806) refer to "stability" and "cross-time stability" in their defense of the original levels index. Their definition of stability is unrelated to the statistical sense of stability. To them, cross-time stability means that cross-sectional surveys show the same relationships at different points in time. Stability, in their sense, is not related to individual change over time. It follows that stability in their sense can exist when stability in the statistical sense is either high or low. This is not to say that their notion of stability is not of interest. Rather, it is not related to the problem of interpreting test-retest correlations and reliability coefficients.

Interpreting the Test-Retest Coefficients

The authors of *The American Voter* clearly saw the levels as fairly permanent individual characteristics. They thought that two fundamental barriers prevent people from developing more sophisticated types of conceptualizations (Campbell et al. 1960, pp. 253–55). First, most people in the lower levels lack both information and the time and motivation necessary to increase their information. Second, most people in the lower levels lack the cognitive ability to understand the abstractions used in the upper levels. On this point, Campbell et al. (1960, p. 255) declared, "[T]here are rather basic limitations on cognitive capacities which are likely to make certain of the most sophisticated types of content [of political debate] remain inaccessible to the poorly endowed observer." In other words, "cognitive limitations" prevent some people from understanding such abstractions as "liberalism" or "conservatism." It is not that these people have never bothered to learn; it is that they are incapable of learning. Some people, according to Campbell et al., simply do not have the "intellectual capacities" necessary to comprehend the abstractions used in political discourse.

Campbell et al. allowed that some change might occur. Alterations in presidential campaign styles and in individuals' political interest and involvement from one election to the next were expected to move some people from one level to another, but not many people. In general, Campbell et al. (1960, pp. 255–56) expected very little change, most of which they thought would occur between adjacent levels in the lower half of the scale.

Field and Anderson (1960, p. 382) interpreted *The American Voter*'s position on the stability of the levels as follows:

In discussing the general applicability of the 1956 findings, Campbell et al. minimized the prospects for variation, particularly at the level of ideology. Their argument rests largely on the proposition that people conceptualize politics in fairly fixed ways and do not adopt new modes of analysis easily. Essentially the same perspectives will be employed regardless of what kinds of appeals the candidates make. Those unaccustomed to thinking in terms of liberal-conservative distinctions are not likely to do so simply because in a given election campaign, stimuli come garbed in ideological terminology.

Field and Anderson argued that some changes in conceptualization levels occur in response to changing presidential campaign styles. Specifically, they found a rise in the proportion of ideologues from 1956 to 1964, which they attributed, in part, to the difference between the bland campaign of Dwight Eisenhower and the ideologically charged campaign of Barry Goldwater. They concluded that, at least to some extent, people evaluate political parties and presidential candidates according to the standards of the current campaign, be they ideological or whatever.

Although Field and Anderson (1969, p. 397) showed that the levels changed over time, they maintained that level of conceptualization has a fairly high level of individual stability: "The Campbell et al. notion of 'cognitive limitations' would seem to apply, but not as rigidly as they surmised on the basis of their 1956 findings." In short, Field and Anderson argued for a weakening of the "conceptual permanence thesis," not its complete rejection.

Nie, Verba, and Petrocik expanded upon the work of Field and Anderson, examining the levels from 1952 to 1976.[8] They found a substantial change in the proportion of ideologues over that period. According to their measure (Nie et al. 1976, p. 115), the proportion of ideologues varied from 12 percent in 1956 to 33 percent in 1972. Contrary to what Campbell et al. had predicted, almost all of the change occurred in the upper levels of the scale, a finding that was supported by Klingemann and Wright's investigations (Klingemann 1973). Nie and his colleagues (1976, p. 117) concluded that cognitive limitations "might inhibit citizens from moving out of the lower reaches of the scale. Indeed, the notion of cognitive limitations may more appropriately apply to the lower half of the levels of conceptualization scale than to the upper." The bottom line was that although Nie et al. agreed that cognitive limitations play an important role in determining the levels, the political environment also plays an important role.

Hagner and Pierce (1982, p. 783) agreed with *The Changing American Voter*'s analysis with one modification. They argued that the levels index does not measure the respondent's capacity for sophisticated conceptualization in general, but rather the conceptual sophistication present in his or her verbal evaluations of the current election. It follows that the individual's capacity for sophisticated thinking may be underestimated because the election may not present the stimuli that would trigger more sophisticated thinking.

In sum, Field and Anderson, Nie et al., and Pierce and Hagner did not so much contradict *The American Voter*'s explanation of the sources of the levels as expand on it. *The American Voter* asserted that the levels were primarily determined by cognitive abilities. Field and Anderson and the others argued that environmental factors form a second set of influences on conceptual sophistication, and that those environmental factors primarily influence those who are already in the more cognitively sophisticated half of the population.

These observations about the sources of the levels are relevant because they speak to the question of the stability of the levels. The terms "cognitive limitations" and "intellectual capacities" imply fixed characteris-

8. The first edition of *The Changing American Voter* stops with 1972. The enlarged edition (Nie et al. 1979) deals with 1976 as well.

tics. In the view of Campbell and his colleagues, these cognitive limitations are the foundations of the levels of conceptualization. Although some aspects of the political environment were thought to influence the levels, the main determinant was the individuals' intellectual capacities. It follows that there should be virtually no change in the levels. That is, the levels should have both high individual and aggregate stability.

The positions of Field and Anderson, Nie et al., and Pierce and Hagner can best be described as moving away from the thesis of fixed levels reflecting cognitive limitations toward the thesis of variable levels that also reflect the environment. Each set of investigators assigned less influence to cognitive limitations and more influence to the changing political environment than the preceding investigators. The implications for the reliability-stability trade-off, however, are not so apparent. Certainly these "environmentalists" found low aggregate stability. But whether they assumed low or high individual stability underlying the aggregate results is not clear. They may well have inferred individual instability from their data showing aggregate instability, but they never had the evidence to prove it. None of the environmentalists looked at any data on individual stability (save for Pierce and Hagner [1982], whose analysis has some serious methodological flaws—see the appendix to this chapter), and the only comments made on the subject were inferences drawn from aggregate data. Thus the question of individual stability remains open.

The Data on Reliability

Let me begin with some standards for comparison to put the data on the levels in context. The best known use of test-retest coefficients to assess the reliability of political items is by Philip Converse (1964, 1970). Converse examined the test-retest correlations (tau-b's) of the Michigan party identification scale and eight issue items (see Figure 2).[9] With party identification, he found a fairly high level of correlation, indicating that the item was fairly reliable. But with the issues items, he found a startling amount of apparently random change.

The four-year test-retest correlations ranged from .20 to .39. Upon

9. Converse discussed both two- and four-year continuity coefficients, but he concentrated on the two-year coefficients. Because the levels measures are basically presidential year measures, Figure 2 reports four-year continuity coefficients.

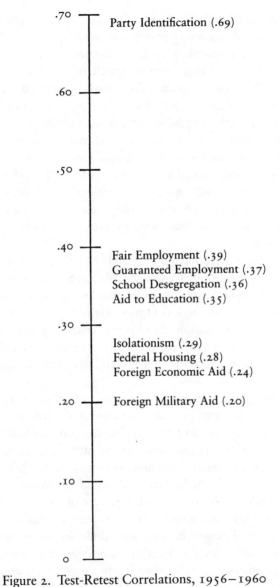

Figure 2. Test-Retest Correlations, 1956–1960

Source. Data are from the CPS 1956–1960 American National Election Studies.
Note: Coefficients are tau-b's.

discovering such distressingly low correlations, Converse (1970, p. 171) concluded, "We were doing a very poor job of tapping the attitudinal dimensions at which we originally aimed, . . . our results . . . give witness to an incredible degree of measurement unreliability." More recently, Converse and Markus (1979) updated their work, showing basically the same patterns in the 1972–1976 panel study. Party identification had high test-retest correlations; candidate evaluations (which were not available in the earlier panel) had moderate test-retest correlations; issue items had low test-retest correlations. Thus once again issue items were found to be far less reliable and stable than our theories about attitudes suggest they should be. Although subsequent investigators have taken a somewhat more lenient view of such low reliability estimates, no one denies the problem. Investigators continue to use the attitude items because they are all that is available.[10]

The principal data for studying the reliability of the levels of conceptualization indexes are from the Center for Political Studies' 1956–1960 and 1972–1976 National Election Panel Studies. In these studies, respondents were interviewed a series of times over four-year periods. Thus the panels allow the examination of individual change as well as aggregate change over the two time periods. With the data on individual change, one can assess the reliabilities and stabilities of the various levels measures.

Table 4 presents the cross-tabulations of the original index across the 1956–1960 and 1972–1976 periods. The test-retest correlation coefficients, Kendall's tau-b's, are identical: .33. These figures indicate a fairly high level of turnover, higher than most of the attitude items Converse examined. Consider, for instance, the number of respondents who moved from the lowest level to the highest and vice versa (the upper right and lower left cells). In the 1956–1960 panel, 8 percent of those who thought about politics with no issue content in 1956 became ideologues four years later; 5 percent of those who were judged ideologues in 1956 were found to conceptualize politics without any issue content in 1960. Moreover, far larger numbers of people moved from the relatively crude "nature of the times" categories to become ideologues and vice versa. The

10. Curiously, political scientists did not turn to multiple item scales when they discovered the unreliability of attitude items. Despite the facts that statisticians clearly point to multiple item scales as a solution to the reliability problem, and that psychologists and sociologists have been using such scales for decades, political scientists have largely ignored the possibility of using them.

TABLE 4. The Stability of the Original Levels Indexes

| | 1956 | | | |
1960	Ideologues	Group Benefit	Nature of Times	No Issue Content
Ideologues	57%	16%	16%	8%
Group Benefit	23	43	19	23
Nature of Times	15	22	40	23
No Issue Content	5	19	25	46
Total	100%	100%	100%	100%
N	(105)	(328)	(160)	(148)
	tau-b = .33		r = .38	

| | 1972 | | | |
1976	Ideologues	Group Benefit	Nature of Times	No Issue Content
Ideologues	46%	19%	15%	10%
Group Benefit	28	48	25	12
Nature of Times	10	19	41	26
No Issue Content	16	14	19	52
Total	100%	100%	100%	100%
N	(91)	(90)	(120)	(58)
	tau-b = .33		r = .37	

Source. Pierce and Hagner 1982, p. 381, t. 2.

extent of movement from one extreme to the other is even greater in the 1972–1976 panel. Ten percent moved from the bottom of the scale to the top; 16 percent moved from the top to the bottom. Thus there was a substantial amount of turnover in the panels, turnover that indicates either fairly unreliable measures or a surprising lack of stability in how people think about and conceptualize politics from one election to the next.

Tables 5 and 6 show the cross-tabulations of respondents' scores on the CAV measure over the 1956–1960 and 1972–1976 periods. Here the reliability coefficients are virtually identical to the original index, .31 and .32.

TABLE 5. The Stability of the Nie,
Verba, and Petrocik Levels Indexes, 1960 by 1956

1960	Apolitical	Party	Groups	Issues	Groups/ Issues	Near- Ideo- logues	Ideo- logues	Total	N
						1956			
Apolitical	38%	10%	7%	8%	1%	5%	1%	8%	94
Party	17	22	14	16	6	9	5	13	158
Groups	16	13	26	10	11	9	9	14	163
Issues	18	28	19	32	23	23	9	23	273
Groups/ Issues	6	9	14	12	31	7	10	14	170
Near- Ideologues	4	12	6	11	6	22	20	11	130
Ideologues	2	6	14	13	21	25	47	18	216
	100%	100%	100%	100%	100%	100%	100%	100%	
Total	7%	17%	17%	21%	18%	7%	13%	100%	
N	84	204	209	253	215	87	152		1,204
	tau-b = .31								

Source. Data are from the 1956–1960 CPS American National Election Studies.

TABLE 6. The Stability of the Nie,
Verba, and Petrocik Levels Indexes, 1976 by 1972

1976	Apolitical	Party	Groups	Issues	Groups/ Issues	Near- Ideo- logues	Ideo- logues	Total	N
						1972			
Apolitical	44%	24%	16%	6%	6%	5%	2%	9%	58
Party	17	36	11	17	17	12	12	15	103
Groups	2	9	26	6	5	3	4	5	34
Issues	12	13	11	20	14	13	8	12	83
Groups/ Issues	6	2	10	13	18	6	8	9	62
Near- Ideologues	8	13	10	19	15	26	18	18	123
Ideologues	10	2	16	18	25	34	47	31	208
	100%	100%	100%	100%	100%	100%	100%	100%	
Total	7%	7%	3%	18%	10%	17%	39%	100%	
N	48	45	19	119	65	113	262		671
	tau-b = .32								

Source. Data are from the 1972–1976 CPS American National Election Studies.

TABLE 7. *The Changing American Voter* Party Component, 1960 by 1956

	1956								
1960	Apoli-tical	Party	Groups	Issues	Groups/ Issues	Near-Ideo-logues	Ideo-logues	Total	N
Apolitical	47%	25%	14%	17%	9%	20%	4%	20%	243
Party	14	22	9	15	8	5	4	11	139
Groups	14	13	33	10	17	10	14	18	213
Issues	11	18	10	28	14	12	6	14	165
Groups/ Issues	6	7	16	10	25	2	10	12	147
Near-Ideologues	5	7	2	7	3	25	13	6	78
Ideologues	4	9	16	14	24	25	50	19	229
	100%	100%	100%	100%	100%	100%	100%	100%	
Total	18%	16%	21%	11%	16%	3%	15%	100%	
N	223	191	254	137	192	40	177		1,214
	tau-b = .35								

Source. Data are from the 1956–1960 CPS American National Election Studies.

Looking now at the party and candidate components of the CAV surrogate measure (shown in Tables 7, 8, 9, and 10), one can examine the
data in more detail. The most striking observation that emerges from an
examination of these data is that the party components are far more reliable than the candidate components. In the 1956–1960 period, the party
component has a test-retest coefficient of .35, and the candidate component has a coefficient of only .15. In the 1972–1976 period, the coefficients are similar to those of the earlier period: .38 and .18 for the party
and candidate indexes respectively. Thus it seems that whatever reliability
and stability these measures have is due mostly to their party components. The obvious inference is that the same holds true of the original
measure, that is, the reliability and stability of the original index are provided largely by the answers to the party like/dislike questions, not the
candidate questions. Unfortunately, because the original index was constructed without separate party and candidate indexes, it is impossible
to tell.

The finding that the party components are more reliable and stable
than the candidate components is consistent with previous analyses,

TABLE 8. *The Changing American Voter* Party Component, 1976 by 1972

	1972								
1976	Apoli-tical	Party	Groups	Issues	Groups/Issues	Near-Ideo-logues	Ideo-logues	Total	N
Apolitical	58%	30%	15%	15%	17%	11%	12%	26%	177
Party	12	15	6	12	2	7	6	9	59
Groups	3	0	21	3	11	5	3	5	34
Issues	7	16	2	12	11	6	4	7	48
Groups/Issues	2	3	8	12	22	7	6	7	44
Near-Ideologues	11	26	21	14	11	23	18	17	115
Ideologues	7	10	28	32	26	40	51	29	194
	100%	100%	100%	100%	100%	100%	100%	100%	
Total	26%	9%	8%	9%	7%	14%	26%	100%	
N	177	61	53	59	46	97	178		671
	tau-b = .38								

Source. Data are from the 1972–1976 CPS American National Election Studies.

TABLE 9. *The Changing American Voter* Candidate Component, 1960 by 1956

	1956								
1960	Apoli-tical	Party	Groups	Issues	Groups/Issues	Near-Ideo-logues	Ideo-logues	Total	N
Apolitical	37%	12%	13%	12%	12%	9%	13%	16%	194
Party	30	41	30	36	24	36	40	36	428
Groups	8	8	10	5	12	9	0	8	92
Issues	17	29	29	32	30	24	0	27	329
Groups/Issues	4	4	9	7	12	6	7	6	67
Near-Ideologues	3	5	6	5	4	6	20	5	58
Ideologues	2	2	3	3	7	9	20	3	36
	100%	100%	100%	100%	100%	100%	100%	100%	
Total	16%	40%	9%	25%	6%	3%	1%	100%	
N	190	483	107	300	76	33	15		1,204
	tau-b = .15								

Source. Data are from the 1956–1960 CPS American National Election Studies.

TABLE 10.   *The Changing American Voter* Candidate Component, 1976 by 1972

1976	1972								
	Apoli-tical	Party	Groups	Issues	Groups/ Issues	Near-Ideo-logues	Ideo-logues	Total	N
Apolitical	47%	24%	13%	10%	14%	16%	5%	16	106
Party	18	49	39	37	33	47	34	36	244
Groups	5	3	13	6	2	4	8	5	36
Issues	20	14	17	22	22	15	23	20	135
Groups/ Issues	4	7	9	8	13	8	8	8	55
Near-Ideologues	4	4	9	10	9	10	11	9	59
Ideologues	1	0	0	7	7	0	11	5	36
	100%	100%	100%	100%	100%	100%	100%	100%	
Total	11%	11%	3%	27%	13%	11%	23%	100%	
N	74	76	23	182	87	74	155		671
	tau-b = .18								

Source. Data are from the 1972–1976 CPS American National Election Studies.

which have shown far more aggregate change in the candidate components than in the party components. Upon examining the separate components of their measure, Field and Anderson (1969, p. 388) concluded that the increase in the combined scale from 1960 to 1964 was due largely to the "threefold increase of Ideologues in the candidate reference." Nie and his colleagues (1976, p. 113) concurred, declaring, "It is the changing candidates rather than the parties that provide the major change in political content."

That conclusion follows common sense. The parties, after all, are a relatively fixed aspect of the political environment. Although evaluations of the parties do change in response to changing issues and new presidential contenders, the candidates change more. Thus changing candidate evaluations provide most of the change in the combined levels indexes.

To summarize the test-retest data, Figure 3 presents the 1956–1960 continuity coefficients for Converse's attitude items (on the right side of the figure) together with the continuity coefficients for the various measures of the levels of conceptualization (on the left side). Clearly, the levels do not fare as well as the attitude items. In particular, the party and com-

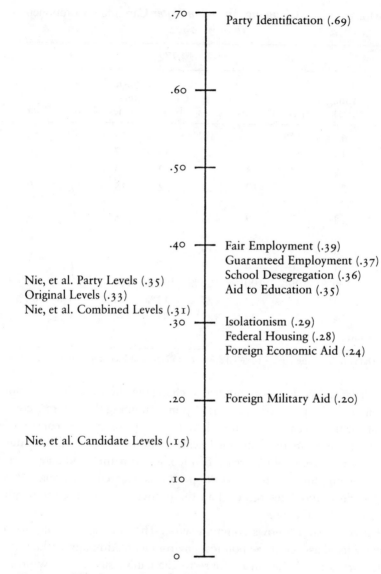

.70 — Party Identification (.69)

.60 —

.50 —

.40 — Fair Employment (.39)
       Guaranteed Employment (.37)
Nie, et al. Party Levels (.35)   School Desegregation (.36)
Original Levels (.33)   Aid to Education (.35)
Nie, et al. Combined Levels (.31)
.30 — Isolationism (.29)
       Federal Housing (.28)
       Foreign Economic Aid (.24)

.20 — Foreign Military Aid (.20)

Nie, et al. Candidate Levels (.15)

.10 —

0 —

Figure 3. Test-Retest Correlations, 1956–1960

Source. Data are from the CPS 1956–1960 American National Election Studies.
Note: Coefficients are tau-b's.

bined indexes fall roughly in the middle of the range of attitude items, but the candidate indexes fall well short of the mediocre standard set by the attitude items. If one were to compare the levels indexes with party identification or candidate evaluations (not shown), the levels indexes would fare very badly. Thus, in some combination, the levels indexes have a serious amount of unreliability and instability.

So how do the various investigators' positions fare in light of these data? *The American Voter* clearly sees the levels as highly stable characteristics. That is, if the levels were reliably measured, one would expect them to have test-retest correlations equal to or, more likely, greater than the test-retest correlation of party identification. The fact that the correlations are so much lower therefore indicates an enormous amount of measurement error—that is, unreliability.

The positions of the "environmentalists" (Field and Anderson, Pierce and Hagner, and Nie et al.) indicate lesser amounts of stability and correspondingly greater amounts of reliability than the position of Campbell et al. The changing environment hypothetically causes instability. The question is, how much? Although the environmentalists argued that the political environment is a major cause of the levels, they did not abandon the cognitive limitations thesis. They agreed with *The American Voter* that cognitive capacity serves as the foundation of the levels. Environmental change causes fluctuation over time in the levels below the individual's cognitive limitations. Thus cognitive limitations introduce at least a moderate amount of stability to the levels. Moreover, because the level of debate changes only moderately from one election to the next, it seems fair to interpret the environmentalists' position as being that the levels are moderately stable, ranging from the middle of the scale to possibly as low as some of the attitude items discussed by Converse.

Given these considerations, I reexamine the data in Figure 3. The test-retest correlations of the levels indexes seem more consistent with the views of the environmentalists than with that of *The American Voter*. However, the test-retest correlations are even lower than those of most of the attitude items (shown on the right half of Figure 3). Therefore they are at least somewhat unreliable. In the case of the candidate component measures, the test-retest correlations are far worse than any of the attitude item correlations. Even allowing for a substantial amount of instability, the Nie et al. candidate component is highly unreliable.

In sum, from the data so far one can conclude three things. First, whether the measures are stable or not, they have substantial measurement error components. If the levels are indeed stable, then the measurement error is huge. Second, the candidate components are enormously unreliable. Although I do not have separate party and candidate component measures of the original *American Voter* index, it seems only reasonable to conclude that because it is based equally on the party and candidate questions, it is seriously flawed. Third, because the findings of Field and Anderson and Nie et al. about aggregate change over time have shown that most of the change in the levels stems from change in the candidate component, I must conclude that the evidence for those changes is flawed. One cannot, of course, conclude that there were no changes over time. However, I can say that my findings have raised some serious questions that must be addressed.

Further Data on Reliability

The test-retest data seem more consistent with the thesis that the levels vary from election to election in response to the changing environmental stimuli than with the "conceptual permanence" thesis of *The American Voter*. Still, I cannot yet draw a conclusion because the data are statistically consistent with either a situation of moderately reliable measures of unstable characteristics or very unreliable measures of stable characteristics. To resolve the question, I consider four further sets of evidence beginning with an assessment of the 1950s.

It seems difficult to argue that the events between 1956 and 1960 were sufficiently turbulent to cause the enormous amount of individual change required to interpret the low test-retest correlations as reflecting individual instability. The 1956–1960 period was a time of relative political calm. The late fifties have often been characterized as the calm before the storm, a time when few political changes were taking place. A popular theme among academics was the "end of ideology."

The data from the CPS 1956 and 1960 National Election Studies confirm this view of the 1950s.[11] The marginal distributions for party identification, the eight attitude items Converse examined, and the levels of conceptualization indexes all remained roughly constant over that four-year period. That is, survey results show no aggregate change in how the public thought about politics.

Speaking of the attitude items, Converse (1970, p. 170) wrote:

11. See Converse (1970) for a similar argument.

The marginal attitude distributions for the various time points were remarkably similar despite high rates of turnover within the tables. It would seem that if national events were exerting systematic forces on opinion in a manner which would produce meaningful evolution of public attitudes, the distributions of opinion should progress in one direction or another over time, rather than remain relatively stable, with almost all of the individual change in one direction being counterbalanced by an equal amount of individual attitude change in the opposing direction.

The point that Converse made about attitudes applies equally well to the levels of conceptualization. Although there was a huge amount of individual change, there was remarkably little aggregate change. If one assumes that environmental forces do indeed have an impact, then one must conclude that whatever environmental forces acted to change people in one direction were balanced by equal and opposite forces acting on other people. The result was no net change.

Given such a description of the 1956–1960 period and such survey results, it is difficult to argue for the environmentalist thesis of highly unstable levels. Even if the levels could easily be changed by the environment, the environment did not change much in the late fifties. Thus the only explanation of the high turnover in the levels would seem to be measurement error and unreliability.

The second set of evidence takes advantage of the design of the CAV levels index. Rather than follow the lead of *The American Voter* and construct a single levels index from the like/dislike questions about both the parties and candidates, Nie and his colleagues chose to construct two separate indexes—one based on the party questions and one based on the candidate questions. Because the party questions were asked not only in the presidential election years of 1956 and 1960, but also in the off-year of 1958, we have measures of the party index in all three waves of the 1956–1958–1960 panel survey.[12] The existence of a third wave allows a substantial increase in the power of the statistical methods I can bring to bear on the reliability-stability problem. To begin with, I can use the estimators of reliability and stability developed by David Wiley and James Wiley (1970).

The Wiley and Wiley method for separating reliability and stability re-

12. The candidate questions, of course, could not be asked in 1958, so we have neither the candidate component nor the combined index. We do not have the same data in the 1972–1976 panel because the party questions were not asked in the 1974 questionnaire.

quires measurements for each respondent at three points in time; therefore it can be applied to the party component index. The party index is an excellent choice for this procedure because it is the best of the levels indexes. Its test-retest correlation is higher than that of any other measure; thus I am giving the levels the best opportunity to demonstrate an acceptable level of reliability.

An assumption that must be made in order to use the Wiley and Wiley method is that the party index is an interval level measure. It is not, of course. The levels indexes are ordinal indexes. The question then is how much difference it will make. The answer seems to be not much. A good deal of research has been done on the question of using interval level statistics with ordinal data. That research suggests that little damage is done (Borgatta and Bohrnstedt 1981; Gaito 1980; Labovitz 1967, 1971). Nevertheless, all of the interval level results contain a certain amount of error caused by use of interval statistics with ordinal data. That is, my results should be viewed as reasonable approximations only.

The results of applying the Wiley and Wiley method strongly support *The American Voter*'s conceptual permanence thesis and reject the environmentalists' position. The reliability of the party index was .33 in 1956 and .50 in 1958 and 1960. The stability coefficients over the 1956–1958 and 1958–1960 periods were a startling 1.00. In other words, according to this model, virtually *all* the change in the observed index over the 1956–1960 period is due to measurement error. The underlying characteristic seems to be almost perfectly stable.

The results of the Wiley and Wiley model should be qualified in two ways. First, sampling error and the assumption that the party index is an interval variable surely introduced some error into the estimates, and that error may have exaggerated the stability of the levels. Second, there is a potential source of bias. Wheaton et al. (1977) show that if any variables that cause the party index exist and if those variables are correlated over time, the stability coefficient will be inflated and the reliability coefficients deflated. Thus the Wiley and Wiley estimates may exaggerate the true stability of the levels. Unfortunately, one cannot tell how much.

For my third set of evidence, I examine the correlations between the party and candidate components of the CAV levels index. In theory, the party and candidate indexes measure the same phenomenon—level of conceptualization. It follows that the correlation between the two indexes at any point in time is a measure of the reliabilities of those two indexes.

TABLE 11.   Correlations Between Party and Candidate Indexes

	1956	1960	1964	1968	1972	1976
Pearson r	.29	.30	.30	.34	.37	.33
N	1,762	1,164	1,571	1,557	1,372	2,248

Source. Data are from the 1972–1976 CPS American National Election Studies.

Strictly speaking, the correlation between the two component indexes is an estimate of the reliability of the indexes only if they measure exactly the same phenomenon and have the same error variances (in technical terms, only if they are "parallel"—see Lord and Novick 1968). Yet we know from the test-retest coefficients for the two indexes that the indexes are not the same. In both panels, the party index has test-retest correlations that are more than twice as large as those of the candidate index. Thus the two indexes either measure different phenomena, or the candidate index has more error variance than the party index. In either event, the result is that the correlation between the two indexes is only a rough estimate of their reliability. More to the point, it is a single estimate for the reliability of both indexes. Given that the two indexes are not equally reliable, one must view their correlation as a rough average of the two reliabilities.

Table 11 shows the correlations between the party and candidate components for each election year from 1956 through 1976. The correlations, ranging from .29 to .37, show the same amount of reliability indicated by the test-retest coefficients in Tables 5 and 6. This time, however, it is not possible to explain away the low correlations by saying that they are partly caused by change over time. These correlations are between variables measured at the same time. Hence the low correlations are caused either by low reliability or by the fact that the two components are measuring different things. Of course, they both claim to measure the same thing—level of conceptualization.

Whether level of conceptualization should be thought of as one or two phenomena is not clear. Campbell et al. and the others who use the original index (e.g., Pierce and Hagner) clearly maintain that there is only one trait, but Field and Anderson and Nie et al. build separate party and candidate indexes and thus implicitly suggest that there are two distinct phenomena. How these investigators think the two are related is not clear because they do not discuss the subject. Certainly, it seems odd that people would think in two different ways about candidates and parties. In general, the whole area is fairly murky. If there are two distinct types of levels, some time should be spent investigating their differences. This inquiry leads toward questions of validity, pursued in Chapter 2.

The data in Table 11 provide further evidence that *The American Voter*'s original idea that the levels are relatively permanent characteristics of individuals is correct and that the environmentalists' argument that conceptual sophistication changes in response to the political environment is wrong. This conclusion follows from the relationship between reliability and stability. As discussed previously, the low test-retest correlations reflect a mixture of unreliability and instability. That is, a trade-off between the two exists. Because the reliability coefficients in Table 11 are roughly as low as the test-retest correlations in Table 7, they account for all the change in the test-retest correlations. It follows that the stability coefficients must be fairly high. Such stability contradicts the environmentalists' position.

For the fourth set of evidence, I look at both indexes over time. Here are the components of a simple two-wave, two-variable multiple indicator (LISREL) model.[13] Each of the two panel studies contains two unobserved variables—the levels of conceptualization at times 1 and 2. There are also two indicators, or observed measures, for each of the unobserved variables at each time point—the party and candidate indexes. These data allow construction of the two-wave, two-variable model shown in Figure 4. The model stems directly from the theory developed by Campbell et al. and others who have worked with the levels. The "true levels" are the latent variables at each time point. The party and candidate indexes are the observed measures of the respondents' true levels. The connection between the observed measures at different time points is solely through the unobserved true levels.

When estimated with the 1956–1960 and 1972–1976 data, the model yields the same answer as before. The true levels are fairly stable, with path coefficients of .72 in the 1950s and .79 in the 1970s. The party in-

---

13. All multiple indicator models discussed here were estimated with LISREL VI (Joreskog and Sorbom 1984). On two-wave, two-variable models, see Costner (1969), Duncan (1975), and Joreskog (1979).

dexes are moderately reliable, with reliability coefficients ranging from .52 to .67. The candidate indexes are quite unreliable, with reliability coefficients ranging from .12 to .24.

The problem with the two-wave, two-variable models is that, as the chi-square statistics report, they fit the data poorly.[14] This is presumably more of a problem for the levels theory than for the models because these models correspond to the theory. However, using the 1958 wave of the 1956–1958–1960 panel survey allows me to revise the model. The addition of the extra wave with its single index provides enough flexibility to improve the model enormously.

Figure 5A shows the model with the addition of the 1958 latent variable and party index. The estimated coefficients are similar to those in the first model. The model still has a poor fit.

If the levels components were measuring exactly the same latent trait, then the model should fit the data. But if the two components are measuring different phenomena, then the two candidate components would be correlated over time independently of the party component. That is, the missing piece of the model would be the correlation between the errors of the two candidate indexes. This correlation bypasses the 1958 wave, which was measured only by the party index. When I reestimate the model (Figure 5B) allowing the candidate index errors to be correlated, the chi-square drops to a mere 1.40, indicating that the revised model fits the data very well.

The interpretation of the correlated errors in the revised model is that there is a second latent factor in addition to the true level. Some other, unknown variable causes respondents' scores on the candidate indexes. The problem is that the writings of the various investigators who have studied the levels of conceptualization make little provision for any second factor. Both party and candidate indexes are supposed to be measuring the same phenomenon—the levels. It turns out, as Figure 5 shows, they are not. The problem is compounded by the fact that the second factor underlying the levels is extremely unstable. Even if one accepts the argument that there are two distinct types of level of conceptualization (party and candidate), it is difficult to believe that the true candidate level could

14. High values of chi-square indicate that we should reject the model because it does not fit the data. Low values of chi-square indicate that the model fits the data.

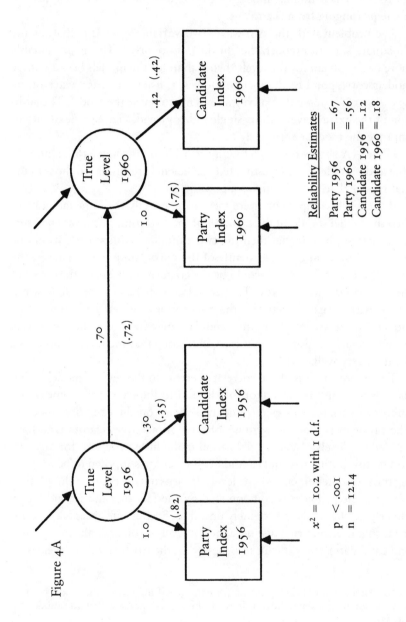

Figure 4A

Reliability Estimates

Party 1956   = .67
Party 1960   = .56
Candidate 1956 = .12
Candidate 1960 = .18

x^2 = 10.2 with 1 d.f.

p < .001
n = 1214

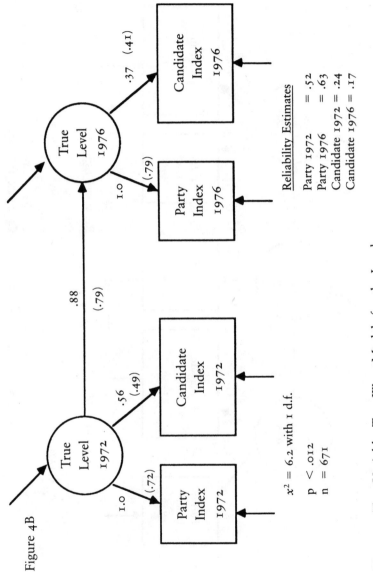

Figure 4B

Reliability Estimates

Party 1972   = .52
Party 1976   = .63
Candidate 1972 = .24
Candidate 1976 = .17

x^2 = 6.2 with 1 d.f.

p < .012
n = 671

Figure 4. Two-Variable, Two-Wave Models for the Levels

Source. Data are from the CPS 1956–1960 and 1972–1976 American National Election Studies.

Note: Coefficients are maximum likelihood estimates. Both standardized and unstandardized coefficients are shown. Standardized coefficients are in parentheses. All coefficients are significant at p < .001.

Figure 5A

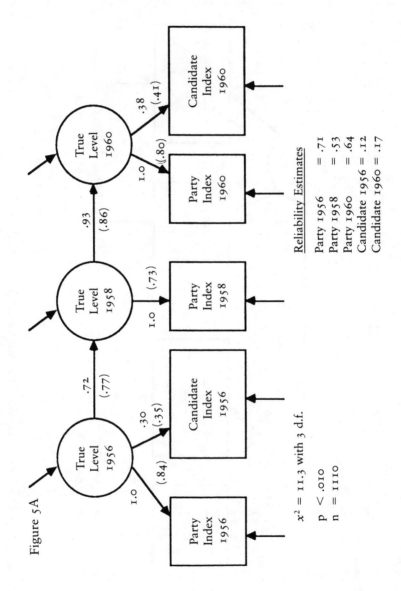

Reliability Estimates

Party 1956 = .71
Party 1958 = .53
Party 1960 = .64
Candidate 1956 = .12
Candidate 1960 = .17

$x^2 = 11.3$ with 3 d.f.

p < .010
n = 1110

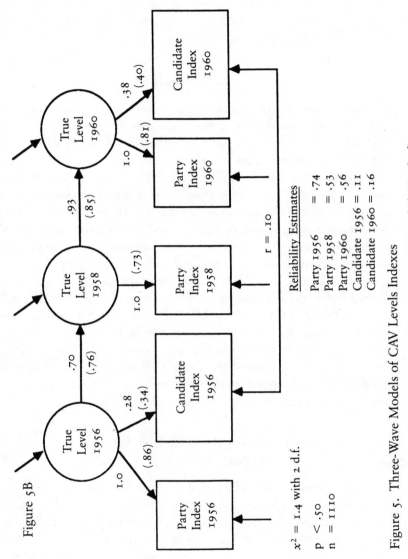

Figure 5B

$x^2 = $ 1.4 with 2 d.f.

p < .50

n = 1110

Reliability Estimates

Party 1956	= .74
Party 1958	= .53
Party 1960	= .56
Candidate 1956	= .11
Candidate 1960	= .16

r = .10

Figure 5. Three-Wave Models of CAV Levels Indexes

Source. Data are from the CPS 1956–1958–1960 American National Election Studies.

Note: Coefficients are maximum likelihood estimates. Both standardized and unstandardized coefficients are shown. Standardized coefficients are in parentheses. All coefficients are significant at p < .001.

be so unstable. Thus one is led to question what the candidate index actually measures. The identity of the second factor remains unknown.

The results in Figure 5B match those of the earlier findings. The levels are highly stable. The party indexes are moderately reliable. The candidate indexes are quite unreliable, seeming to be mostly random noise, unrelated to sophistication or anything else.

Conclusions

The four major sets of evidence—the history of the 1956–1960 period, the Wiley and Wiley reliability and stability estimates, the party-candidate index correlations, and the multiple indicator models—provide the same conclusion each time. The levels of conceptualization show a high level of individual stability. The observed measures of the levels change a great deal, but the evidence shows that that variation is caused almost entirely by random measurement error. All the evidence points to the conclusion that the underlying latent trait is very stable. Therefore the evidence supports *The American Voter*'s conceptual permanence thesis and rejects the environmentalists' argument.

Because most of the evidence was about the CAV indexes, not the original index, my conclusions about the original index must be more tentative. But what is true of the CAV indexes is probably also true of the original because the original index seems to be just like the CAV combined index. That is, the two indexes are highly correlated, and the test-retest correlations are about the same. Moreover, the two indexes are based on the same questions. Therefore the original index, like the CAV counterpart, is probably stable and unreliable.

Appendix: Reliability Under the Assumption of Nominal Variables

In response to my earlier criticism of the surrogate levels indexes (Smith 1980), Pierce and Hagner argued that although the surrogate indexes may be unreliable, the original index of Campbell et al. (1960) (which Pierce and Hagner had replicated by the original method) was reliable and valid (Hagner and Pierce 1982; Pierce and Hagner 1982). In support of their argument, they presented data from the CPS 1956–1960 and 1972–1976 panel studies.

In each of the panels, they cross-tabulated respondents' levels in the first wave of the panels with their levels in the second wave. The test-retest reliability coefficients that they report (tau-b = .33 for both panel studies) are essentially the same as the ones for the Nie et al. indexes (.31 and .32). Thus it would seem that the Nie et al. surrogate measure is about as reliable as the original measure, which is to say not very reliable.

Pierce and Hagner took a different view of the matter. Although they reported the tau-b coefficients in their table, they completely ignored them in the text. Instead, they discussed the percentage of respondents who are in the same level after four years (i.e., the percentage in the main diagonal of the table). That percentage is a measure of test-retest reliability for nominal or categorical variables, not for ordinal variables. Pierce and Hagner subsequently explained that they were tending toward the view that the levels index is actually a nominal variable.[1] This hypothesis deserves some consideration because Nie et al. (1981) also suggest this possibility. However, neither Pierce and Hagner nor Nie and his colleagues provided any arguments or evidence to support their suggestion.

Assuming for the moment that the levels index is nominal, one can examine its reliability using more appropriate methods than those used by Pierce and Hagner. In their analysis of the index's reliability, they compared the percentage in the main diagonal of the original four-category index to the percentage in the main diagonal of the CAV seven-category index. Obviously, the percentage in the main diagonal of the surrogate index is likely to be less than the corresponding percentage from the original index because the surrogate index has more categories. The same number of "reliable" respondents is being spread over more categories in the CAV index and so they have a much greater chance of switching categories. Thus Pierce and Hagner's (1982, pp. 380–81) finding that the original index places 45 percent in the main diagonal in the 1956–1960 panel and 46 percent in the 1972–1976 panel, while the Nie et al. index places only 31 percent in the main diagonal in the 1956–1960 panel, reveals little about how the reliabilities of the two indexes differ.[2]

One way to compare the reliabilities of the two indexes is to collapse the surrogate index into four categories matching the original index as closely as possible. The problem with doing this is that the categories do not match exactly. For instance, Nie et al. put "nature of the times" com-

1. Personal communication to the author.
2. Pierce and Hagner did not examine the 1972–1976 CAV index because Nie et al. had not yet produced the 1976 coding instructions (the source of Pierce and Hagner's CAV data) when my 1980 article was published.

ments together with apolitical comments at the bottom of their index—below party comments. Campbell et al., on the other hand, make nature of the times their third level, above both apolitical and party comments.[3] For these reasons, several different methods of collapsing the CAV index were examined. These methods yielded from 41 to 45 percent in the main diagonal. Comparing these figures to the 45 and 46 percent for the Pierce and Hagner original index shows that there is little difference.

An alternative way to compare the reliabilities of the two indexes is to use a formal test of reliability. Goodman and Kruskal's (1954, pp. 757–58) "reliability index for unordered variables" is such a measure. Their reliability index is superior to the crude method of adding up the percentages in the main diagonal because their method takes advantage of the information in the main diagonal. Specifically, the Goodman and Kruskal index is a proportional reduction in error (PRE) index. It uses the additional information to calculate the percentage improvement in the prediction by using the first test (i.e., the first application of the measure) to predict the second test over using the modal class of the first test to predict the second.

Goodman and Kruskal's reliability provides a somewhat different result from that of Pierce and Hagner. The reliabilities of both the original and the surrogate indexes over the 1956–1960 panel are identical: .12.

Thus whether one chooses to assume that the indexes are ordinal (the conventional assumption) or nominal, the outcome is the same. The indexes are equally reliable.

3. I discuss this peculiarity in Chapter 3.

Two

The Validity of the Levels

The validity of a measure is both more important and more difficult to assess than its reliability. In general, a measure's validity is the degree to which it reflects the theoretical construct of interest. That is, validity is the degree to which a variable measures what it is supposed to measure. In statistical terms, validity is usually taken to be the absolute value of the product-moment correlation between the observed measure and the unobserved criterion of interest.[1] Thus social scientists often speak of "validity coefficients" when they mean Pearson r's between observed indexes and "true" scores.

The idea of validity and the practice of validating measures are elementary topics in virtually every introductory social science textbook. Yet when Angus Campbell and his colleagues set to work upon the research that eventually led to *The American Voter* and the levels of conceptualization index, they gave scant attention to testing and validating their measure of ideological thinking. They examined the relationship of their new levels index to only two other variables—education and interest in politics (which they called "sense of political involvement"). This hardly

1. This is sometimes referred to as the "theoretical validity." There are other useful ways to explicate the concept of validity (see Lord and Novick [1970, ch. 12]). Carmines and Zeller (1979, ch. 2 and p. 53, nn. 6 and 8) give a somewhat different definition, namely, that validity is the correlation between the true score of the observed measure (i.e., the score corrected for random measurement error) and the unobserved variable of interest (also measured without error). This has the advantage of separating two distinct concepts—reliability and validity. However, it has the disadvantage of relying on two unobserved variables. I use Lord and Novick's definition.

45

constitutes a thorough testing of a newly developed index of a complicated phenomenon. Instead, Campbell et al. relied on what might be called the "face validity" or "content validity" of the levels indexes (Carmines and Zeller 1979; Nunnally 1967).

Essentially, Campbell et al. assumed that when people were asked what they liked and disliked about the parties and candidates, they responded with their basic, innermost likes and dislikes. Because the reasons for liking and disliking the parties and candidates were on display in the responses, Campbell et al. decided that they could assess the ideological sophistication of those reasons. In short, everything was as it seemed; the measures were assumed to have face validity.

Apparently, it never occurred to Campbell and his associates that people might be responding with transitory likes and dislikes—superficial comments that reflected not innermost feelings, but casual likes and dislikes picked up from television, newspapers, recent conversations, and the like. The authors of *The American Voter* did not raise the possibilities that people either were not able to look within themselves and know why they liked or disliked the parties and candidates, or did not feel prompted to do so by the questions. The failure to consider these possibilities is especially peculiar because elsewhere Campbell et al. recognized the difficulty of tapping the original sources of partisan preferences. In discussing the sources of party identification, they declared, "Partisan choice tends to be maintained long after its nonpolitical sources have faded into oblivion" (1960, p. 118). Thus the sources or causes of party identification were thought to be lost to the individual, but the reasons one liked or disliked the parties were thought to be readily available. On the one hand, we have failure in introspection; on the other hand, we have success in introspection—an apparent contradiction.

In defense of *The American Voter*, one might respond that it is not necessary that the evaluations be basic sources. They can just as well be superficial. The crucial assumption is that the evaluations (whether basic or superficial) be in language that reflects the respondent's conceptual framework. The question is, then, whether those who think in ideological terms use ideological labels, whether those who think in terms of group benefits talk about groups, and so on. Thus introspection may not be necessary. Yet having one without the other seems questionable. This is surely something that should be examined. One should not rely on face validity alone.

The Question of Validity

The difficulty in assessing the validity of the levels indexes arises from the fact that we do not have an established criterion variable against which to test the indexes. We cannot check the validity of the levels measures against some previously validated measure of the levels because none exists. Therefore we must rely on the limited and less direct method of construct validation.

The method of construct validation is to correlate a test variable (e.g., the levels index) with a variety of other variables with which, according to theory, the test variable should be correlated. If the strength and direction of all the correlations are as theoretically predicted, then one can infer that the test variable is a valid measure of the construct it is supposed to measure. If the strength and direction of the correlations are not as predicted, then one infers that the test variable is not valid. Construct validation is a limited method because one is forced to rely heavily upon theory. If the theory specifying the correlates of the levels is wrong, the test will not work. This is especially troublesome because none of the theoretical criterion variables (e.g., education, interest in politics, and so forth) comes close to the characteristic I really want to measure—conceptual framework. Moreover, because the state of the theory about the levels is so imprecise (as are most social science theories), I cannot say how strongly the levels indexes would covary with the criterion variables if the levels indexes were perfectly valid. The best I can do is say that the test variable should covary with the criterion variables. Consequently, this method forces me to draw fairly crude conclusions of this form: The measure is valid or the measure is not valid. That is, the method makes me speak of validity as if it were a dichotomy instead of a matter of degree.

Another important aspect of construct validity methods is that they are one sided. Assuming the theory is correct , one can prove that a measure is not valid by showing that the correlations fail to behave as predicted. However, even if the correlations are as predicted, one cannot prove that a measure is valid. Many measures might have the same predicted correlations as the test measure. For instance, almost any measure of political knowledge should correlate with other measures as the levels index does. Thus showing that the levels indexes behave as predicted is consistent with the hypothesis that the indexes are valid, but it does not prove it. For a stronger confirmation, one would have to develop tests of discriminant validity. That is, one would have to identify the variables with which the levels might be confused and show that the levels indexes measured the levels, not the other variables (Campbell and Fiske 1959; Nunnally 1967, ch. 3).

Table 12 presents a set of validity coefficients between four measures of the levels and several criterion variables. The levels indexes are the principal ones discussed in Chapter 1: (1) the original index built by Pierce and Hagner, (2) the surrogate index built by Nie et al., (3) the party component of the Nie et al. index, and (4) the candidate component of the Nie et al. index. The criterion variables are (1) education (scored 1–5), (2) whether the respondent voted and was politically active in any one of four ways (scored 0–2), (3) the number of media in which the respondent followed politics (scored 0–4), (4) external political efficacy (scored 0–2), (5) the CPS political involvement index based on questions about how much the respondent cared who won the presidential race and how interested the respondent was in the campaign (scored 1–8), (6) a political information scale based on whether the respondent knew which party controlled the House before and after the election (scored 0–2), and (7) a party difference scale based on the number of differences be-

TABLE 12.   Correlations Between
Levels Indexes and Criterion Variables

	1956				1960			
	Original Index	Total	Party	Candidate	Original Index	Total	Party	Candidate
Education	.25	.26	.26	.08	.24	.29	.26	.20
Activity	.25	.24	.25	.12	.14	.15	.18	.10
Media	.27	.28	.27	.17	.31	.35	.34	.22
Efficacy	.24	.29	.27	.14	.19	.31	.26	.23
Involvement	.34	.37	.36	.23	.30	.38	.21	.29
Information	*	*	*	*	.32	.39	.37	.23
Party difference	.10	.26	.27	.13	.09	.25	.26	.13
Mean	.24	.28	.28	.14	.23	.30	.29	.19

TABLE 12.   (*continued*)

| | 1964 | | | | 1968 | | | |
	Origi-nal Index	Total	Party	Candi-date	Origi-nal Index	Total	Party	Candi-date
Education	.26	.23	.29	.10	.26	.28	.27	.16
Activity	.22	.23	.27	.12	.23	.24	.27	.17
Media	.27	.10	.10	.05	.27	.30	.29	.19
Efficacy	.16	.14	.17	.09	.17	.15	.16	.10
Involvement	.29	.32	.33	.22	.27	.30	.32	.22
Information	.28	.29	.31	.18	.26	.31	.30	.19
Party difference	.10	.12	.17	.04	.28	.36	.34	.31
Mean	.23	.20	.23	.11	.25	.28	.28	.19

| | 1972 | | | | 1976 | | | |
	Origi-nal Index	Total	Party	Candi-date	Origi-nal Index	Total	Party	Candi-date
Education	.11	.22	.21	.22	.27	.28	.26	.17
Activity	.16	.28	.26	.22	.29	.29	.31	.14
Media	.19	.27	.23	.22	.35	.39	.38	.21
Efficacy	.13	.16	.16	.13	.20	.23	.21	.15
Care	.15	.20	.24	.15	.23	.28	.29	.15
Interest	.20	.31	.28	.26	.33	.38	.37	.24
Information	.18	.29	.32	.23	.35	.40	.42	.20
Party difference	.38	.40	.44	.31	.45	.48	.50	.29
Mean	.19	.27	.27	.22	.31	.34	.34	.19

tween the parties that the respondent sees on the issues (scored 0–10).[2]

The criterion variables were previously used by Hagner and Pierce (1982) in their work on the validity of the original index. Their argument,

2. For details on these variables, see Appendix 2, Hagner and Pierce (1982), and the 1956–1976 CPS American National Election Study codebooks. The

which is certainly correct, is that one should expect those who have better educations, who are politically active, who follow politics through several media, who feel politically efficacious, who feel involved with politics, and who have a good deal of political information to have higher levels of conceptualization than those who are less educated, active, and so forth.

The criterion variables can be roughly grouped into two categories—causes of sophistication and direct measures of sophistication. The causes are education, activity, media attention, involvement, and efficacy. The information and party difference scales measure political knowledge, which is an aspect of sophistication. The causes are something of a mixed bag. Only education is just causally prior to sophistication. The others are probably both causes of and caused by sophistication. For instance, political activity, media attention, and interest in politics all undoubtedly cause people to learn more about politics because they bring people into contact with politics. Greater sophistication also seems likely to lead to more interest, activity, and so forth. Thus two-way causation probably holds for all variables but education.

Although many consider education one of the best measures of sophistication (and it is one of the only two variables that Campbell et al. examine in their efforts to validate the levels index), Converse (1975, 1979, 1980), Wray (1979), and others have found that it is not related to attitude consistency—the other principal measure of political sophistication. This finding is controversial because others who have examined the matter have shown that education is related to consistency if consistency is measured by another, arguably better method (Barton and Parsons 1977; Smith 1982). Moreover, no one has alleged that education is not closely associated with the levels of conceptualization. Still, the status of education as a criterion variable may be challenged. In the articles in which Converse attempts to explain why education and attitude consistency are unrelated, he argues that political interest and involvement are the most important causes of sophistication. So although education has been challenged, interest and involvement have been praised. I use both here.

The two direct measures of political knowledge I use are fine as far as

---

response categories of the questions used to build the involvement scale were changed in 1972; therefore the two questions (care who wins and interest in the outcome) were used in 1972 and 1976. Also, the party difference scale is based on the placement of the two parties on seven point issue scales in 1972 and 1976. The 1972–1976 version of the party difference scale works better than the earlier version.

they go, but they do not go very far. The problem is that the levels indexes supposedly measure the nature of the concepts and abstractions people use when they think about politics, but the information indexes measure knowledge—knowledge of who controls the House of Representatives and of differences between the parties. One may think of knowledge and conceptual sophistication as parts of a broader idea of political sophistication, but the two are theoretically distinct. This is the fundamental problem of using construct validation methods. Because one does not have any direct measures of conceptual sophistication, one must rely on assumptions about the relationships between the observed criterion variables and the unobserved characteristic of interest—conceptual sophistication. For instance, one must assume that those who are conceptually sophisticated will see lots of differences on issues between the two parties, but those who are not sophisticated will not see them. I have no doubt that this assumption is correct, but some may dissent. More to the point, this is an assumption I cannot prove with available data.

The source of the problem is that the CPS National Election Studies do not have an adequate set of information items. Scholarly interest in information questions is weak. Moreover, asking information questions can be difficult because respondents do not like it when they do not know the answers. The NES solution to these problems has been to avoid asking such touchy questions. The result of this policy is that both this study and many others have awkward gaps. (See Chapter 4 for a full discussion of this problem.)

All the correlation coefficients in Table 12 are in the predicted direction, and most are in the moderate to low range of strength.[3] Determining how strong a correlation must be to validate a measure is always difficult. Whether these correlations are high enough to justify saying that the levels indexes are valid is debatable because we do not know how high they would be if the measure were perfect. Correlations averaging .25 provide support for a claim of validity, but not very strongly. Yet given that none of the criterion variables directly measures the use of abstractions in political thinking, which is supposedly what the levels indexes measure, one should probably conclude that these data support the claim that the levels indexes are valid.

Two points about the correlations in Table 12 should be made. First, the candidate component is clearly the weakest of the indexes. Although

3. If these correlations were corrected for unreliability, they would be higher.

comparing correlation coefficients is a crude method of assessing validity, the differences nevertheless seem substantial. Correlations are the standard statistic to use in assessing validity, but comparing them is a method with many weaknesses. Differences in the distributions of either measure or differences in the reliabilities of either measure can cause changes in the correlations. For instance, it seems likely that the low candidate component correlations are mostly the product of the measure's low reliability, rather than the product of a weak underlying relationship. For my purposes, however, a crude method such as comparing correlations is sufficient.

Second, the original levels index does not differ much from either the surrogate overall index or the surrogate party index. The average correlations of the three indexes are virtually identical. Moreover, the original index does not correlate more or less strongly with any of the criterion variables over the six election years. No pattern emerges with which one can distinguish the original index from the surrogates. Therefore I must conclude that the original and surrogate indexes are equally valid measures of the levels of conceptualization.

The finding that the surrogate indexes are as valid as the original index contradicts Pierce and Hagner's position. They maintained that, lacking proof to the contrary, one must assume that the surrogate indexes are invalid versions of the original because the surrogates were built from the CPS Master Codes in a two-step process instead of directly from the interview transcripts, as was the original index.

However, the data indicate that the two measures are equally valid. Moreover, as Table 3 shows, the original level is strongly related to the Nie et al. party level and combined index. Thus Pierce and Hagner's argument that the original level differs from the Nie et al. surrogates is wrong.

An Alternative Hypothesis

Despite these data, the question of validity is not yet settled. That the levels indexes vary with several criterion variables as predicted does not prove validity because many measures vary with the criterion variables in the same way. That is, I do not yet know whether the levels indexes are measuring the "levels of conceptualization" or some related phenomenon.

Before one can safely conclude that the levels indexes are actually measuring the levels, one must consider what else they might be measuring. The most likely alternative is some other aspect of political sophistication. This may seem to be a subtle and unimportant distinction. Subtle it

is, but unimportant it is *not*. Whether one concludes that the public's sophistication did or did not change during the 1960s depends on this critical distinction. The aspect of political sophistication that apparently underlies the levels index is measured by the number of responses given to
the like/dislike questions used to build the indexes.

The case for the number of responses as a measure of political awareness and sophistication is fairly strong. In his classic paper, "The Nature
of Belief Systems in Mass Publics," Converse (1964) argued that the belief systems of ideologues have four characteristics: a great deal of information about politics, a wide range of opinions on political issues, a high
level of attitude consistency, and a high level of conceptualization. The
number of things a person likes and dislikes about the parties and candidates is closely related to the first two characteristics: information and
range of opinions. That is, those who have more to say about the parties
and candidates are more knowledgeable and have more opinions than
those who have less to say. This argument is not new. Kessel (1980,
pp. 275–76) made precisely this argument when he used the number of
responses as his "information level" measure in his study of presidential
voting.

Yet the number of responses may not be a simple measure of political
knowledge and range of opinions. First, as Kessel pointed out, another
variable, how talkative people are, may be a confounding factor. That is,
some people will have more to say because they know more about politics; other people may have more to say because they always have more to
say about everything—whether they know much about it or not. Second,
as Shapiro (1970) showed, some of the variation in number of responses,
or verbosity, can be accounted for by differences in interviewer behavior.
Some interviewers probe more and elicit more responses than others.
These are probably only minor sources of error.

The alternative hypothesis about the number of responses and the levels indexes is that as respondents make more comments about the parties
and candidates, they increase their chances of saying the things that will
raise their scores on the levels indexes. That is, the more one says, the
more likely one will be to mention an issue or say something ideological.
And saying something ideological (even a single comment) makes one at
least a near-ideologue on the CAV scale.

To state the hypothesis more formally: The total number of responses
of any given type (e.g., ideological, group benefit, etc.) can be decom-
posed into the product of the number of responses of all types an individual gives and the probability of a response being of a given type. That is:

$$\begin{vmatrix} \text{Number of} \\ \text{Type X} \\ \text{Responses} \end{vmatrix} = \begin{vmatrix} \text{Total} \\ \text{Number of} \\ \text{Responses} \end{vmatrix} \times \begin{vmatrix} \text{Probability} \\ \text{of Type X} \\ \text{Response} \end{vmatrix}$$

The hypothesis is that political sophistication is measured almost entirely by number of responses, the first term on the right-hand side of the equation.

The alternative hypothesis can best be illustrated by presenting two hypothetical alternatives. First, respondents might consistently evaluate the parties and candidates in language reflecting a single level of conceptualization. For instance, one respondent might talk only about how the parties and candidates help certain groups; another might talk only about how the times have been bad during the past year. In this case, no matter how much a respondent said, he or she would still be placed in the same level on the index. The number of responses would be unrelated to the score on the index.

Second, in each given comment, all respondents might have roughly equal probabilities of giving the various types of responses (e.g., ideological comments or group benefit comments). In this case, as respondents say more things, they steadily increase their chances of saying something that will place them in higher levels on the index. A respondent who makes ten comments has twice the likelihood of saying something ideological as one who makes only five. The greater the number of responses, the higher the probability of saying something ideological and being coded as an ideologue.

My alternative hypothesis, based on the latter possibility, consists of several interrelated propositions, as shown in Figure 6. First, the model states that sophistication causes the number of responses. That is, the number of responses is a measure of political sophistication. The notion of sophistication is information and range of opinions, not the use of abstractions in political thinking. Second, sophistication is also a cause of the content of what people say in their responses to the like/dislike questions. However, this is hypothesized to be a very weak causal connection, as indicated by the broken line. Third, various short-term forces—such as recent news items or political conversations—are the main causes of the content of what people say in evaluating the parties and candidates. These are hypothesized to be the principal causes of response content. In other words, the content of what people say reflects the rhetoric, themes, issues, and controversies of the current campaign. Fourth, the number of

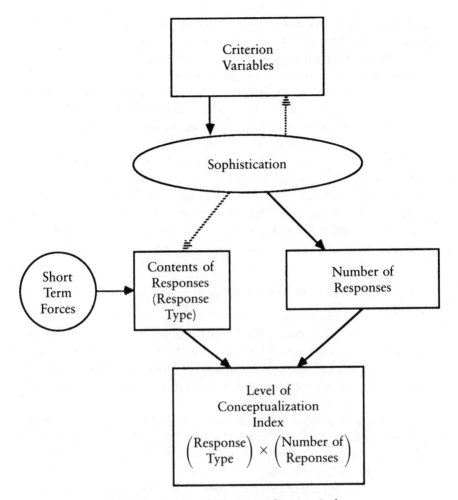

Figure 6. Model of the Levels of Conceptualization Index

Note: Solid lines indicate principal effects. Broken lines indicate weaker effects (including feedback over time).

responses and the content of those responses cause the scores on the levels indexes. Fifth, the criterion variables are both causes of and caused by political sophistication. The direction of the causal connections between the criterion variables and sophistication is not clear. Here I assume that the main causal direction is from the criterion variables to sophistication.

The principal implication of this model can be summed up as follows: The number of responses is the main measure of sophistication, and as such, it is the primary causal link between the criterion variables and the levels indexes. The content of the responses is largely noise (at least insofar as one is interested in measuring sophistication).[4]

The alternative hypothesis may strike some as an ad hoc explanation of the levels index. It is not. To the contrary, it has a solid foundation in psychological theory. Specifically, a great deal of work in the area of attribution theory and its offshoots addresses the problem of how people explain their own behavior—that is, how people answer such questions as, "What is it that you like about So-and-So that might make you want to vote for him?" The findings from these studies indicate that the content of the answers will tell us very little. In other words, the basic premise underlying the levels index—that the answers to the like/dislike questions reveal how people think about politics—is refuted by a good deal of psychological research. I shall return to this subject later.

Anomalous Findings on the Levels

The alternative hypothesis is supported by several findings in the literature. To begin with, about half the population understands the terms "liberal" and "conservative." Converse (1964, pp. 218, 222) reports that only 11.5 percent of the population are ideologues or near-ideologues, but slightly over half the population recognizes and understands the term "conservative."

In the 1960 CPS/SRC study, respondents were first asked to identify the more conservative party and then asked, "What do you have in mind when you say that the Republicans (Democrats) are more conservative than the Democrats (Republicans)?" (Converse 1964, p. 219). On the basis of their responses, Converse developed a measure of "strata of knowledge and understanding" and concluded that about half the population reasonably understood the liberal-conservative distinction.

Following Converse, Pierce (1970) updated Converse's "strata of knowledge and understanding" measure for 1964. The results were the same: Slightly over half the respondents understood the meaning of "conservative." More recently, Luttbeg and Gant (1985) reported that 49 percent of the respondents to the 1980 CPS National Election Survey could come up with reasonable definitions of "conservative," and 42 percent could

4. The content of the responses may be important for many other purposes. The sole concern here is with measuring sophistication.

come up with adequate definitions of both "liberal" and "conservative." Thus knowledge of ideological labels—and hence potential use of them—vastly exceeds their actual use.

Given that the number of people who might use ideological labels is so high, it is easy to suppose that the more comments one makes in response to the like/dislike questions, the more likely one will be to use an ideological label (at least for those who know what the labels mean). People are clearly not using the most sophisticated language at their disposal. Whether they use language reflecting the conceptual frameworks they use in evaluating the parties and candidates or language reflecting what they have heard or read lately is not so clear.

This evidence suggests that the truth falls somewhere between the two hypotheses. The fact that half the population does not understand ideological labels supports the original hypothesis that the levels indexes are valid. Yet the fact that the other half of the population chooses not to use ideological labels is consistent with the alternative hypothesis. The question is, do they not use ideological labels because they do not think in those terms (as the original hypothesis would have it) or because of some more or less random process (as the alternative hypothesis would have it)?

Beyond the matter of the number of people who understand ideological terms is the question of how that number has changed over time. Specifically, as Pierce discovered, it did not change from 1960 to 1964 or from then until the 1980 CPS survey. The interesting aspect of this is that the levels of conceptualization index did change over that period. The great surge in ideological thinking supposedly occurred between 1960 and 1964. Yet while the levels index showed a sharp increase in the number of ideologues, the number who understood this liberal-conservative distinction remained unchanged. In explaining this peculiar disparity, Pierce (1970, p. 34) wrote,

The explanation is probably found in the divergent character of the phenomena examined by the two measures. That is, it would take much less psychological effort for an individual to merely reflect campaign rhetoric emphasizing the ideological character of political agents . . . than for him to increase the mass of information he holds.

In other words, changes over time in the levels result from changes in the campaign rhetoric that one chooses to repeat in one's responses to the like/dislike questions. Such changes are more superficial than changes in the informational base from which the responses are drawn. Thus the content of the responses (i.e., the rhetoric) is a poor indicator of sophistication.

A related finding that supports the same conclusion comes from Field and Anderson. When they built their measure of the levels, they distinguished between those who made explicit and implicit ideological remarks, as well as between ideologues and nonideologues. The "explicit ideologues" were those who used ideological labels; the "implicit ideologues" were those who discussed ideological issues (e.g., government intervention in the market) without using ideological labels. Field and Anderson's (1969, p. 388) distinction led them to an interesting finding: "While the proportion of Implicit Ideologues remains quite stable from one election to the next, the number of people volunteering the actual language of ideology is subject to considerable fluctuation. This suggests that terminology is more easily adopted than is concern for substantive ideological problems."

In other words, Field and Anderson found that there was no increase in the number of those who evaluated the parties and candidates in terms of ideological concerns, only an increase in the number of those who used ideological rhetoric. In light of the fact that the data cover the period from the bland Stevenson-Eisenhower campaign of 1956 to the fiery Johnson-Goldwater campaign of 1964, one must wonder whether there was an increase in the ideological sophistication of the electorate or only an increase in the sophistication of its rhetoric. Aside from the issue of change in sophistication over time, evidence again suggests that the use of ideological rhetoric may not measure political sophistication. This evidence gives further credence to the alternative hypothesis that the number of responses, not the content of those responses, is the key to the levels indexes.

Testing the Alternative Hypothesis

The first step in testing the alternative hypothesis is to assess the number of responses as a measure of political knowledge and sophistication. To do this, I use the same approach used for testing the levels indexes. I begin by looking at the reliability of the number of responses. Rather than examine all the data in detail, I focus on the three most important sets of data—the test-retest correlations, the correlations between the number of party responses and the number of candidate responses, and the multiple

TABLE 13.   Test-Retest Correlations for
Levels Indexes and Number of Responses

	1956–1960	*1972–1976*
Number of party responses	.50	.56
Number of candidate responses	.48	.47
Total number of responses	.57	.60
CAV party levels	.44	.46
CAV candidate levels	.18	.22
CAV total levels	.41	.41
Original levels	.38	.37
N	1,214	671

Source. Data are from the CPS 1956–1960 and 1972–1976 American National Election Studies.

Note: Cell entries are Pearson r's.

indicator models. The first of these, the test-retest correlations, are shown in Table 13.

The test-retest correlations (Pearson r's) for both the levels indexes and the number of responses are presented in Table 13 to facilitate comparison. What stands out most is that all the continuity coefficients for the number of responses are larger than any of the continuity coefficients for the levels indexes. The party questions yield the closest match. Although the continuity coefficients for the number of responses to the party questions are greater than those for the party levels indexes, the differences are modest (.50 versus .44 and .56 versus .46). The differences between the total number of responses and the combined levels indexes are larger; the differences for the candidate questions are larger still.

The most important difference between the number of responses and the levels indexes lies with the candidate questions. With the levels indexes, the candidate measures are far less stable and reliable than the party measures, but with the number of responses, there is little difference. In the 1950s panel, the party and candidate indexes differ by only .02, in the latter panel, by .09. Thus it seems that whatever causes the unreliability and instability in the candidate questions is mostly contained in the content of the questions, not in the number of responses to the questions.

TABLE 14.   Split-Half Reliability Coefficients
for Levels and Number of Responses

	1956	1960	1964	1968	1972	1976
Levels	.29	.30	.30	.34	.37	.33
Number of responses	.55	.51	.50	.53	.52	.56
N	1,762	1,164	1,571	1,557	1,372	2,248

Source. Data are from the 1956–1976 CPS American National Election Studies.

Note: Cell entries are Pearson r's between the indexes (levels or number of responses) based on the party questions and the indexes based on the candidate questions.

Table 14 presents rough split-half reliability coefficients for the levels indexes and the number of responses—that is, the correlations between the party and candidate levels indexes (top row) and between the party and candidate number of responses (bottom row). The number of responses perform far better than the levels indexes. The former have correlations ranging from .50 to .56; the latter have correlations ranging from .29 to .37. Clearly, the number of responses is doing a much better job of measuring the same thing (whatever that is) than the levels indexes are.

The two-wave, two-variable multiple indicator models for the number of responses (shown in Figure 7) yield results that support the conclusions drawn from Tables 13 and 14. The number of responses to the candidate questions are less reliable than the responses to the party questions, but the differences are far smaller than the huge differences found with the levels indexes (see Figure 4). Unfortunately, like the analysis of the levels, the models do not fit the data very well.

In order to investigate the problem further, I use the full three waves of the panel study, with all five measures of the number of responses. The simple three-wave model is shown in Figure 8A. Like the earlier model for the levels indexes, the simple model for the number of responses has a poor fit. In analyzing the levels indexes, I suggested that the most likely theoretical problem with the model was that a separate component influenced the candidate index. This indicated that the two candidate index residuals would be correlated over time. That idea proved correct. The same solution seems likely here. Indeed, when I allow the correlated errors, the model fits quite well (see Figure 8B).

Examination of the final three-wave model and comparison to the earlier model for the levels indexes reveals several important findings. The party levels indexes and the number of responses to the party questions are about equally reliable. But the responses to the candidate questions, on the other hand, behave differently in the two models. In the levels index model, the candidate indexes are very unreliable, with reliability coefficients of only .11 and .16. In the number of responses model, the candidate questions are moderately reliable, with reliability coefficients of .44 and .42. I have already shown that the candidate levels indexes basically do not work. Here the number of responses to the candidate questions work, but not as well as the number of responses to the party questions.

Moreover, the correlated errors between the two candidate response measures indicate the existence of another unobserved variable influencing the candidate measures. Just as with the levels indexes, such a second unobserved variable causing the number of responses does not seem to be consistent with a simple interpretation of the number of responses as a measure of sophistication. The numbers of responses to the party and candidate questions are caused by two distinct latent variables— so which one is the real sophistication? It is a question I cannot answer.

The principal latent variable underlying the number of responses in the three-wave model is very stable, even somewhat more so than the latent variable underlying the levels indexes. This stability is a characteristic that *The American Voter* would associate with sophistication; it is consistent with the conceptual permanence thesis.

As a second step in considering the plausibility of the alternative hypothesis, Table 15 presents the correlations between the number of responses (to the party questions, to the candidate questions, and to all the questions) and the four levels indexes. In general, the correlations are in the moderate to high range. The correlations between the party index and the number of party responses range from .71 to .79 across the six survey years. The correlations for the candidate indexes range from .45 to .64 (again the weakest set of correlations). The correlations between the overall surrogate index and the total number of responses range from .65 to .72. And the correlations between the original index and the total responses range from .32 to .61. The original index correlations for 1972 are far lower than any of the others (all of which cluster around .60). So for some reason, 1972 is an aberrant case.[5] Given the level of the correlations between the indexes and the number of responses, which (with the

5. The most likely reason is the enormous jump in the frequency of issue comments about candidates in 1972.

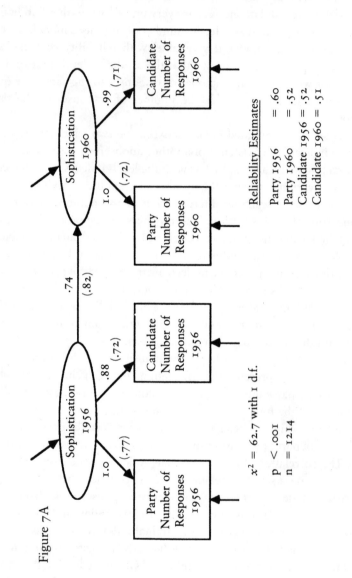

Figure 7A

Reliability Estimates

Party 1956 = .60
Party 1960 = .52
Candidate 1956 = .52
Candidate 1960 = .51

$x^2 = 62.7$ with 1 d.f.

$p < .001$
$n = 1214$

Figure 7B

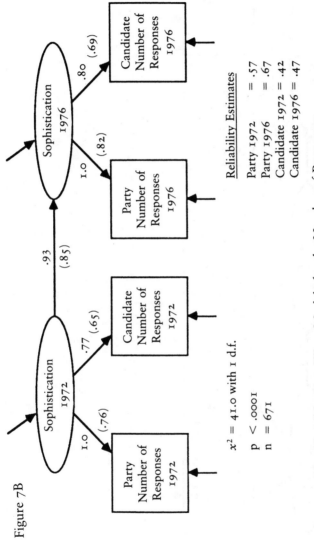

Reliability Estimates

Party 1972   = .57
Party 1976   = .67
Candidate 1972 = .42
Candidate 1976 = .47

$x^2 = 41.0$ with 1 d.f.

p < .0001
n = 671

Figure 7. Two-Variable, Two-Wave Models for the Number of Responses

Source. Data are from the 1956–1960 and 1972–1976 CPS American National Election Studies.

Note: Coefficients are maximum likelihood estimates. Both standardized and unstandardized coefficients are shown. Standardized coefficients are in parentheses.

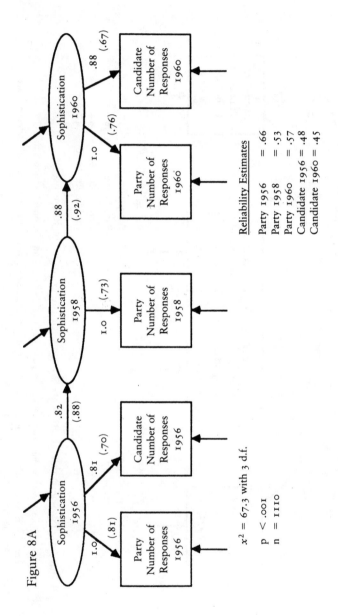

Figure 8A

$x^2 = 67.3$ with 3 d.f.

p < .001
n = 1110

Reliability Estimates

Party 1956 = .66
Party 1958 = .53
Party 1960 = .57
Candidate 1956 = .48
Candidate 1960 = .45

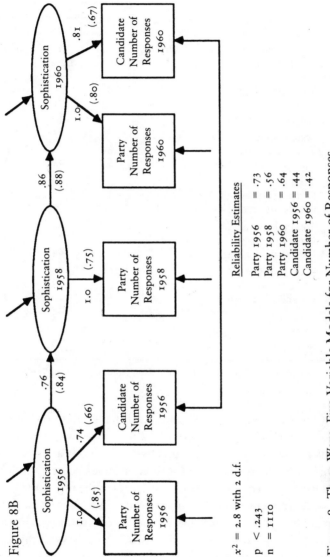

Figure 8B

Reliability Estimates

Party 1956   = .73
Party 1958   = .56
Party 1960   = .64
Candidate 1956 = .44
Candidate 1960 = .42

$x^2 = 2.8$ with 2 d.f.

p < .243
n = 1110

Figure 8. Three-Wave, Five-Variable Models for Number of Responses

Source. Data are from the 1956–1958–1960 CPS American National Election Studies.
Note: Coefficients are maximum likelihood estimates. Both standardized and unstandardized coefficients are shown. Standardized coefficients are in parentheses.

TABLE 15.   Correlations Between the Levels Indexes
and Number of Responses

		Levels Indexes			
Year	Number of Responses	Original Level	Total Level	Party Level	Candidate Level
1956	Total responses	.61	.65	.65	.40
	Party responses	.63	.63	.71	.26
	Candidate responses	.45	.51	.44	.45
1960	Total responses	.60	.70	.71	.45
	Party responses	.60	.64	.74	.26
	Candidate responses	.43	.57	.48	.52
1964	Total responses	.59	.65	.68	.45
	Party responses	.55	.57	.75	.30
	Candidate responses	.45	.55	.43	.49
1968	Total responses	.58	.66	.66	.47
	Party responses	.57	.63	.71	.32
	Candidate responses	.37	.52	.44	.51
1972	Total responses	.32	.68	.70	.56
	Party responses	.25	.58	.78	.35
	Candidate responses	.30	.61	.44	.64
1976	Total responses	.60	.72	.72	.45
	Party responses	.59	.69	.79	.29
	Candidate responses	.48	.58	.48	.51

Source. Data are from the CPS 1956–1976 American National Election Studies.

Note: Cell entries are Pearson r's.

exception of the 1972 original index) are much higher than the validity coefficients shown in Table 12, the alternative hypothesis looks plausible.

As an illustration of the relationship between the levels and the number of responses, Figure 9 shows the mean levels index score by number of responses for 1956. The very small sample sizes at the top of the range of number of responses causes the curve to be a little ragged. Still, the relationship holds over the entire range of number of responses. The relationship in 1956 is typical of that in other years. All behave in the same way, and all are consistent with the hypothesis that the number of responses causes the levels index.

The data on the relationship between the number of responses and the set of criterion variables (shown in Table 16) are similar to the data on the

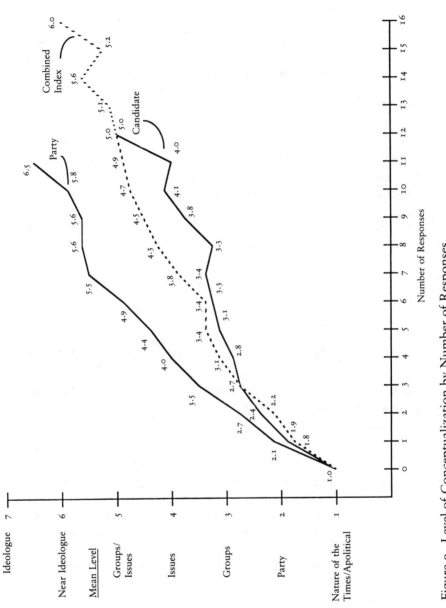

Figure 9. Level of Conceptualization by Number of Responses

TABLE 16. Correlations Between N
of Responses and Criterion Variables

	1956			1960			1964		
	Total	Party	Candi-date	Total	Party	Candi-date	Total	Party	Candi-date
Education	.37	.27	.39	.29	.18	.33	.36	.27	.35
Activity	.34	.30	.31	.18	.14	.16	.26	.26	.19
Media	.40	.33	.38	.38	.29	.35	.10	.10	.07
Efficacy	.34	.27	.33	.30	.22	.31	.22	.17	.20
Involvement	.50	.45	.44	.45	.39	.39	.39	.35	.31
Information	*	*	*	.41	.33	.37	.34	.31	.28
Party difference	.27	.24	.23	.27	.22	.24	.10	.13	.04
Mean	.37	.31	.35	.33	.25	.31	.25	.23	.21

	1968			1972			1976		
	Total	Party	Candi-date	Total	Party	Candi-date	Total	Party	Candi-date
Education	.34	.27	.33	.33	.24	.34	.39	.31	.38
Activity	.30	.26	.26	.35	.30	.32	.33	.31	.26
Media	.37	.32	.33	.34	.27	.32	.46	.39	.43
Efficacy	.18	.15	.16	.21	.16	.21	.24	.19	.23
Involvement	.42	.37	.36	*	*	*	*	*	*
Care	*	*	*	.25	.23	.20	.27	.28	.19
Interest	*	*	*	.40	.32	.38	.44	.40	.39
Information	.33	.29	.28	.34	.28	.32	.45	.42	.38
Party difference	.36	.33	.30	.49	.45	.41	.52	.51	.41
Mean	.33	.28	.29	.34	.28	.31	.39	.35	.33

Source. Data are from the CPS 1956–1976 American National Election Studies.

Note: Cell entries are Pearson r's.

Key: Total = total number of responses to like/dislike questions, 0–24. Party = number of responses to party questions, 0–12. Candidate = number of responses to candidate questions, 0–12. * = data not available.

levels indexes in Table 12. The data support the interpretation of the number of responses as measures of political knowledge and sophistication, although again not very strongly. All the correlations are in the predicted direction and roughly of the same magnitude as the correlations between the levels indexes and the criterion variables. I have now traced a potential causal path from the criterion variables to the number of responses and then to the levels indexes.

The alternative causal path from the criterion variables to the levels is through the content of the responses. The question one must ask when assessing that path is, given that a person says something that he or she likes or dislikes about a candidate or party, does it matter what that thing is? An important breakthrough on the problem of interpreting the substantive content of the responses to the like/dislike questions was recently made by David Glass (1985). Glass examined what sorts of people talk about personalities in their evaluations of presidential candidates. He was testing the widely held belief that because comments about the candidates' personalities are supposedly "less sophisticated" than comments about controversial issues and ideological matters, those who are more educated and more knowledgeable about politics are less likely to talk about personalities than those who are less educated and knowledgeable.

Glass made two important discoveries. First, he found that the better educated and more sophisticated generally say more about everything. They say more about personalities, issues, and everything else than do the less educated and sophisticated. It follows that by counting the number of comments a respondent makes about personalities or issues, the investigator confuses the likelihood that a respondent will mention something on any given response with the number of things the respondent mentions. Thus to make sense of the data, one must calculate types of responses as percentages of the total number of responses given by each respondent (e.g., what percentage of a respondent's comments were about issues, about group benefits, etc). That way the number of responses and their substantive content can be distinguished. The substantive content is thus measured as the probability that the respondent will give a response of a particular type.

Second, Glass found that the better educated and more sophisticated make a higher percentage of their comments about personalities than the less educated and sophisticated. More important, there are no differences in the likelihoods of talking about issues. That is, the more educated are more likely to say things about issues because they say more about everything, not because a higher percentage of their responses is about issues. When we look at each respondent's percentages of comments about issues, the well-educated are no more likely to talk about issues than the poorly educated.

At another electoral level, Fuchs and Shapiro (1983, p. 546) had a similar finding. In their analysis of a 1975 survey of voting in Chicago city elections, they examined the responses to open-ended questions that sought voters' explanations for their choices. The best educated were most likely to cite candidates' personal qualities in explaining their votes; the least educated were most likely to cite political experience and performance in office. Thus the least educated use what are normally considered more sophisticated standards than the best educated.

The implication of Glass's and Fuchs and Shapiro's findings is that the more educated and politically aware receive higher scores on the levels indexes because they talk more, not because a higher percentage of their responses is about issues and other supposedly "sophisticated" subjects. Moreover, there may not be any difference between the more and less politically aware in their probabilities of talking about supposedly sophisticated things.

In order to examine the substantive content of the responses with respect to the levels, I created a set of variables that are the types of responses as percentages of each respondent's total number of responses. The types of responses are the six categories developed by Nie et al. (1976) for use in building their levels indexes. The types are (1) explicit ideological references (e.g., using terms such as "liberal" or "conservative"), (2) implicit ideological references (e.g., comments on such implicitly ideological topics as big government or the welfare state), (3) issue references (i.e., comments about issues), (4) group references (e.g., comments about blacks or unions), (5) party references (i.e., comments about the two parties), and (6) nature of the times references (e.g., comments about whether the times have been good or bad lately).[6]

Given these measures of the content of the responses, a third step in testing the alternative hypothesis is to examine the correlations between the response types and the criterion variables. The model predicts that they will be weak or nonexistent. As Table 17 shows, that is the case.

---

6. For a description of the types, see Nie et al. (1976, ap. 2). The exact codes stated in the appendix are incorrect. For the actual codes, contact Nie, Verba, or Petrocik.

TABLE 17. Correlations Between Criterion Variables
and Response Types

Responses to Party Questions

	Edu-cation	Activ-ity	Care	Inter-est	In-volve-ment	Me-dia	Infor-ma-tion	Party Differ-ence	Effi-cacy	Mean
Explicit	.20	.13	.09	.10	.13	.14	.14	.16	.12	.13
Implicit	.19	.14	.11	.15	.14	.15	.21	.20	.13	.16
Issues	.03	.05	.14	.12	.12	.08	.09	.15	.04	.09
Groups	−.04	.05	.10	.09	.07	.05	.05	.00	.03	.09
Nature of times	−.09	−.02	.06	.04	.00	−.02	.02	.00	−.04	−.01
Parties	.03	.04	.07	.08	−.02	.04	.03	.04	.03	.04

Responses to Candidate Questions

	Edu-cation	Activ-ity	Care	Inter-est	In-volve-ment	Me-dia	Infor-ma-tion	Party Differ-ence	Effi-cacy	Mean
Explicit	.09	.06	.04	.07	.06	.06	.10	.04	.05	.06
Implicit	.01	.04	.06	.06	.07	.03	.03	.07	.01	.04
Issues	.04	.03	.05	.09	.01	.05	.07	.07	.05	.05
Groups	−.13	.02	.02	.01	.02	−.02	−.05	.00	−.04	−.02
Nature of times	−.02	−.02	.00	−.02	.00	−.04	−.03	−.02	.00	−.02
Parties	.02	.03	.08	.08	.02	.03	.05	.04	.06	.05

Source. Data are from the CPS 1956–1976 American National Election Studies.

Note: Cell entries are average correlations between the criterion variables and the response types. The response types are the percentage of each respondent's comments that are explicitly ideological, implicitly ideological, about issues, groups, and so forth.

Because presenting all the correlations from each of the six sample years would take so much space, Table 17 presents the average correlations between the response types and the criterion variables (mean r from the six samples 1956–1976). The party comments in the top half of the table reveal that only the implicit and explicit ideological comments show any sort of consistent relationship with the criterion variables, and that

TABLE 18. Regression of Response Types on Criterion Variables

Responses to Party Questions

	Education	Activity	Care	Interest	Involvement	Media	Information	Party Difference	Efficacy	R̄²	Net Impact
Explicit	1.2	0.9	0.6	-0.3	0.2	0.4	0.5	0.5	0.6	.06	16.8%
Implicit	1.2	1.2	0.2	0.2	0.4	0.2	2.4	0.9	0.5	.08	25.6
Issues	-0.6	-0.2	2.2	0.4	1.1	0.7	0.8	0.9	-0.2	.03	17.9
Groups	-1.6	1.4	0.9	0.4	1.1	0.4	0.6	-0.8	0.4	.04	-0.3
Nature of times	-1.0	-0.1	0.4	0.2	0.3	-0.1	0.6	0.1	-0.7	.01	0.3
Parties	0.2	-0.4	0.9	0.9	0.8	0.1	0.2	0.3	-0.2	.00	9.0

Responses to Candidate Questions

	Education	Activity	Care	Interest	Involvement	Media	Information	Party Difference	Efficacy	R̄²	Net Impact
Explicit	0.3	0.2	0.0	0.1	0.0	0.0	0.4	0.0	0.2	.02	2.8%
Implicit	-0.1	0.4	0.4	-0.1	0.2	-0.1	0.1	0.2	-0.2	.01	3.2
Issues	0.1	0.0	-0.1	0.8	0.1	0.1	0.2	0.4	0.7	.01	7.3
Groups	-1.4	0.2	0.3	0.4	0.2	0.1	-0.4	0.0	-0.2	.03	-4.6
Nature of times	0.0	0.1	0.0	0.0	0.1	-0.3	-0.2	0.0	0.2	.00	-0.3
Parties	-0.2	0.3	1.2	0.5	0.4	0.0	0.8	-0.1	1.0	.00	5.2

Source. Data are from the CPS 1956–1976 American National Election Studies.

Note: Each row is an equation. The coefficients (unstandardized b's) are the averages for the six surveys. The dependent variables are the percentages of each respondent's comments that are explicitly ideological, implicitly ideological, about issues, groups, and so forth.

relationship is not very strong. The other response types show smaller correlations, many of which are substantively trivial. Moreover, many of the individual correlations from the different samples that went into the average correlations were statistically insignificant (in general, correlations had to be .05 or greater to be significant at the .05 level).

The candidate comments in the lower half of Table 17 indicate that none of the response types shows a consistent relationship with the criterion variables. The explicit ideological comments work best, but correlations ranging from .04 to .10 are substantively trivial. In other words, the content of the responses to the candidate questions is just barely related to the criterion variables.

Before discussing the implications of these data, I take the analysis one step further by regressing each of the percentage response type variables of the set of criterion variables. These data are shown in Table 18. Again, because six sets of equations would take so much space, Table 18 reports average regression coefficients (the mean of the coefficients from the six equations).

Because the dependent variables are percentages, the coefficients are easy to interpret. Consider, for instance, the coefficient in the upper left-hand corner of the table. On average, a one-unit change in education yields a 1.2 percent change in the percentage of ideological comments. Because education is scored 1-5, it follows that the difference between the most and the least educated (holding all other variables constant) is 4.8 percent (i.e., the range, 4, times the coefficient, 1.2, equals 4.8). Multiplying the range and the coefficient for each variable in an equation and adding up the results yields the difference between the most educated, active, involved, and so forth and the least educated, active, involved, and so forth respondents.

In Table 18, this difference between the most and least sophisticated respondents is called the "net impact" of the equation. That piece of information is shown in the rightmost column in Table 18. Thus for the first equation, the most sophisticated are 16.8 percent more likely than the least sophisticated to make an explicit ideological comment on any given response.

Several observations should be made about Table 18. First, the party response variables work far better than the candidate variables. The party coefficients are larger than the candidate coefficients, the explained variances in the equations are larger, and the net impacts of the equations are larger. Second, few of the equations work well. The explicit and implicit party response equations work the best, explaining 6 and 8 percent of the variance, respectively, and accounting for changes of 16.8 and 25.6 percent in the dependent variables. Yet even with these two equations, many of the individual coefficients are not statistically significant, and two of the significant coefficients are in the wrong direction.

Beyond these two equations, little else works at all. The adjusted R squares range from 0 to .04. Few of the coefficients are statistically significant. The net impacts are substantively trivial. Consider, for instance, the percentage of explicitly ideological comments made in response to the candidate questions: 2 percent of the variance is explained by the equation, seven of the forty-three coefficients are statistically insignificant, and the impact is only 2.8 percent.

The last statistic deserves special attention. The net impact is the difference between the most and least sophisticated. The most sophisticated are the college educated who are politically active, who are interested in politics, who follow politics in all four media, who know which party controls Congress, who both have opinions on the major issues of the day and see differences between the parties on those issues, and who feel politically efficacious. The least sophisticated are those who did not finish the eighth grade, who are inactive, who are not interested, who do not follow politics in any media, who do not know which party controls Congress or have opinions on any of the leading issues, and who feel politically inefficacious. Yet the difference between these two types of people, who are worlds apart, is a mere 2.8 percent in their likelihoods of making explicit ideological comments. The only reasonable conclusion is that the percentage of explicit ideological comments made when evaluating the candidates tells us nothing.

Scanning the column of net impacts shows that only the top three party categories—ideological comments and issue comments—are influenced much by the criterion variables. A few of the categories are not influenced at all. Specifically, party group benefits comments and both party and candidate nature of the times comments show no change at all. That is, all types of respondents, from the most to the least sophisticated, are equally likely to make such comments.

Looking at the column of adjusted R squares yields another disturbing finding. Many of the equations fail to explain any variance at all. There is simply no statistically significant difference between the most and least sophisticated respondents according to the criterion variables. Specifically, none of the twelve equations predicting party responses to either

the party or candidate questions or the six equations predicting party responses to either the party or candidate questions works. For that matter,
a majority of the thirty-six equations (six years with six dependent variables per year) explaining responses to the candidate questions fail to explain anything.

The failure of these equations to predict anything indicates a serious
validity problem. Consider people who referred to parties in their responses to either the party or candidate questions. These responses are
supposedly the least sophisticated type of comments possible. Yet people
who are very sophisticated or very unsophisticated are equally likely to
make those responses. The adjusted R squares of zero for those equations
indicate that there are no differences other than random ones. Why then
are these comments and the associated type of thinking considered unsophisticated? The answer is because of a mistake. The validity of the levels index was never adequately investigated. It was built on a foundation
of untested assumptions.

Both the adjusted R squares and the net impacts reveal that a general
validity problem confronts the levels indexes. Several of the response
types—each of which is associated with a level—are indistinguishable
from one another. Thus even if these questions might yield a valid measure of sophistication, this index and these levels do not appear to correspond to any real differences in conceptualization.

Stop and think about these findings for a moment. This is the most
important evidence about the validity of the levels indexes that we have.
Consider the candidate questions. Can the responses to the candidate
questions really measure anything about ideological thinking and sophistication if they are so weakly related to the criterion variables? The criterion variables do not measure the precise aspect of sophistication that the
levels indexes are supposed to measure, but can the relationship really be
so weak (and nonexistent in many cases)? I believe the answer is no.

The inevitable implication of these data is that the levels indexes are
based on a false assumption, namely, that the content of the responses to
the like/dislike questions reveals the frame of reference or level of conceptualization in which the respondents think when they evaluate the parties
and candidates. The data certainly support the much weaker assumption
that people who make explicit or implicit ideological comments and issue
comments about the parties are more sophisticated than those who
do not, but that seems to be all. The other types of party comments and
all types of the candidate comments are more or less evenly distributed

throughout the population. Thus building an index of sophistication on the *content* of the like/dislike responses to the party question seems difficult. Building an index based on the content of the candidate questions seems impossible.

Discussion

To summarize the findings up to this point, the levels indexes were designed as measures of ideological thinking. The assumption underlying the design of the indexes was that people would reveal their levels of sophistication, or ways of thinking about politics, in what they said about the parties and candidates. The previous data show that the assumption was wrong. The substantive content of the responses reveals little about the respondents' sophistication. In fact, comment by comment, the more informed, interested, active, and educated citizens are only sightly more likely than the less informed and interested citizens to say "sophisticated" things in response to the party questions. There is no substantive difference at all in the responses to the candidate questions.

On the other hand, the more informed and interested are more likely to have many more things of all types to say about the parties and candidates. Given that most response types are about equally likely throughout the population (especially in response to the candidate questions), the more one says, the more likely one will be to say something that will move one up the levels index. Thus the levels indexes are associated with other measures of political sophistication mainly because they reflect the number of responses to the like/dislike questions.

Given these findings, it follows that the levels indexes are not measuring the "levels of conceptualization." They are not valid measures. The explanation is simple. Separating the content of the responses from the number of responses reveals that the content of the party responses is very weakly related to sophistication, and the content of the candidate responses is not related at all. Yet the number of responses is related to sophistication. Thus the number of responses accounts for the correlation between the levels indexes and the criterion variables.

The levels indexes do measure sophistication, albeit crudely. But the levels measure sophistication only because they reflect the number of responses, which measure sophistication. What the levels indexes do not measure is the "levels of conceptualization"—that is, the different modes of thinking. In that sense and that sense alone, the levels indexes are not valid.

There are two reasons that the indexes do not measure the level of conceptualization construct. First, the levels indexes are supposed to measure the level of abstract thinking by analyzing the content of the responses to the like/dislike questions. They do not. In fact, the levels indexes largely reflect the number of responses, not the content. The number of responses is a *continuous* measure of political knowledge and range of opinions. The theory of the levels implies that there is some sort of discrete difference in ways of thinking about politics between one level and another. So if the indexes are a continuous function of knowledge and range of opinions, they are not measuring the levels of conceptualization.

Second, this examination of the response types revealed little support for the hierarchy of levels assumed in the levels index. People who commented on parties in their responses, for instance, were not detectably more or less sophisticated than those who did not, or who made other types of responses. Because party, nature of the times, and group benefit responses are not distinct and are not related to sophistication (as measured by the criterion variables), it would seem that the levels associated with each of these response types are really not distinct. That is, the data show that there are no differences among most of the levels.

This analysis explains the difference between *The American Voter*'s original four levels and *The Changing American Voter*'s seven levels. The shift from four levels to seven is certainly peculiar. If there were really four modes of thought, why did a different group of investigators find seven? (Nie, Verba, and Petrocik offer no explanation.)

Even more puzzling is the change in the order of the levels. According to *The American Voter,* "nature of the times" thinking characterizes the third level, and thinking about politics without any issue content (including using party labels) characterizes the lowest level. Yet according to *The Changing American Voter,* nature of the times thinking and apolitical thinking characterize the lowest level, and thinking in terms of parties characterizes the next higher level. That is, comments about nature of the times and about parties are reversed in the scale of levels from *The American Voter* to *The Changing American Voter.*

Both the change in the number of levels and the change in the order of the levels indicate a validity problem. Obviously, if the levels measure ways of thinking about politics, one of the scales has to be wrong. Despite the change in the number of levels and the change in the order of the levels, however, both measures seem to work equally well. This paradox requires an explanation.

If the levels indexes measure the number of responses, rather than the levels of conceptualization, the explanation is easy. Because the number of responses is a continuous variable, it does not matter how many levels are included in the index. The number of levels is arbitrary.[7]

Moreover, if the more sophisticated respondents are more likely to give all types of responses, then the order of the levels is also partly arbitrary. Giving more responses should move one up the scale no matter what the order of categories on that scale. Consider, for instance, Glass's finding that the most educated and sophisticated are more likely to talk about personalities than the less educated and sophisticated. Both Campbell et al. and Nie et al. raised respondents to the highest level justified by their most sophisticated responses. Ideological comments were defined as the most sophisticated. Because knowledgeable and sophisticated respondents talk the most, they are most likely to say something ideological and are thus most likely to be raised to the highest level. However, had personality comments been defined as the most sophisticated, the same outcome would have resulted. The most sophisticated are most likely to say things about the candidates' personalities, and thus would be most likely to be raised to the highest level.

Let me raise a question about the burden of proof. Some may not find the evidence sufficient to convince them that the levels indexes measure sophistication, but not the levels of conceptualization per se. They may decide that because no direct measures of abstract thinking were included among the criterion variables, it follows that nothing has disproven the validity of the levels indexes. (The point that no measures of abstract thinking are available in the data sets in which the levels indexes exist and thus no such test can be made would, I suppose, have to be deemed irrelevant.) According to this view, the burden of proof lies with the critic of the levels. In effect, the null hypothesis is that the levels indexes are valid. The critic must provide a thoroughly convincing case before he or she is taken seriously.

Although I certainly think I have provided a convincing case that the levels are not valid, I also think that the burden of proof should lie more with the defenders of the levels than with its critics. To see why, recall the logic of hypothesis testing. Two types of errors are possible when testing

7. The precise location of the levels is also arbitrary. Hagner and Pierce (1982, p. 785) argue that because the original and surrogate indexes yield different numbers of ideologues, the surrogate index must not be valid. However, if the indexes reflect a continuous variable, the boundaries separating the levels are arbitrary. Any set of demarcations will yield an ordinal scale.

hypotheses. A "Type I" error is to conclude that a hypothesis is true when it is, in fact, false. A "Type II" error is to conclude that a hypothesis is false when it is, in fact, true. The scientific method is to lean toward making Type II errors. The justification for this is that we do not wish to add false hypotheses to our accumulation of knowledge. As in Mark Twain's famous line, what worries us most is what we know that ain't so.

To assume that the levels indexes are valid and to accept findings based on them runs the risk of making a Type I error. One risks making "findings" that are not true and building theories on a false foundation. To put first things first, one must be certain that the levels indexes can be trusted before accepting findings that depend on their validity. Simply because the levels indexes have been in use for some time does not eliminate the need to know that they are measuring what they are supposed to measure.

Probably the main reason some will assume the levels indexes are valid until proven otherwise is the enormous prestige of *The American Voter.* Yet what did Campbell et al. do? They relied on face validity. They accepted the levels indexes as valid because they believed that when people said that they liked or disliked a candidate or party for some reason, there was no cause to doubt them. Beyond saying that the levels indexes were valid because the measurement process seemed like a reasonable one to them, Campbell and his colleagues did little to validate the indexes. They examined the relationship of the levels indexes with only two other variables—education and involvement in politics.

Had Campbell and his colleagues tested the levels indexes more extensively, they would have found that while the number of responses covaried with all the criterion variables, the content of the responses was only weakly related to the criterion variables. What would they have done? I believe they would have decided that the levels indexes did not work. Before they or anyone else invested the time, effort, and resources in developing and using the levels indexes, they would have approached the problem differently. Upon seeing the evidence presented here, they would have rejected the indexes because they could not be certain that they were valid.

This is the key to the defense of the levels. An enormous amount of time and resources was invested in the assumption that the levels indexes are valid. Many articles scattered over a dozen or more journals and books represent a great investment by scholars. To conclude that the levels indexes are not valid is, in some sense, to lose that investment. Thus the burden of proof, some will argue, must lie with the critic.

That is not an acceptable argument. The logic used to justify the preference for Type II errors remains unchallenged. If there is some serious doubt as to the validity of the levels indexes, one must assume that they do not work. The alternative is to run the risk of investing still more time and resources in a faulty foundation and throwing good research dollars after bad.

Explaining the Failure of the Levels Indexes

The failure of the levels indexes raises the problem of what went wrong. Two hypotheses deserve consideration. First, the levels of conceptualization might not exist. Second, the levels indexes might not work because the like/dislike questions might not be capable of measuring the levels.

The Existence of the Levels of Conceptualization

There is no evidence, aside from the levels indexes themselves, that there is such a phenomenon as level of conceptualization. That is, we have no independent verification that there are different modes of thinking, as Campbell et al. claimed.

There are two types of independent verification that someone might be able to produce. First, investigators could develop measures so that one could directly validate the levels index. The key difficulty facing this approach is that discriminating between the levels of conceptualization and virtually any other measure of political sophistication is extremely difficult.

Several investigators have put forth data analyses that they claim validate the levels index (Cassel 1982; Hagner and Pierce 1982, 1983; Jacoby 1986). These analyses are similar to the one presented in Table 12. (They differ only in that they are less extensive. They use fewer variables and cover fewer years.) Like the analysis of Table 12, their shortcoming is that they only manage to show that the levels index covaries with other measures of sophistication. Thus they demonstrate only that the levels index measures sophistication; they do not demonstrate that the levels index actually measures different ways of thinking about politics. To validate the levels index, one must show that the levels measure distinct ways of thinking about politics—ideological conceptualization, group benefits conceptualization, and so forth. This is a problem of discriminant validity, and so far no one has come up with a way of solving it.

The second way to provide independent verification of the levels' existence is to identify some highly similar findings in another field. Suppose, for example, that cognitive psychologists had developed a theory of "levels of abstraction," had argued that these levels represent different modes of thinking about events, and had found that there happen to be four or seven such levels (ideological abstractions, group abstractions, and so forth). Psychologists might have done so by nonsurvey methods—experimentation, clinical observation, or whatever. Given such similar findings from a parallel field, one could conclude that one had found independent verification.

Indeed, when one thinks about the focus of cognitive psychology on learning, memory, thinking processes, and related topics, one should positively *expect* cognitive psychologists to come up with independent verification of the existence of the levels if they do, in fact, exist. After all, there are far more psychologists working on such matters than political scientists, and the problem properly falls within the range of problems psychologists deal with. Therefore the lack of such supporting evidence from psychology would indicate that the levels indexes are not valid. In light of this point, let us see what psychologists have to say about the levels.

To begin with, when Campbell, Converse, Miller, and Stokes devised their level of conceptualization theory, they did so without recourse to any existing psychological theory. There is but one single reference to any psychologists in the chapter in which Campbell et al. develop their theory of the levels, and that reference just calls up an anecdote to serve as the starting point of the discussion (Campbell et al. 1960, pp. 218–19).[8] So the theory of the levels is not taken from any previous work in psychology.

Does psychological theory have anything to say about how people think about politics? A great deal has been written in the field of cognitive psychology about how people learn and organize their thinking. In fact, what are probably the two predominant models of political thinking in use by political scientists today—schema theory (Bartlett 1932; Bobrow

---

8. The reference is to Smith et al. (1956). Campbell et al. recited the tale of "Sam Hodder," a factory worker with a grade school education who was unfamiliar with such terms as "socialism," "liberalism," and "veto." Campbell et al. did not cite any theories in relation to Sam Hodder; they merely related his description to serve as a starting point for their discussion of the levels.

and Norman 1975; Kelly 1955; Markus 1977; Neisser 1976; Piaget 1951; Rumelhart and Ortony 1977) and information processing theory (Lachman et al. 1979; Miller 1974; Neisser 1967; Newell and Simon 1961, 1972, 1976; Simon and Newell 1964) are both taken from cognitive psychology.

In addition, the question of cognitive limitations on the ability to think abstractly is one of the major focuses of research in educational psychology (Bruner et al. 1956; Flavell 1963; Gagne 1970; Guilford 1967; Lerner 1976; Meeker 1969). Thus a great wealth of knowledge has been accumulated by other fields in the social sciences, especially psychology, that is relevant to studying the levels of conceptualization and how people think about politics.

Yet virtually none of the findings and theories developed in other fields have found their way into discussions of the levels of conceptualization. Campbell et al., and the many others who used the levels indexes later, largely ignored the other relevant fields such as psychology. Throughout the literature on the levels, there are astonishingly few references to the literature outside of political science. The scholars who studied the levels, and for that matter those who studied most aspects of belief systems, independently developed a political psychology that was isolated from mainstream psychology. In effect, political scientists reinvented the study of psychology. Indeed, political scientists have only fairly recently brought some psychological theories to bear on political thinking and the study of belief systems (e.g., Axelrod 1973; Conover and Feldman 1980, 1984; Graber 1984b; Zaller 1984), and none of these investigators deals with the levels of conceptualization.

What one can learn from psychology is that political scientists are alone in their belief that the levels of conceptualization exist. No support can be found for the theory at all. There are theories that explain the same subjects as the levels of conceptualization theory (e.g., schema theory), but they are not the same as the levels theory.[9] There is just no corresponding model.

___

9. If anything, schema theory is a replacement for levels theory and much of the rest of belief systems theory. For an excellent description of schema theory and its application to political thinking, see Conover and Feldman (1984). Occasionally, one hears people grumble that the innumerable studies of attitude consistency and the levels have not provided much new information about how people think about politics. In response to this, Conover and Feldman suggested that schema theory may provide a way to move beyond our current limitations. I have no doubt that they are right.

The bottom line is that there is no independent verification for the existence of the levels from psychology or from any other discipline. The entire basis of support for the levels theory comes from the fact that when Campbell et al. looked at the responses to the like/dislike questions from 1956, they believed that they could distinguish four different types of responses, and that those response types could be ordered in terms of degree of abstraction. When cognitive psychologists studied the same problem, they drew much different conclusions. They found evidence for schema theory, information processing theory, and other related theories, but nothing that resembles level of conceptualization theory. In other words, they answered the same question in a very different way.

To summarize, there is no evidence that the levels of conceptualization exist. Direct attempts to validate the levels indexes have done no more than show that the indexes measure sophistication. There has been no evidence to show that the levels reveal different ways of thinking about politics. Moreover, there have been no attempts to validate the levels indexes by producing supporting evidence from another discipline. Campbell et al. did not draw upon any existing psychological theory when they devised their levels of conceptualization theory, and for that matter, no psychological theory supports the levels theory anyway.

We believed that the levels of conceptualization exist because the authors of *The American Voter* told us that it was so. They believed because the levels indexes had face validity. It made sense that people voted for the candidates because of the reasons that they gave in response to the like/dislike questions. Those reasons seemed to group into four types, which became the levels of conceptualization.

Face validity alone is not enough. Given the findings presented previously, Campbell et al. would probably have abandoned the idea of levels of conceptualization. So we, too, should abandon it. The evidence that the levels exist is too slim. Unless someone presents new support for the levels, we should conclude that their existence is an interesting but unproven hypothesis.

The Failure of the Like/Dislike Questions

The second general explanation for the failure of the levels indexes is that the questions used to measure the levels might not work. Another set of questions might be needed. Indeed, the assumption that the answers to the like/dislike questions reveal much of interest about the respondent might be wrong. That is, there might be a general problem with the like/dislike questions.

The Superficial Content Hypothesis.   The assumption underlying most interpretations of the questions is that when respondents are asked what they like and dislike, their answers will reveal some fundamental attitudes about the parties and candidates. The authors of *The American Voter* examined these supposedly fundamental attitudes in order to infer the conceptual level at which the respondents thought about politics. But suppose that respondents briefly search their memories for a few things that they like and dislike. More politically astute respondents search their memories longer and have more to say, but no matter how sophisticated they are, the comments do not reveal their fundamental attitudes. Instead, the responses reveal more casual likes and dislikes, such as what the respondent has read in the papers recently or heard on television or in a conversation with a friend. Such superficial comments would not yield much explanatory power about anything. This would explain why the content of the responses to the like/dislike questions is so weakly related to the criterion variables.

If the content of the questions has some explanatory power when used in another setting, one would have to conclude that the superficial content hypothesis is false. Finding that the content did not explain anything in another context, however, would lend support to the superficial content hypothesis.

One well-known use of the questions in a different context is the Michigan Six Component Model of presidential voting (Campbell et al. 1960; Stokes 1966; Stokes et al. 1958). The Six Component Model divides responses to the like/dislike questions into six dimensions—attitudes toward the Democratic candidate, attitudes toward the Republican candidate, attitudes related to group benefits, attitudes on domestic policy issues, attitudes on foreign policy issues, and attitudes toward party performance and the parties as managers of government. The number of comments both for and against the parties and candidates are counted for each dimension, and net partisan scales are calculated. That is, each scale is equal to the number of pro-Democratic comments and anti-Republican comments minus the number of anti-Democratic and pro-Republican comments. The six scales, or components, are then used to predict presidential voting.

The question here is whether the Six Component Model has any greater predictive power than a single scale constructed by adding up all the comments.[10] More precisely, the content of the responses would be ignored, and the simple scale would be the number of pro-Democratic comments plus the number of anti-Republican comments less the number of pro-Republican comments and anti-Democratic comments. Such a single scale model of presidential voting has been used before. Kelley and Mirer (1974) developed a model in which the vote was predicted to be either for the candidate who received the higher score or, in the event of a tie, for the candidate of the voter's party identification.[11] Thus I shall be using the Kelley-Mirer model without party identification as a tiebreaker.

If separating the responses into six components yields a more accurate prediction of the vote than using all the responses indiscriminately in a single scale, the substantive content of the responses (as defined by the six components) has some predictive power. If, however, the single scale predicts as well as the six scales, then the substantive content of the responses has no predictive power.

Michael Kagay (1983) performed such an analysis for the 1952–1968 CPS National Election Studies. Kagay's interest in comparing the Six Component Model to the Kelley-Mirer rule was different from mine. He sought to show that the two seemingly different models are basically the same and can be used interchangeably. I offer an alternative interpretation of his data.

Kagay's data strongly support the hypothesis that there is no predictive power in the substantive content of the responses. Kagay reported two findings of interest. First, he compared the predictive power of the two models, as measured by adjusted R squares, for the five presidential elections from 1952 to 1968 (see Table 19). He found that in 1952 and 1956, there were no statistically significant differences in the predictive power of the two models. Separating the responses into six components made no difference whatsoever. In 1960, 1964, and 1968, statistically significant differences did exist; however, they were so small as to be completely unimportant. The differences in adjusted R square between the two models ranged from .003 to .006 percent—statistically significant to be sure, but substantively trivial.

Second, Kagay examined the regression coefficients of the Six Component Model for the five years (see Table 20). If the substantive content of the responses were meaningless, the responses would be interchangeable across the six dimensions. For instance, a comment about a candidate

10. The Six Component Model has been questioned before (Shaffer 1972), but the critique had shortcomings (Fiorina 1976; see also Shaffer 1976).

11. See also Kelley (1983).

TABLE 19. Comparison of Six Component
and Kelley-Mirer Models

Year	$\bar{R}^2$ for Component Model	$\bar{R}^2$ for Kelley-Mirer Model	Significance of Difference
1952	.531	.530	n.s.
1956	.508	.507	n.s.
1960*	.571	.568	p < .05
1964	.543	.537	p < .05
1968	.547	.543	p < .05

Source. Kagay 1983.
*The 1960 sample is weighted. Weighted n = 1406; raw n = 885.

TABLE 20. Regression Coefficients from the Six Component Model

Component	Mean	Minimum	Maximum	Range
Democratic candidate	.048	.034	.054	.020
Republican candidate	.066	.047	.076	.029
Group benefits	.054	.035	.063	.028
Domestic issues	.047	.039	.053	.014
Foreign issues	.047	.028	.063	.035
Party performance	.052	.047	.060	.013

Source. Kagay 1983.
Note: The mean coefficients are averages across the five sample years, 1952–1968.

would have the same ability to predict the vote as a comment about foreign policy or the parties as managers of government. It follows that the regression coefficients (unstandardized b's) should all be about equal. Indeed, Kagay found that the regression coefficients were all about the same, .05 ± .026. (Kagay did not test the coefficients to find out if the difference was statistically significant.) Because my investigation of the levels shows some predictive power in the substantive content of the responses, albeit very little, Kagay's finding of small differences is consistent with my findings.

Kagay's analysis forces us to reevaluate our understanding of past elections. The six components are apparently superficial characteristics of elections. They may mirror the campaign themes and election controversies, but they have no power to predict the elections. Insofar as they reflect the themes and issues of the campaign, the six components are of interest, but they can no longer be taken at face value.

The importance of Kagay's work for my purposes is that it allows me to look at a different way in which the like/dislike questions are used. Two different coding schemes—the levels indexes and the Six Component Model—are used to predict two different things—conceptual sophistication and presidential voting. Both coding schemes attempt to use the substantive content of the responses to generate predictions. Neither scheme works. Consequently, Kagay's analysis confirms the conclusion drawn from the analysis of the levels indexes: The substantive content of the responses to the like/dislike questions holds little predictive power. What people say in response to the questions is superficial. The real predictive power of the questions lies in the number of answers respondents give.

The evidence I have just presented is of a decidedly limited nature. The superficial content hypothesis is not just a challenge to the use of the like/dislike questions in explaining sophistication and vote choice; it is a challenge to the use of the questions in other contexts as well. Although the evidence presented here supports the hypothesis, the evidence is far too narrow to confirm it. Such a conclusion is just not warranted by these data.

In order to claim that the hypothesis is confirmed, at the very least, one would have to examine all the uses to which the content of the like/dislike questions have been put. There have been a number of other uses (e.g., Kelley 1983; Miller et al. 1986). Showing that the levels indexes and the Six Component Model do not work does not prove that other uses do not work. My hope here is not that readers will be persuaded that the hypothesis is right, but that they will be persuaded to consider the hypothesis seriously and thus carefully test the validity of other uses of the like/dislike questions.

The Wrong Question Hypothesis.   I hypothesize that the number of responses drives the levels indexes and that the content of the responses to the like/dislike questions is only weakly related to political sophistication because people respond to the questions with fairly casual, superficial likes and dislikes. They search their memories briefly and come up with things they have seen on recent television news broadcasts or read in the newspapers or heard in recent conversations. As far as that goes, the hypothesis certainly seems to fit the data. The problem is that it does not go as far as one would like it to. One needs to see how this hypothesis fits with other work on question wording and related matters.

Another explanation for the failure of the like/dislike questions is that the questions may not work simply because they fail to ask for sophisticated evaluations. Nothing in the questions even vaguely hints that "sophisticated" responses are valued more highly than unsophisticated ones. The candidate question, for instance, just asks, "Is there anything in particular about [candidate's name] that might make you want to vote for him?" The questions do not even ask for the "most important" things about the candidates and parties.

Many years ago, Paul Lazarsfeld (1935) declared that we cannot simply ask respondents why they behaved as they did and expect to learn much from their answers. Lazarsfeld argued that in explaining everyday behavior, a "respondent not only has reasons for his actions; he usually knows, also, in which reason we might be especially interested, and it is upon this assumption that he bases his answer" (p. 32). The problem that arises when asking about less common forms of behavior (e.g., voting) is that the respondent does not know what we are interested in. Respondents guess at our motives when we ask "why" questions, and base their answers on tacit assumptions about what we want to hear. The result, according to Lazarsfeld, is that "We cannot leave it up to respondents to tell us whatever they are inclined. The average consumer is not trained to survey off-hand all the factors which determine his [behavior] . . . and he usually has a very hazy understanding of the 'why' question" (p. 32).

In practice, this means that some respondents will interpret the like/dislike questions as referring to personality characteristics and will respond accordingly. Other respondents will think that the questions are directed at the candidates' issue stands and will respond with issue evaluations. Still other respondents will make other assumptions, and so on. The responses to the questions may well depend as much on what the respondents think we want to hear as on what the respondents actually like and dislike about the parties and candidates.

Lazarsfeld was one of the first to observe that in order to answer most questions, one must make some assumptions about the questioner, but he was not the only one. More recently, a number of scholars have made similar points about answering questions (Lehnert 1978; Norman 1973). Norman (1973, p. 156) provided a reasonably thorough statement of the problem:

In order to answer a question appropriately, it is necessary to have a model of the knowledge of the listener, including knowledge of why the question was asked. . . . Basically, a person who is giving a serious answer to a question must consider the developing network of information owned by his listener and attempt to fill the gaps. To do this well requires reasonable depth of knowledge about the listener, or perhaps a sophisticated understanding of the reason that certain questions get asked.

As an example of the ambiguities posed in even a seemingly straightforward question, Norman suggested the question "Where is the Empire State Building?" The answer, as Norman (1973, p. 156) explained, requires some knowledge about the questioner and the context:

If I were asked this question in Russia, I might well respond "In the United States." If I were asked by an adult in Europe, I would probably respond "In New York City." In the United States—especially in New York City, I would respond "On 34th Street." Finally, if asked in the New York subway system, I would not answer with a location, but rather with instructions on how to get there.

The point is that many seemingly simple questions require the answerer to make some assumptions about the questioner. The like/dislike questions, of course, are not simple questions at all. A glance at the Master Codes showing the wide array of answers should convince the reader of that. So the answers to the like/dislike questions are based on unstated assumptions about the questioner and the intent of the questions.

How, then, should we interpret the answers? What does a response reveal? Does it reveal the level at which the answerer conceptualizes politics? Or does it reveal the assumptions that the answerer made about our intent in asking the like/dislike questions? When someone says, "I don't like Dick Nixon because I think he's a crook," do we conclude that the person conceptualizes politics in terms of personalities and without any issue content, or do we conclude that the person thought we wanted to hear about Nixon's character or lack thereof? We cannot easily answer this question. Certainly the respondents' implicit assumptions influence their answers, but what shape that influence takes is not clear. This is potentially an explanation for the failure of the questions, but whether it is the correct explanation is impossible to tell.

In looking for an explanation for the failure of the like/dislike questions, one should also think about the context in which the respondent faces the questions. During presidential election campaigns, the public is hit with a torrent of political stimuli. Even slightly attentive people hear enough television newscasts so that they have a huge potential array of things to like and dislike. Out of the flow of news and conversations, they remember a few items.

What happens when respondents are asked about likes and dislikes? The things they are likely to remember first, and thus to say, are those that are most salient (Jones and Nisbett 1972; Kanouse 1972; Taylor and Fiske 1978). These are things on which their attention was focused for some reason—possibly because they learned them recently or because they were reminded of them recently. The predominant sources of political items coming to people's attention are, of course, the news media.

There is abundant evidence that the news media guide people in deciding what political issues are most important (Behr and Iyengar 1985; Higgins and King 1981; Iyengar and Kinder 1987; Iyengar et al. 1982; MacKuen and Coombs 1981; McCombs and Shaw 1972). That is, the news media perform an agenda setting function. By focusing on some issues and ignoring others, the media identify important topics and thus steer people toward using those topics as the bases for evaluating the candidates and parties.

In one of the best studies in this field, Iyengar et al. (1982) conducted two experiments on agenda setting by television. They experimentally manipulated the content of the network news to emphasize or ignore various topics (defense, pollution, and inflation). Their data show that the selection of stories on the nightly news strongly influences what topics people name as the most important problems facing the nation and that those topics, in turn, influence evaluations of the president.

As the news media swing their spotlight from topic to topic—focusing on the Middle East one day and on George Bush's image as a wimp the next—the things that people think of when asked the like/dislike questions will likewise swing back and forth. What people think of ends up as the content of the responses to the like/dislike questions. Content that can be so easily manipulated is, of course, not likely to reflect fundamental standards of evaluation; rather, it is likely to be superficial.

Consider next the type of news that people are likely to hear from the media. Studies of both television and newspapers have categorized and counted different types of news stories and have come up with unpleasant findings. If one divides news coverage into three categories—campaign activities, personal characteristics of the candidates, and issues—one finds that the bulk of the coverage goes to campaign activities (Graber 1984a; Patterson 1980; Patterson and McClure 1976). That is, the news media focus most of their attention on campaign rallies, speeches, whistle-stop tours, strategy, and the horserace aspects of the contest. The remainder of the coverage seems to be directed more at candidate personalities and characteristics than issues.

In her analysis of the media coverage of the 1968–1980 presidential elections, Graber (1984a, p. 195) finds that on average, "60 percent of the comments refer to personal and professional qualifications of the candidates and 40 percent to issues." Graber qualifies this somewhat by noting that this may underestimate the coverage of issues because some "professional qualifications" touch on issues. In addition, Patterson and McClure (1976) find that issues received more coverage than candidate characteristics on television in 1972. Thus the actual mix of personal characteristics and issues seems to favor characteristics, but the evidence cannot provide a precise answer as to how much.

Although the findings on the mix of candidate and issue stories are a little ambiguous, one must keep in mind that characteristics form a more tightly related, homogeneous set of considerations than do issues. For instance, Jimmy Carter's trustworthiness and compassion are far more closely linked than, say, his Middle East policies and his inflation fighting program. So from the point of view of the voters, a great deal of coverage focuses on the candidates, while only a little focuses on any given issue or cluster of closely related issues (e.g., the economy). In other words, not only do candidate characteristics receive more coverage than issues, but the coverage given to candidates is more concentrated.

Given that campaign activity stories are not likely to serve as the basis for evaluations (except insofar as they reflect on personalities), one is left with personality stories as the largest category. Who, then, should be most likely to raise personality characteristics? Drawing on social learning theory, one might speculate that the most sophisticated would be most likely to mention personalities (e.g., Chong et al. 1984; DiPalma and McClosky 1970; Gamson and Modigliani 1966; Sniderman 1975; Zaller, 1984).

The argument is that those with the greatest exposure to television (with its emphasis on personalities) and those with the greatest capacities to understand what is being said are the most sophisticated. (The capacity to learn is especially important here because exposure to television is so widespread. Those with the greatest capacities to learn will be more likely to understand and remember what they hear on television so that they can later use it in evaluations.) Those with the greatest capacities to learn and most exposure to society's mainstream channels of communication are most likely to acquire the norms, standards, and attitudes being communicated.

In the case of presidential elections, the standard being communicated is that the candidates' personal characteristics are extremely important. As the agenda setting literature discussed previously shows, when the media focus on something, people conclude that it must be important. Thus social learning theory implies that the most sophisticated should be the most likely to discuss personality characteristics in their answers to the like/dislike questions.

In fact, that is exactly what happens. As Glass (1985) demonstrated convincingly, the more educated and sophisticated respondents are, the more likely they are to talk about candidate personalities.[12] Not only do the better educated make a greater number of comments about candidate characteristics, but a higher percentage of their comments are about personalities as well. Moreover, when Glass separated personality comments into those that could be deemed rational considerations (e.g., experience) and those that could be deemed obviously frivolous (e.g., good looks, the quality of one's movies), the more educated respondents were still more likely than the less educated to make frivolous personality comments.

Fuchs and Shapiro (1983) found a similar pattern among voters in the 1975 Chicago mayoral race. In discussing responses people gave when asked why they voted for a particular candidate, Fuchs and Shapiro (1983, p. 546) wrote,

Of those voters with less than high school education, the largest group (41%) explained their preference in terms of political experience and performance criteria. In contrast, the largest group of college educated voters (37%) cited personal qualities of the candidate in explaining their votes. . . . low-SES [socioeconomic status] voters . . . appear to have been more concerned with a collective benefit (performance) than the high-SES antimachine voters, who seem to have largely reduced their concerns to nonsubstantive personal qualities.

In sum, the more sophisticated, not the less sophisticated, talk more about personalities and other frivolous matters.

12. For further evidence, see also Graber (1984b) and Miller et al. (1982).

If one were to take the evidence at face value, one would have to conclude that sophisticated voters are more concerned with and influenced
by personal characteristics and other nonsubstantive matters than are unsophisticated voters. But that conclusion is just not believable.

An alternative explanation is that sophisticates are indeed more aware
of personalities than nonsophisticates, but that they are not more influenced by them. Certainly sophisticates are more likely to know about the
personal characteristics of the candidates because they are more likely to
follow the campaign news. Knowing about candidate personalities leads
to talking about candidate personalities, but it does not necessarily lead
to conceptualizing politics in simplistic personality terms or to being influenced by candidate personalities in voting decisions. That is, people respond to the like/dislike questions with currently salient likes and dislikes, not necessarily with what influences them the most.

Apparently, the questions did not elicit the answers that Campbell and
his colleagues expected. The questions originally appeared to be valid
methods for finding out why people voted as they did, but the questions
were not valid after all. They did not put the things that influenced
people's voting decisions on display.

The Limited Introspection Hypothesis.   The third possible explanation
for the failure of the like/dislike questions is an extension of the first. Although it may seem more speculative, there is a substantial body of evidence to support it. The explanation is that the questions may not work
because people may not have the insight needed to know why they like or
dislike a party or candidate. In other words, introspection into the original sources for liking or disliking may be limited.

The source of the limited introspection hypothesis is attribution theory
and its offshoots. In general, attribution theory deals with how people
attribute causes to events.[13] That is, when something happens, how do
people decide what caused it?

One major application of attribution theory has been in the area
of explaining one's own behavior. This line of research largely developed from the work of David Bem (1965, 1967, 1968, 1970; Bem and
McConnell 1970) and Stuart Valins (Nisbett and Valins 1971; Reisman
et al. 1970; Valins 1966, 1967, 1970, 1974). What Bem and Valins and
others discovered was that internal cues are often ambiguous. The result

13. For an excellent summary of the current state of attribution theory, see
Ross and Fletcher (1985).

is that in assessing how they feel or why they behave as they do, people are often in the same position as external observers. People do not immediately "know" why they behave as they do; they must look at the evidence and figure out the causes. In Bem's (1970, p. 50) words, "In identifying his own internal states, an individual partially relies on the same external cues that others use when they infer his internal states." In other words, people do not look within themselves to find out how they feel.

The idea that introspection is a limited ability has been around for some time. Miller (1962, p. 56), for instance, declared, "It is the result of thinking, not the process, that appears spontaneously in consciousness." Yet not until a series of clever experiments by Valins was a great deal of attention focused on the problem.

Attempting to explain the effects of autonomic changes (e.g., changes in heart rates, breathing, perspiration, etc.) on emotions, Valins theorized that people treat autonomic changes exactly as they do other salient external events. That is, when people observe autonomic changes (e.g., an increased heart rate), they search for explanations of those changes and may infer that alterations in their internal states were the causes of the autonomic changes. In short, changes in emotional states are not directly felt, they are inferred by observing one's own behavior. People infer the causes of their own behavior in much the same way as they infer the causes of other people's behavior.

In Valins's (1966) original experiment on introspection, male subjects were shown photographs of women and asked to rate their looks. The subjects were told that the experiment was designed to measure physiological changes in response to the pictures, and for that reason, the subjects' heart rates were being recorded, and they were allowed to hear their heartbeats during the recording. In fact, the heartbeats the subjects heard were faked by the experimenter. The result was that if a subject heard the fake heartbeat change when he was shown a photograph, he would rate the woman as looking far better than if the fake heartbeat did not change. In other words, the subjects looked at (false) external cues to see how they felt.

Valins's work was bolstered and extended by many other studies. These studies eventually carried beyond the focus on autonomic responses to general introspective ability. Recent work points toward the conclusion that people have little introspective ability of any kind. Gergen and Gergen (1980, p. 204), for instance, wrote that there "appears to be growing agreement among cognitive psychologists that most cognitive processing takes place at a level well below conscious awareness." On a similar note,

Mandler (1975, p. 33) argued, "The analysis of situations and appraisal of the environment . . . goes on mainly at the nonconscious level." That is, people cannot look within themselves to find out why they came to decisions; they can only know what decisions they made. The impression that they know *why* they decided as they did stems from external cues.

Building on the work of Valins and others, Nisbett and Wilson (1977) put forward the argument in a clear theoretical statement. They came to their conclusions after an exhaustive review of dissonance and attribution theory studies by social and cognitive psychologists. In those studies, subjects were divided into experimental and control groups and exposed to various stimuli to test a wide variety of hypotheses in dissonance and attribution theories. The relevant phenomena (e.g., attitude change, learning, etc.) were measured, and then the subjects were asked to explain why they behaved as they did. Nisbett and Wilson (1977, p. 231) concluded:

Subjects are sometimes (a) unaware of the existence of a stimulus that importantly influenced a response, (b) unaware of the existence of the response, and (c) unaware that the stimulus has affected the response. It is proposed that when people attempt to report on their cognitive processes, that is, on the processes mediating the effects of a stimulus on a response, they do not do so on the basis of any true introspection. Instead, their reports are based on a priori, implicit causal theories, or judgments about the extent to which a particular stimulus is a plausible cause of a given response.

This sweeping statement perhaps went a little further than it should have. As a number of critics have pointed out, there are instances in which people seem to have better access to their own mental processes than observers do (Bowers 1981; Ericsson and Simon 1980; Ross and Fletcher 1985; Smith and Miller 1978; White 1980). Indeed, Nisbett subsequently backed off from his declaration that there was no true introspection at all (Nisbett and Ross 1980).

Nevertheless, the general conclusion that introspection is a limited ability—Bem's original position—is now widely accepted. Moreover, it is precisely in areas such as politics—areas that people are unaccustomed to and about which they do not have intense feelings—that introspection is supposed to be weakest.

To put the introspection argument in the context of my problem, when respondents are asked what they like about a candidate that might make them want to vote for him or her, they do not look within themselves and report the factors that influenced them. Instead, they call up implicit theories that explain how people make voting decisions, and they select a few of their likes and dislikes that are consistent with their theories. Rather than identify real causes, people are likely to identify the most salient things that their theories tell them might be causes. In other words, they may know what they like and dislike, but they do not know how their likes and dislikes influence their choices or whether some other causes, of which they are unaware, are the principal influences on their choices.

The notion that we do not have much introspective ability may be new to political science, but it can find some support in voting behavior studies. Consider, for instance, the statement by Campbell et al. (1960, p. 118) quoted at the beginning of this chapter: "Partisan choice tends to be maintained long after its nonpolitical sources have faded into oblivion." Party preferences are socialized into most children long before they have any idea of how parties and elections work. What children like and dislike about parties thus has relatively little to do with *why* children like or dislike parties.

For a second example, consider the influence of party identification on voting. There is no doubt that party identification has an enormous influence on such things as candidate evaluations, issue positions (which in turn influence candidate evaluations), the incumbent administration's performance handling the economy, and so forth (Fiorina 1981; Markus and Converse 1979). It follows that if respondents had a good deal of insight, when asked what they liked about a candidate, many of them would say that they liked the person because he or she was a Democrat or a Republican. The fact of the matter, however, is that identifying a candidate's party as a reason for liking him or her is a fairly rare comment. For instance, of the 1,372 people who were asked what they liked about George McGovern in 1972, only 34 (2.5 percent) said that they liked him because he was a Democrat. Similarly, only 21 people (1.5 percent) said they liked Richard Nixon because he was a Republican. These data do not seem consistent with the notion that people have much insight.

The problem with these examples is that their interpretation is not clear-cut.[14] They suggest that people are not aware of the influence of party identification. Yet the problem could be that the right questions were not asked. People could assume that we are interested in personalities and issues when they answer the questions. They may be aware of

14. For similar arguments in rebuttal to Nisbett and Wilson, see Smith and Miller (1978) and Zajonc (1980).

the influence of party identification and just not think that it is worth mentioning because party identification is constant to them while the personalities and issues are not. That is, personalities and issues are new and thus more salient.[15] The most salient influences, of course, will be named in response to the like/dislike questions.

In sum, it is true, as Gergen and Gergen say, that there is a growing consensus among psychologists that people have limited introspective abilities. Whether that means little ability or no ability is not yet clear. What is clear, however, is that researchers must use extreme caution when interpreting the results of self-reports on motives.

Probably the most reasonable conclusion to draw on the subject is that Elizabeth Martin's (Turner and Martin 1984, p. 300) statement in the report of the Panel on Survey Measurement of Subjective Phenomena is correct:

Caution should be exercised when interpreting respondents' reports of their own reasons or motives. When asked to explain themselves, respondents may give reasons that seem plausible or socially acceptable, or they may report salient features of a situation or object, without really knowing why they act, feel, or think as they do. These accounts certainly provide valuable data on the perspective or frame of reference that respondents adopt when answering a question, but it is suspect to accept self-reported reasons as valid measures of underlying motives without other evidence.

For my purposes, Martin's statement cuts directly to the core of the problem. To accept the levels of conceptualization indexes, and indeed the very existence of the levels, one must accept self-reports of motives at face value, without any supporting evidence. Such acceptance is not justified in light of the findings of psychologists.

To summarize, there are three basic hypotheses to explain why the like/dislike questions fail—the superficial content hypothesis, the wrong questions hypothesis, and the limited introspection hypothesis. At present, we do not have sufficient knowledge to decide which one is correct or, for that matter, if any of them is correct. Yet strong arguments can be made for all three. Therefore the best that can be done here is to say that these matters warrant further research.

---

15. The fact that novelty elicits spontaneous attention and thus makes novel things salient is well established. See Berlyne (1960), Jefferies (1968), and Taylor and Fiske (1978).

The Great Leap Forward That Never Was:
1960–1964

The primary thesis of *The Changing American Voter* is that the sophistication of the electorate can change. People can learn to think about politics in more sophisticated, ideological ways if they are given the right stimuli from politicians. According to Nie and his colleagues, that is exactly what happened in the 1960s. Between 1960 and 1964, there was a great leap forward in sophisticated thinking by the public. This sudden change was caused by changes in the political environment. Beginning with the 1964 presidential candidacy of Barry Goldwater, the ideological tone of political debate became more polarized and ideological. Politicians began to talk in ideological terms. The different sides in the major issues of the time (civil rights, the war in Vietnam, the Great Society welfare programs) were more distinct than those of the 1950s. Thus voters had a clearer picture of politics, one that presented them with more well-defined choices. This new political environment led people to think in more structured, ideological ways. In short, the people became more sophisticated because their environment made it easier for them to do so.

One of the principal pieces of evidence that Nie and his colleagues put forward to support their explanation of what happened during the 1960s was the enormous change in the number of ideologues in the population according to the levels of conceptualization index. Between 1960 and 1964, there was a great leap forward in ideological thinking—or so it seemed.

That change deserves a closer look. An examination of the Nie et al. party and candidate levels over time (shown in Figure 10) reveals that the changes in the number of ideologues in the levels from 1960 to 1964 were caused *entirely* by changes in the candidate index. The party index was quite stable over that period, while the candidate index showed a huge increase in the number of ideologues and near-ideologues. The number of ideologues in the candidate index jumped from 3 to 13 percent; the combined number of ideologues and near-ideologues jumped from 8 to 31 percent. Of course, because each respondent's overall levels index score is merely the higher of his or her party and candidate scores, the overall index reflected the increase in the candidate index. Thus we see that the 1960–1964 surge in the levels was reflected only in the candidate like/dislike questions.

The number of ideologues in the candidate index increased either be-

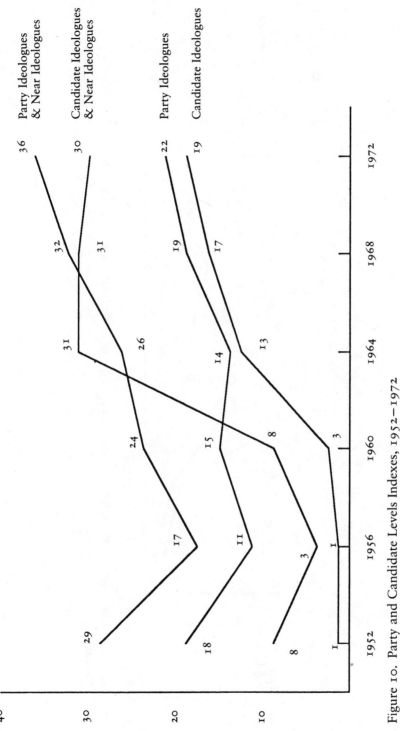

Figure 10. Party and Candidate Levels Indexes, 1952–1972

Source. Nie et al. 1976 (figs. 7.1 and 7.2, pp. 112, 113).

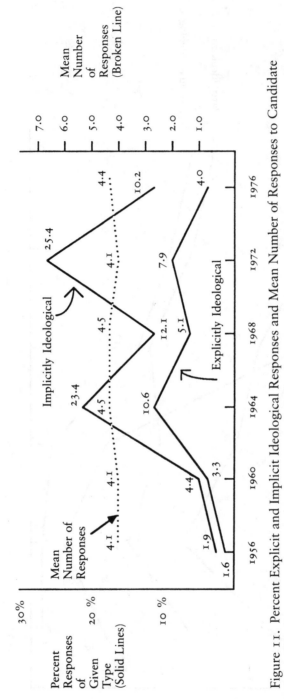

Figure 11. Percent Explicit and Implicit Ideological Responses and Mean Number of Responses to Candidate Questions

Source. Data are from the CPS 1956–1976 American National Election Studies.

cause the number of responses increased or because the content of the responses changed so that more respondents made ideological remarks. Figure 11 shows the mean number of responses given to the candidate questions, the percentage of respondents who gave at least one explicitly ideological response to the candidate questions, and the percentage who gave at least one implicitly ideological response. Those data demonstrate that while the number of responses remained roughly constant over the 1960–1964 period (and, indeed, over the entire 1956–1976 period), the number of people who made ideological comments rose sharply. The biggest jump occurred between 1960 and 1964, when the number of people making explicitly ideological comments rose from 3.3 to 10.6 percent, and the number making implicitly ideological comments rose from 4.4 to 23.4 percent. Thus it was the content of the responses, not the number, that caused the rise in the number of ideologues according to the levels index.

The conclusions one must draw from these data do not support *The Changing American Voter*'s thesis. The great leap forward from 1960 to 1964 does not seem to have happened. The key measure of sophistication, the number of responses, did not change.[16] Instead, the content of the responses to the candidate questions changed.

Yet we now know that that change does not indicate a change in sophistication. In the first place, as shown in Chapter 1, the candidate indexes are unreliable. They reflect seemingly random noise far more than anything else. In the second place, the content of the responses to the candidate questions is almost completely unrelated to political sophistication. Whatever the content of the candidate questions measures, it does not seem to be any aspect of sophistication or ideological thinking. Therefore the inevitable conclusion is that the 1960–1964 great leap forward was just a leap in the level of rhetoric, not a leap in the level of conceptualization.

What the Levels Can Tell Us

So far, many pages have been spent discussing the levels indexes and explaining why they do not work as they were supposed to. One might conclude that the levels indexes are hopeless and that the work based on them is all wrong. That is not the case.

16. Chapter 4 examines a full range of information items across time and comes to the same conclusion: Nothing changed.

The party index seems to work as a measure of political sophistication for some purposes. It is about as reliable and almost as stable as the number of responses to the party questions. Moreover, it correlates with the criterion variables at about the same level as do the number of responses, and it correlates strongly with the number of responses.

The candidate index does not perform as well. The candidate index has a very low reliability. The three-wave multiple indicator model shows that the latent factor underlying the candidate index has a remarkably low stability. The correlations with the criterion variables are quite weak. In fact, nothing about this index seems to work very well. Thus unlike the party index, the candidate index seems to be a very poor measure of sophistication.

The combined CAV index and the original seem to fall somewhere in between the party and candidate indexes. The CAV combined index is, of course, nothing more than the higher of the respondent's scores on the party and candidate component indexes. Although the original index was not built from a set of codes, as the CAV indexes were, it is similar to the CAV combined index. After all, the CAV index was designed to measure the same phenomenon with the same questions. The two indexes differ only by their coding schemes. In addition, the way in which the CAV component indexes were put together into the combined index—by giving the respondent the higher score on either component as the combined index score—followed *The American Voter*'s procedure of giving respondents' scores as high as any portion of their responses justified. Thus it should not be surprising that the text statistics of the combined and original indexes fall in between those of the two CAV component indexes.

Fortunately for those who use the combined and original indexes, they are much closer to the party indexes. The reliabilities are not as high as those of the party indexes (judging from the test-retest correlations), but they are close. The same is true of the correlations with the criterion variables. Thus although the combined and original indexes do not seem to work as well as the party index, they are almost as good. If the levels indexes (other than the candidate index) are so much like the number of responses, why do they not work? Two questions must be answered: What limitations must we put on their interpretations? What can they tell us?

The problem with the party index and the original and combined indexes is that they seem to be little more than error-laden proxies for the number of responses. Although ideological content contributes somewhat to these indexes, the major driving force is clearly the number of responses. As argued before, this means that the indexes do not measure the "levels of conceptualization." Instead, they measure whatever the number of responses measures, and that seems to be some function of political information and range of opinions. Thus the indexes are measures of what one might call general political sophistication.

The practical implication is that although the number of responses works better, the indexes can be used for some purposes. There are, however, two important limitations. The first is that statements citing specific percentages of the population as being ideologues or near-ideologues are not justified. The "levels" of the levels indexes are arbitrary. One cannot use the levels indexes to tell how many ideologues there are in the population any more than one can use the number of responses. Whatever percentages one claimed would be no more than arbitrary choices.

The second limitation on interpreting the levels indexes is in making comparisons across time. Consider the two sources of the scores on the levels indexes—the number of responses one gives to the like/dislike questions and the content of those responses. I have shown that the number of responses is a reasonable (although hardly perfect) measure of political sophistication. The content of the responses, however, reflects mostly short-term forces unrelated to sophistication.

Those short-term forces come out of elections. Much of the content of the like/dislike questions is set by the candidates, the news media, and other leading political figures during each presidential campaign. The candidates choose their election themes; and in the jousting among the candidates, journalists, and other political figures, other themes may arise. Thus some elections focus on ideological themes (e.g., as with Barry Goldwater's call for a choice, not an echo), but other elections focus on personalities (e.g., as did Jimmy Carter's campaign of confidence and trust). In short, political elites set the rhetorical tone of the election, which is reflected back in the content of the responses to the like/dislike questions.

These campaign themes are roughly constant over the span of a single election. However, they are not constant across elections. One campaign may see the candidates running on themes of youth or experience; the next may see the candidates running on calls to true believers. There lies the source of the problem. The campaign themes and rhetoric are reflected back in the content of the like/dislike questions, and that content is not related to sophistication. The result is that two distinct phenomena are mixed up in comparisons over time—the number of responses and the content of the responses. Because the content does not measure so-phistication, but does change from one election to the next, interelection comparisons do not work. An increase in the percentage of ideologues in the levels index from one election to the next could mean one of two things: The public became more sophisticated. Or the candidates used ideological rhetoric more frequently in their campaigns, and the public repeated what they heard.

The implication is that the levels indexes cannot be compared across time because there is no basis for assuming that the rhetorical content of different elections is the same. One can, however, use the levels indexes for comparisons within a single election. One need merely assume that the ideological tone of the campaign is the same all across the nation. Given the nationalization of campaigns and the nationalization of the mass me-dia in the last few decades, that seems like a reasonable assumption.

Taken together, the two limitations on interpreting the levels indexes are enormously important. The principal uses of the levels indexes have been to assess the number of ideologues in the population and to assess the change in that number over time. Neither use is justified. The remain-ing uses to which the levels indexes have been put are not nearly as im-portant. In sum, for virtually everything that we judge important, the lev-els indexes do not work.

Three

Attitude Consistency

A foolish consistency is the hobgoblin of little minds,
adored by little statesmen and philosophers and divines.
With consistency a great soul has simply nothing to do.
—Ralph Waldo Emerson

Aside from level of conceptualization, the characteristic of people's political thinking that has drawn the most attention from political scientists is attitude consistency or attitude constraint. The basic idea of attitude consistency is that one is consistent if one's opinions on political issues are all at the same point on the ideological spectrum. That is, if one holds all liberal opinions or all conservative opinions, then one is consistent. If one holds a mixture of liberal, moderate, and conservative opinions, one is inconsistent. Although holding consistent attitudes is not the same as ideological thinking or political sophistication, it is generally thought to be closely related to them.

Attitude consistency became a major focus of research by political scientists when Philip Converse (1964) used it to show that most people do not organize their attitudes coherently and are therefore not ideological thinkers. Interest in consistency increased when researchers discovered that between 1960 and 1964 there was a sudden growth of consistency. It seemed that the public had become far more ideological. This surge in consistency came at the same time as the surge in the levels of conceptualization, and together these two measures fueled the *Changing American Voter* thesis.

There are two important reasons why one might suspect that the 1960–1964 rise in consistency was not real. First, between 1960 and

1964 there was a change in how the questions used to measure attitude consistency were worded. A great deal has been written about this question wording controversy, and although I have a number of points to add to the debate, much of this section is a review. Second, since the 1950s, and especially between 1960 and 1964, there have been changes in the attitude items used to measure consistency. In addition, there were changes in how the political leaders and the public stood on these issues. For the investigator, these changes cause problems of item selection (i.e., what items should be used, and, if necessary, should they be treated equally, or should some be weighted more heavily than others). This subject has barely been touched by researchers.

Together these two problems destroy the possibility of comparing attitude consistency levels across the 1960–1964 gap. It is not clear what such comparisons are telling us. When consistency rose in the early sixties, was it because people began to organize their thoughts more coherently, because the questions were worded differently, or because some of the questions were on different subjects, and the other questions were about subjects that had changed? We cannot tell.

The Nature of Attitude Consistency

Attention to attitude consistency stems largely from Philip Converse's path-breaking article, "The Nature of Belief Systems in Mass Publics" (1964). In that article, Converse defined a belief system as a "configuration of ideas and attitudes in which the elements are bound together by some form of constraint or functional interdependence" (p. 207). Expanding upon his general definition, he defined two cases of constraint— "dynamic" and "static": "In the dynamic case, 'constraint' or 'interdependence' refers to the probability that a change in the perceived status (truth, desirability, and so forth) of one idea-element would psychologically require, from the point of view of the actor, some compensating change(s) in the status of idea-elements elsewhere in the configuration" (p. 208). In other words, a person's ideas are constrained if the person understands how the ideas are connected with one another. To take the classic example, cutting taxes, increasing spending, and balancing the budget all at the same time is generally conceded to be a fairly difficult trick. Yet some people favor all three policies. With the exception of a few sophisticates who understand and believe in Reaganomics, most of these people are confused. They favor all three policies because they do not realize that there are trade-offs among them. If the budget is going to be balanced, increasing spending generally means that taxes must be increased as well. Understanding the connections between different policies and tailoring one's ideas so that they fit together and make sense constitutes constraint.

Clearly, dynamic constraint is closely related to political knowledge and sophistication. If one knows a good deal about politics and if one understands how ideas relate to one another, then one will probably be constrained. For instance, a knowledgeable voter is not likely to favor cutting taxes, increasing spending, and balancing the budget. Something has to give. For instance, if one favors increasing spending, one might favor increasing taxes to pay for the extra spending. Thus dynamic constraint can be taken as an indication of political knowledge.

Converse (1964, p. 207) defined static constraint somewhat differently: "In the static case, 'constraint' may be taken to mean the success we would have in predicting, given initial knowledge that an individual holds a specified attitude, that he holds certain further ideas and attitudes." To understand the definition of static constraint, one must understand the basis for prediction. Knowledge of an individual's attitude on one issue allows prediction of the individual's attitudes on other issues because the rest of the population shares the same sets of attitudes. That is, the basis for prediction is the predominant pattern of beliefs in society. If most people who, say, favor busing to end segregation also favor spending less on defense, and most of those who oppose busing also favor more defense spending, then to be constrained, one must hold one of those two sets of positions. The combinations of favoring both busing and defense spending or opposing both are defined as inconsistent, unconstrained positions.

On the surface, dynamic and static constraint seem quite different. Dynamic constraint focuses on the individual's process of thinking about politics; static constraint focuses on how the individual's attitudes relate to those of the rest of the population. In fact, Converse argued, the two cases of constraint are merely different ways of getting at the same concept. His theory of constraint explains the connection.

Converse argued that there are three sources of constraint: (1) logical (in the sense of formal, symbolic logic), (2) "psycho-logical" (in the sense of the rationality of a coherent, persuasive argument), and (3) social (in the sense of social pressures to accept certain ways of thinking about things regardless of their logical or psycho-logical relationships). Converse (1964, p. 211) maintained that the social sources of constraint are by far the most important, and the primary source of social constraint

lies in two simple facts about the creation and diffusion of belief systems. First, the shaping of belief systems of any range into apparently logical wholes that are credible to large numbers of people is an act of creative synthesis characteristic of only a miniscule proportion of any population. Second, to the extent that multiple idea-elements of a belief system are socially diffused from such creative sources, they tend to be diffused in "packages," which consumers come to see as "natural" wholes, for they are presented in such terms ("If you believe this, then you will also believe that, for it follows in such-and-such ways").

This statement is part of the foundation of Converse's theoretical approach. Ideologies are not worked out by people on their own; rather, ideologies are learned.[1] Although many individuals may add their own personal touches to the ideologies they learn, only a handful of the most sophisticated elites make basic changes in ideological frameworks. For the rest of the population, ideologies are institutionalized sets of beliefs that are out there to be learned. Some people learn them quite well (and thus can explain why, for instance, conservatives favor cutting welfare spending), others learn only bits and pieces of them, and still others learn nothing at all about them.

Having laid the foundations for his argument, Converse (1964, p. 213) declared his intentions for "Mass Belief Systems":

It is our thesis that, as one moves from elite sources of belief systems downwards on . . . an information scale, several important things occur. First, the contextual grasp of "standard" political belief systems fades out very rapidly, almost before one has passed beyond the 10% of the American population that in the 1950s has completed standard college training. Increasingly, simpler forms of information about "what goes with what" (or even information about the simple identity of objects) turn up missing. The net result, as one moves downward, is that constraint declines across the universe of idea-elements, and that the range of relevant belief systems becomes narrower and narrower. Instead of a few wide-ranging

---

1. The view that ideologies are independent of individuals is a widely held one (Adorno et al. 1950, p. 2; Campbell et al. 1960; Rokeach 1960, p. 35). Other investigators (Brown 1970; Lane 1962) argue that each individual has his or her own ideological perspective on politics. This debate over the existence of idiosyncratic ideologies has been going on for some time (e.g., Achen 1975; Converse 1964, 1970), but it is not relevant to the present discussion.

belief systems that organize large amounts of specific information, one would expect to find a proliferation of clusters of ideas among which little constraint is felt, even, quite often, in instances of sheer logical constraint.

To support his thesis, Converse presented a set of correlations (gammas) among seven issue items that were asked of a 1958 national cross-section sample and of a 1958 sample of congressional candidates.[2] The items were a "purposive sampling of some of the more salient political controversies at the time of the study" (Converse 1964, p. 229). The questions were about federal aid to education, government guarantee of full employment, federal fair employment and fair housing laws for blacks, government intervention in housing and electric power, foreign economic aid, foreign military aid, and isolationism.

The correlations were intended to measure static constraint. That is, if two attitudes correlate strongly, then one attitude item can be used to predict the other. Thus strong correlations indicate high constraint, and low correlations indicate low constraint.

The data solidly supported Converse's position. The average correlation for the elite sample was .34; the average for the mass sample was only .11. When Converse divided the issues into domestic and foreign, he found that the average domestic issue correlations were higher, but the elite-mass differences remained. The average correlation among domestic issues in the mass sample was .23; in the elite sample, it was .53. The average correlation among foreign issues in the mass sample was also .23, but the elites were still higher with an average of .37. Thus in 1958, the congressional candidates had far more constrained, organized belief systems than did most members of the mass public, and presumably so too did other elites—journalists, academics, political activists, and so on.

The Rise of Constraint

Converse's description of the American public's political sophistication was basically an extension of the account presented four years earlier in *The American Voter*. The public neither knew nor cared much about politics, and this was unlikely to change much with the passing years. So

2. The questions asked of the mass sample and the elite sample were slightly different (Converse 1964, p. 229, esp. n. 21). The differences in question wording may have influenced the resulting correlations, but how is not clear.

strong and convincing were Converse's arguments that little was done to find out whether that description did, in fact, continue to hold in the next decade. There were, to be sure, a number of investigations of other aspects of attitude consistency (Axelrod 1967; Brown 1970; Eitzen 1972–1973; Jones and Rambo 1973; Kirkpatrick 1970; Luttbeg 1968; Luttbeg and Zeigler 1966; Aberbach and Walker 1973), but nothing was done to replicate Converse's analysis in the years immediately following publication of "Mass Belief Systems." As Nie and Andersen (1974, p. 543) put it, "The initial questions about the nature of mass political beliefs had been answered in a way which foreclosed continued research on the question."

The first indications that low constraint might not be an unchanging characteristic of the American population came years later from Gerald Pomper (1972). In "From Confusion to Clarity," Pomper examined six policy questions that the SRC/CPS National Election Surveys had asked in each presidential year from 1956 through 1968.[3] The questions were about federal aid to education, government provision of medical care, government guarantee of full employment, federal fair employment and fair housing laws, federal enforcement of school integration, and foreign aid. Three important findings emerged from the data.

First, between 1960 and 1964, the relationship between party identification and attitudes on each of the six issues substantially strengthened. In 1956 and 1960, there were either only very weak or no relationships between party identification and policy preferences. Starting in 1964, relationships suddenly grew so that Democrats were more likely to be liberal, and Republicans were more likely to be conservative.

Second, awareness of party differences on the six issues grew. After being asked what they thought about the issues, respondents were asked whether there were any differences between the parties on them. The number saying that there were indeed differences markedly increased across the four elections, with the biggest increase for five of the six issues occurring between 1960 and 1964.

Third, the recognition that the Democratic party was more liberal than the Republican party also grew across the four elections. Those who saw differences between the parties were asked which party took which position on each of the issues. The number correctly identifying the Democratic party as taking the more liberal stand rose between 1956 and 1968,

3. Four of the six items were the same as those used by Converse (1964). There were, however, changes in both question wordings and formats over the years.

and again the largest increases for most of the policies happened between 1960 and 1964.

Pomper investigated several possible causes of these shifts (generational changes, rising education, race, and region), but he was unable to account for much change. Pomper (1972, p. 421) finally concluded that the cause must have been change in the political environment: "The events and campaigns of the 1960s, I suggest, made politics more relevant and more dramatic to the mass electorate. In the process, party differences were developed and perceived. Democrats divided from Republicans, Democrats became more liberal, and voters became more aware."

Although Pomper's data did not deal directly with constraint, the implications were readily apparent. If the public's views on the issues were becoming more closely aligned with party identification, then they were probably also becoming more closely aligned with one another.

Bennett (1973) and Nie and Andersen (1974) were the first to reexamine attitude consistency. Bennett analyzed four social welfare policy items in the 1964 and 1968 SRC/CPS surveys: federal aid to education, federal guarantee of full employment, government provision of medical care, and the size of the federal government. The first two of these items were substantively the same as two of Converse's items (the questions were worded differently); the second two items were new. Bennett discovered that there had been a huge increase in constraint between 1958, the year of Converse's data, and the 1960s. Whereas Converse had found an average gamma of only .23 among domestic issues, Bennett found average gammas of .54 and .51 in 1964 and 1968. It was an enormous change. As Bennett (1973, p. 559) pointed out, to appreciate the change fully, one had to compare the masses in the 1960s to the elites in the 1950s:

The dramatic rise in the level of consistency among the mass public's domestic policy attitudes is highlighted by the fact that the average gamma coefficients for the populace's attitudes in the four issues in the 1960s were almost identical with the mean coefficient for the 1958 sample of congressional candidates studied by Converse. In other words, the mass public's attitudes on the social welfare policy issues were as tightly constrained in the mid- and late-1960s as had been the congressional elite's in the late 1950s.

In short, the evidence suggested a staggering increase in the public's ability to organize its opinions about politics.

Bennett proposed several hypotheses to explain the jump in consistency, but none of them panned out very well. His principal problem was that he examined only 1964 and 1968 data. Because he did not cover the 1960–1964 gap in his analysis, he was limited in what he could prove.

Bennett began by looking at the hypothesis that rising education had caused the increase in constraint. He rejected it upon discovering that in 1964 and 1968, the better educated did not have higher levels of consistency than the less well educated (a finding later confirmed by several others, including Converse [1975]).

Bennett next examined interest in politics, as measured by a question asking how much people followed "government and public affairs."[4] The hypothesis was that politics had become more salient in the 1960s. Again he met with disconfirming data. Although consistency was associated with interest in 1964, it was not in 1968. Because the data did not confirm the relationship between interest and consistency, the hypothesis had to be rejected.

Bennett also looked at the hypothesis that greater participation in the 1960s brought about the rise in constraint. His participation measure had three levels: (1) no participation at all, (2) voted but did not otherwise participate, and (3) participated in one of several activist roles.[5] That hypothesis, too, had to be rejected because, although the 1968 data behaved as expected, the 1964 data failed to perform as the hypothesis demanded. Nonparticipants were far more constrained than those who voted.

Finally, Bennett looked at a narrower type of participation, attempting to influence others' votes. Here the data were consistent with the hypothesis. In both years, those who were "opinion leaders" had higher levels of constraint than those who did not attempt to influence others. Still, as Bennett pointed out, the average gamma coefficients of the noninfluencers were .46 and .47 in the two sample years—both averages far higher than the entire mass public in 1958. Moreover, Bennett had no evidence to show that attempts to influence had increased between 1958 and 1964.

Thus Bennett's attempts to explain the surge in attitude consistency

4. The question was: "Some people seem to follow what's going on in government and public affairs most of the time, whether there's an election going on or not. Others aren't that interested. Would you say you follow what's going on in government and public affairs most of the time, some of the time, only now and then, or hardly at all?"

5. The possible means of participation were attempting to influence the votes of others, wearing a campaign button or putting a bumper sticker on a car, going to a campaign rally or meeting, working for a candidate or party, and belonging to a political club or organization. The coding scheme is from Campbell et al. (1954, pp. 28–31).

failed. In the end, all he could do was argue that the ideologically charged 1964 election and the turbulent 1960s had increased the salience of politics for the electorate, and thereby had increased attitude consistency. He was not able to come up with any direct measures of the salience of politics that supported his explanation.

Following closely behind Bennett, Nie and Andersen looked at a somewhat wider range of items. They divided the issue questions into five areas: social welfare (aid to education, guaranteed employment, government medical care), welfare measures specific for blacks (federal fair housing and fair employment laws), the size of government (federal intervention in housing and electric power in 1956 and 1960, the power of the federal government from 1964 on), racial integration in the schools (federal enforcement of integration), and the cold war (should the United States send soldiers abroad to fight communism, should the United States talk to communist leaders, Vietnam). Where two or more questions were available for an area in a survey, Nie and Andersen looked at the average of the inter-item gammas rather than at each individual coefficient.[6] Aside from their choice of items and decision to average coefficients for policy areas, Nie and Andersen's analysis was similar to Converse's and Bennett's.

Nie and Andersen found that between 1960 and 1964, there had been a huge increase in attitude consistency. Although the size of the increase varied from one pair of issues to the next, all the correlations between issue pairs strengthened substantially. More important, with one exception, the higher level of attitude constraint held constant from 1964 through 1972. These data allowed Nie and Andersen to argue that there were two distinct political periods: 1956–1960, when constraint was low and the public seemed to be almost completely unideological, and 1964–1972, when constraint was high and the public seemed at least somewhat ideological.

The exception to Nie and Andersen's general finding that constraint remained high after 1964 was the size of government question. In 1964, 1968, and 1972, SRC/CPS respondents were asked, "Some people are afraid the government in Washington is getting too powerful for the good of the country and the individual person. Others feel that the government in Washington is not getting too strong for the good of the country. Have you been interested enough in this to favor one side over the other?" Be-

6. For a complete description of their methods, see Nie and Andersen (1974, pp. 545–47, 588–90).

tween 1968 and 1972, the correlation between this item and each of the other attitude items dropped sharply, almost disappearing.

Why did the size of government question stop being constrained? Nie and Andersen's (1974, pp. 554–57) explanation is straightforward. Size of government was a basic liberal-conservative issue until the late 1960s. Conservatives opposed big government solutions to problems; liberals favored them. But some time between 1968 and 1972, this ceased to be true. For whatever reasons (Vietnam, the feeling that aspects of the Great Society were not working, etc.), liberals moved away from their belief in big government solutions. In 1964 and 1968, liberals had been most likely to say they did not feel that the government was getting too big; conservatives had been most likely to take the opposite stand. In 1972, however, all that changed. Moderates became the most likely to say that the government was not too big. Liberals had actually become more likely than conservatives to think the government was too big. In short, the liberal ideology—at least insofar as it was reflected in public opinion—changed.

Nie and Andersen (1974) concluded that the appropriate way to deal with the size of government question was to exclude it from the analysis when it ceased being part of the liberal ideology. That is, they argued that the fact that the correlations between that question and the others fell should not be interpreted as a drop in constraint, but as a "redefinition of the liberal and conservative positions on this issue" (p. 557). Given this redefinition, one should not expect any constraint, so including the question would be a mistake.

The problem of how to deal with the size of government question is a difficult one. Nie and Andersen's solution certainly makes sense, but it is an ad hoc solution. If one is going to exclude a question from an analysis because of a change in the liberal and conservative ideologies, one should see how that exclusion principle applies to other questions as well. One should not just apply the principle to a single item. I will return to this problem later in this chapter.

Like Pomper and Bennett, Nie and Andersen examined various possible explanations for the sudden surge of constraint. In a footnote, they examined and dismissed the possibility that a change in how issue questions were worded might have caused the change. As did their predecessors, they also looked at rising education as a possible explanation and concluded that education had nothing to do with the rise of constraint. Finally, they turned their attention toward Pomper's and Bennett's answer.

Nie and Andersen's tentative explanation for the rise in constraint was that it was brought about by changes in the political environment. They maintained that the civil rights struggle, the Vietnam War, the Great Society programs, and other aspects of the turbulent sixties caused the public to become more politically aware. But beyond the general argument, Nie and Andersen provided some specifics that can be measured with surveys.

Two variables were said to hold the key to the transformation: interest in politics (as measured by interest in the outcomes of presidential elections) and trust in government. Interest alone is not sufficient to explain the rise in constraint. As Nie and Andersen showed, interest increased between 1956 and 1960—four years too early to account for the 1960–1964 rise in constraint—and then fell between 1968 and 1972—a period during which there was no corresponding drop in constraint. Moreover, constraint increased among both the interested and the uninterested across the 1960–1964 gap. Thus the growth of constraint does not seem to have been caused by a simple increase in interest in politics.

After further investigation, Nie and Andersen (1974, pp. 571–78) concluded that the most likely explanation involves both interest and trust in government. They distinguished three groups for analysis: those who were interested in politics; those who were not interested, but who trusted government—labeled the "quiescent"; and those who were not interested and who did not trust the government—labeled the "disenchanted."

In 1964 and 1968, the interested were the only ones who had high levels of constraint. But by 1972, the disenchanted had also developed a fairly high level of constraint. To explain this, Nie and Andersen noted that between 1968 and 1972, the number of interested declined, and the number of disenchanted rose by the same amount; while the number of quiescent remained constant. From this, they inferred that many of those who were interested in 1964 and 1968 became disenchanted. Moreover, the disenchanted "underwent a fundamental change. . . . The high levels of ideological constraint displayed by the disenchanted in 1972 suggest that politics has remained central to these individuals but has turned from a politics of positive salience to one of negative salience" (Nie and Andersen 1974, p. 578). Exactly what Nie and Andersen meant by this statement is a little difficult to say, but the general idea is that as trust in government declined in the late sixties and early seventies, many people said that they were not interested, but in fact they still cared and still followed politics enough to maintain ideological points of view.

Nie and Andersen (1974, p. 579) emphasized that their explanation that the "heightened salience of politics produced higher levels of attitude constraint" was tentative, based on fairly thin data. They were certainly right. There are two glaring weaknesses in their argument. First, they have no way of explaining the 1960–1964 jump in constraint. They suggested that the rising salience of politics caused constraint to increase. Yet the principal measure of salience, interest in elections, fails to explain it because interest remained unchanged across the 1960–1964 gap. Although Nie and Andersen did not mention it, the other available measure of salience, how much people care about the outcome of the presidential election, also remained unchanged across the 1960–1964 gap (see Table 35). Second, Nie and Andersen's explanation for the 1968–1972 discrepancy, when interest fell but constraint did not, is very weak. The problem is that their discussion of the disenchanted rests on a single time point, 1972. Because they wrote before any other data were available, they were unable to give their explanation the test of time by seeing whether the disenchanted still behaved in the same way in 1976 and later years. In fact, the explanation breaks down. Between 1972 and 1976, interest rose, returning to its original level. Attitude constraint, however, fell (Nie et al. 1979, p. 369).

In sum, the Pomper/Bennett/Nie and Andersen explanation was similar to the arguments put forward to explain the rise in the levels of conceptualization. The political environment did it. The exact mechanism, however, was unclear. Everyone pointed at the salience of politics, but the survey data failed to provide the necessary confirmation. Three survey items were available to measure salience: interest in the current elections, the extent to which one followed politics and public affairs, and how much one cared about the outcome of the presidential election. The "follow public affairs" item was not asked before 1964 and was thus not available over the critical 1960–1964 period. The other two items did not change over those years. In short, the explanation sounds persuasive, but the evidence to back it up is not there.

Following the work of Bennett and Nie and Andersen, a number of other researchers investigated changes in attitude constraint over time (Hagner and Pierce 1983; Kirkpatrick 1976; LeBlanc and Merrin 1977; Nie et al. 1976; Piereson 1978). The most important of these were Nie, Verba, and Petrocik, the authors of *The Changing American Voter*.

The data and arguments presented by Nie and his coauthors were virtually identical to those offered by Nie and Andersen two years earlier. *The Changing American Voter*'s important contribution was to present a new explanation for the growth of constraint. Instead of pointing to the rising salience of politics (a rise for which no survey evidence could be found), Nie et al. (1976, p. 139) identified two possibilities: "Increased issue consistency can result from changes in the stimuli the citizen receives from the political world or from changes in the way he or she processes these stimuli."

The second possibility, that increased consistency resulted from changes in how people processed the stimuli, is just the original salience hypothesis restated. Politics became more salient, which caused people to learn more and understand more about politics. In other words, the growing salience of politics caused people to become more sophisticated about politics, and that sophistication was reflected in attitude consistency. More people learned what issue positions went with what other issue positions and why.

The first possibility, that people received different stimuli from the political world, was new. The idea was, of course, that the political environment had changed. The two parties became more distinct. Politicians began to send clearer, more understandable messages to the people. Because the people were given clearer messages about what issue positions went together, they were able to put them together more consistently. That is, constraint did not rise because people understood politics better, but because politics was easier to understand. It was not necessary for the salience of politics to increase. People did not have to be more interested in or pay more attention to politics. What the politicians were saying to the people was so much clearer that people got the message without any extra effort. It was as if the political leaders of this country took the marbles out of their mouths. They spoke more clearly.

The beauty of the new explanation was that it did not depend on any increase in the salience of politics. Nevertheless, Nie et al. maintained that both explanations were at work. Not only did the environment change so that politics became easier to follow, but politics became more salient, and people became more sophisticated as a result.

The Question Wording Controversy

The findings about the sudden rise of issue constraint were an exciting new development for those who studied political behavior. For a few brief years, those findings became the accepted knowledge. Even Converse (1975, pp. 89–93) allowed that he had been mistaken about the extent of stability in consistency. In 1978, however, questions began to be raised.

In several articles published almost simultaneously, critics challenged the findings that consistency had increased (Bishop et al. 1978a, 1978b; Brunk 1978; Sullivan et al. 1978). They argued that the surge of consistency was the result of a previously unrecognized methodological flaw, namely, a change in the wordings and formats of the SRC/CPS issue questions between 1960 and 1964. There was, the critics said, no increase in consistency; instead, survey respondents were presented with different types of questions that made them answer in a more consistent way. The great leap forward in constraint was really a great methodological mistake.

The old question format—used in 1956, 1958, and 1960—was to ask whether a respondent agreed or disagreed with a given policy position. The new format was to ask whether a respondent favored one position or another. Thus the old format (subsequently referred to as the 1950s format) was one sided; the new format (the 1960s format) was two sided or balanced. As an illustration, consider the two versions of the guaranteed jobs question:

1950s format: "The government in Washington ought to see to it that everybody who wants to work can find a job. Now would you have an opinion on this or not? [If Yes] Do you think the government should do this?" Response categories: Agree strongly, Agree, Not Sure, Disagree, Disagree Strongly.

1960s format: "In general, some people feel that the government in Washington should see to it that every person has a job and a good standard of living. Others think the government should just let each person get ahead on his own. Have you been interested enough in this to favor one side over the other? [If Yes] Do you think that the government should see to it that every person has a job and a good standard of living or should it let each person get ahead on his own?" Response categories: Government should see to it that each person has a job, Depends, Gov't should let each person get ahead on his own.

The 1950s question presents people with a goal that sounds praiseworthy and asks them if they agree with it. Some respondents, of course, may not immediately recognize that the goal is controversial. They may fail to recognize the ideological conflict hidden in the question. The 1960s question makes the conflict more obvious. Two opposing positions are stated, an argument and a counterargument, and the respondent is asked to choose between them. The quick, unthinking agreement brought out by the first question is not elicited by the second question because the respondent must think about two conflicting ideas rather than one. Thus the question makes sure that the respondent thinks about both sides of the question.

SRC's change in question format was motivated by research into question wording. A host of studies (Bass 1955, 1956; Couch and Keniston 1960; Cronbach 1946, 1950, 1958; Jackson and Messick 1958) had found that asking questions in an agree/disagree, or Likert, format biases the results. The problem is that some people have what psychologists call a "response set." That is, some people tend to agree with the statements posed in questions irrespective of the content of those statements (agreement response set or acquiescence bias), but other people tend to disagree with questions irrespective of the content (disagreement response set).[7]

Because "yeasayers" are far more common than "naysayers," agree/disagree questions bias the results in favor of the position stated in the question. That is, a question that asks whether the respondent agrees with a liberal policy position, such as the first version of the employment question, has a liberal bias. A question that asks about agreement with a conservative position has a conservative bias.

Between 1960 and 1964, the SRC principal investigators decided to convert the issue items from the old agree/disagree format to a balanced format. This set the stage for the question wording controversy. When the new balanced questions were asked, some of the results differed substantially from the results of the earlier questions. Thus the dilemma: Were the new results caused by real changes in the public or by the change in question format?

Some of the issue items showed, or seemed to show, huge shifts in public opinion between 1960 and 1964. The two questions on guaranteed jobs, for instance, got quite different responses. In 1956, 63 percent of the respondents agreed that the government should see to it that people get jobs; but in 1964, only 36 percent of the people took that position.

Old Question Wording (1956)	New Question Wording (1964)
Economic Welfare	
The government in Washington ought to see to it that everybody who wants to work can find a	In general, some people feel that the government in Washington should see to it that every person

---

7. Not surprisingly, the well educated (e.g., academics) are the most likely to be the perverse sorts who enjoy disagreeing with everything.

job. Now would you have an opinion on this or not? [If Yes]: Do you think the government should do this?

48.0% Agree strongly
14.7 Agree, but not very strongly
7.6 Not sure; it depends
11.5 Disagree, but not very strongly
18.2 Disagree strongly
(N = 1,587)

has a job and a good standard of living. Others think the government should just let each person get ahead on his own. Have you been interested enough in this to favor one side or the other? [If Yes]: Do you think that the government should see to it that every person has a job and a good standard of living or should it let each person get ahead on his own?

36.4% Govt should see to it that every person has a job and a good standard of living
13.0 Other, depends
50.6 Govt should let each person get ahead on his own
(N = 1,338)

Medical Welfare

The government ought to help people get doctors and hospital care at low cost. Do you have an opinion on this or not? [If Yes]: Do you think the government should do this?

43.6% Agree strongly
17.5 Agree, but not very strongly
9.4 Not sure, it depends
8.9 Disagree, but not very strongly
20.6 Disagree strongly
(N = 1,554)

Some say the government in Washington ought to help people get doctors and hospital care at low cost; others say the government should not get into this. Have you been interested enough in this to favor one side or the other? [If Yes]: What is your position? Should the government in Washington help people get doctors and hospital care at low cost or stay out of this?

59.3% Govt should help people
7.3 Other, depends
33.4 Govt should stay out
(N = 1,312)

Black Welfare

If Negroes are not getting fair treatment in jobs and housing,

Some people feel that if Negroes (colored people) are not getting the government should see to it that they do. Do you have an opinion on this or not? [If Yes]: Do you think the government should do this?

49.3% Agree strongly
21.0   Agree, but not very strongly
7.5   Not sure, it depends
7.5   Disagree, but not very strongly
14.7   Disagree strongly
(N = 1,522)

fair treatment in jobs the government in Washington ought to see to it that they do. Others feel that this is not the federal government's business. Have you had enough interest in this question to favor one side over the other? [If Yes]: How do you feel? Should the government in Washington see to it that Negroes get fair treatment in jobs or leave these matters to the states and communities?

45.2% Govt should see to it that Negroes get fair treatment
8.5   Other, depends
46.3   Leave these matters to the states and communities
(N = 1,352)

Federal Aid to Schools

If cities and towns around the country need help to build more schools, the government in Washington ought to give them the money they need. Do you have an opinion on this or not? [If Yes]: Do you think the government should do this?

52.6% Agree strongly
21.7   Agree, but not very strongly
9.4   Not sure, it depends
5.8   Disagree, but not very strongly
10.5   Disagree strongly
(N = 1,593)

Some people think the government in Washington should help towns and cities provide education for grade and high school children; others think that this should be handled by the states and local communities. Have you been interested enough in this to favor one side over the other? [If Yes]: Which are you in favor of: getting help from the government in Washington or handling it at the state and local level?

38.0% Getting help from the govt
5.7   Other, depends
56.3   Handling it at the state level
(N = 1,289)

School Integration

The government in Washington should stay out of the question of whether white and colored children go to the same school. Do you have an opinion on this or not? [If Yes]: Do you think the government should stay out of this question?	Some people say that the government in Washington should see to it that white and Negro (colored) children are allowed to go to the same schools. Others claim that it is not the government's business. Have you been concerned enough about this question to favor one side over the other? [If Yes]: Do you think that the government in Washington should: see to it that white and Negro children go to the same schools or stay out of this area as it is none of its business?

39.7% Agree strongly
 9.3 Agree, but not very strongly
 7.1 Not sure
10.5 Disagree, but not very strongly
33.4 Disagree strongly
(N = 1,550)

47.5% See to it that white and Negro children go to the same schools
 8.3 Other, it depends
44.2 Stay out of this area
(N = 1,362)

If we accept the questions at face value, that would mean that there was a 27 percent shift to the right over those years—a lurch to the right during a period in which the liberal Lyndon Johnson buried his conservative foe, Barry Goldwater, in one of the greatest electoral landslides in American history. It is just not believable.

Certainly there may have been some real shift in opinion, but a shift of that magnitude just did not happen. An examination of questions from Gallup, Harris, and other surveys that were worded identically over time leaves no doubt that little changed in the early 1960s (Erskine 1971, 1972; Gallup 1972; Mueller 1973). Simon's (1974) extensive review of opinion trends reveals only small shifts back and forth on most issues. Trends were found in attitudes on civil rights and civil liberties, but these were liberal trends, contrary to the findings of the SRC questions.[8]

The work of Page and Shapiro and their associates (Page and Shapiro

8. The SRC questions on government intervention in fair housing and fair jobs for blacks showed a 25 percent shift to the right over the 1960–1964 period. Other SRC questions also showed shifts to the right.

1982; Shapiro and Patterson 1986) provides evidence for this conclusion. Over the past few years, Page and Shapiro have been collecting survey data on trends in policy preferences. Their data set consists of over thirty-three hundred survey questions. Their goal in this massive data collection project is to describe and explain changes in policy preferences over time. Their first major discovery, however, was that there is not a great deal of change. To the contrary, the best description of change in public opinion is that it is minimal. Page and Shapiro (1982, p. 26) wrote, "The first question of interest is just how much change and how much stability are found in the data. To us, the striking finding is one of stability in Americans' policy preferences." In short, there were no such massive swings in opinion between 1960 and 1964. There were occasional small shifts, but nothing on the order of the changes suggested by the SRC questions. The explanation is clearly that the changes in question format caused the changes in the marginal distributions.

The pattern shown in the guaranteed jobs questions is not repeated by all the pairs of questions previously listed. The federal aid to education and federal enforcement of fair housing and fair employment for blacks items show the same huge shift in public opinion. According to the questions, there is a 36 percent drop in support for aid to schools (during a period in which Congress passed an aid law), and there is a 25 percent drop in support for fair housing and fair employment (during a period in which civil rights laws were passed to cover those areas). There were only 2 percent changes in the school integration item and the government medical care item.

There is no way to tell exactly why the responses to some items changed while others did not, but based on the question wording literature, one can make some educated guesses. The most likely explanation is that the three questions that changed provided solid counterarguments, while the two that did not change much were only "formally balanced."

To see the difference in counterarguments, compare the aid to education and school integration items. The aid item identifies states and local communities as the responsible parties in the conservative alternative. The integration item does not suggest such an alternative. It just says that other people think that integration is none of the government's business. The same lack of a strong counterargument may have influenced the medical care item. If the conservative alternative in the 1960s question suggested that medical care was properly left to the private sector or the free enterprise system, the question might very well have produced more conservatives. The other two pairs of items that produced strong differences also had solid counterarguments. The jobs item raised the theme of individualism by saying that others thought that each person should get ahead on his or her own. The fair jobs and housing item, like the aid to education item, suggests that those matters might properly be left to the states and local communities. In sum, the two items showing little or no difference are the items without counterarguments. The three items that yield large differences all have counterarguments.

The relationship between counterarguments and the extent of change in the results found in the SRC questions matches what one would expect based on the literature. Schuman and Presser (1981, ch. 7–8) carried out a number of experiments on question format, balancing arguments, and so forth. They found, as did everyone else, that acquiescence bias exists. More important for my purposes, they found that formal balancing of questions does not have any effect on the resulting marginal distributions, but including substantive counterarguments in the questions does.

By "formal balancing," Schuman and Presser mean asking a question of the form, "Some people think thus-and-so; others disagree. What do you think?" That is, the question says that others disagree, but it does not say why or offer a counterargument. Although the medical care item is not exactly formally balanced because it suggests as the alternative that the government "should stay out," it is very close to being formally balanced. It certainly does not go so far as to suggest a substantive counterargument, as do the employment item (which suggests individualism) and the aid to education item (which suggests local control). There is no reference to the private sector or free enterprise. Thus it should be no surprise that the medical care item fails to show any change, but the other items do.

These comments on what might have occurred had the 1960s questions been worded differently are speculative, but they bring out a basic problem in measuring public opinion. It is impossible to know exactly what the correct opposing alternatives are. One version will yield one answer; another version will yield a different answer.

The standard advice given by those who study question wording applies. One cannot interpret the answers to these questions as exactly reflecting public opinion. One should treat results as ranges rather than as exact reflections of public opinion. As many investigators have demonstrated (Cantril 1944; Schuman and Duncan 1974; Schuman and Presser

1981; Sudman and Bradburn 1974), subtle changes in question wording can produce substantial changes in the distribution of responses. In Davis's (1971, p. 20) words, "You should always be suspicious of single-variable results. . . . It is well known that the distribution of answers on attitude and opinion questions will vary by 15 or 20 percent with apparently slight changes in question wording."

Here there are enormous changes in the question wordings. To conclude that the changes in responses coinciding with the changes in the question wordings are real is just not acceptable. Some portion of that change may be real, but there is no way of finding out what that portion is. In the end, the only choice is to accept Schuman and Presser's (1981, p. 188) conclusion that "the effects of adding counterarguments are too pervasive and too large to allow the question forms [agree/disagree and balanced with counterarguments] . . . to be treated as interchangeable, for example, in studies of trends over time."

Another serious problem with the analysis by Nie and his colleagues is that some of the supposedly interchangeable questions were, in fact, substantively different. The previous list presents only five of the seven question areas dealt with by Nie et al. The questions were worded differently, but they were on substantively identical matters. To be sure, there were changes in the question wordings that twisted the meanings in ways that go beyond a shift from Likert to balanced questions (Bishop et al. 1978a). Nevertheless, the questions were clearly asking about the same issues.

The following two questions were used for the other two policy areas in the attitude consistency studies.

Old Question Wording (1956)	New Question Wording (1964)
Cold War	
The United States should keep soldiers overseas where they can help countries that are against communism. Do you have an opinion on this or not? [If Yes]: Do you think the government should do this?	Some people think our government should sit down and talk to the leaders of the communist countries and try to settle our differences, while others think we should refuse to have anything to do with them. Have you been interested enough to favor one side over the other? [If Yes]:
49.0% Agree strongly	
23.7 Agree, but not strongly	

11.1   Not sure, it depends
6.5   Disagree, but not very
       strongly
9.7   Disagree strongly
(N = 1,405)

What do you think? Should we: try to discuss and settle our differences or refuse to have anything to do with the leaders of communist countries?

84.3% Try to discuss
       differences
4.3   Other, depends
11.4   Refuse to have anything
       to do with communist
       leaders
(N = 1,334)

Size of Government

The government should leave things like electric power and housing for private businessmen to handle. Do you have an opinion on this or not? [If Yes]: Do you think the government should leave things like this to private business?

43.0% Agree strongly
15.5   Agree, but not very
       strongly
9.6   Not sure, it depends
10.6   Disagree, but not very
       strongly
21.3   Disagree strongly
(N = 1,249)

Some people say that the government in Washington is getting too powerful for the good of the country and the individual person. Others feel that the government in Washington has not gotten too strong for the good of the country. Have you been interested enough in this to favor one side over the other? [If Yes]: What is your feeling? Do you think the government is getting too powerful or do you think the government has not gotten too strong?

43.6% Govt is getting too
       powerful
4.5   Other, depends
51.9   Govt has not gotten too
       powerful
(N = 1,084)

Here the questions are just not about the same issues. The cold war question for the 1950s is whether the United States should keep soldiers overseas to fight communism. The 1960s question is whether the United States should sit down and talk to communist leaders. True, both questions deal with communists, but the similarities end there. Fighting and talking (about what? trade? nuclear weapons?) are just not the same. Indeed, U.S. policy since World War II has always been to keep soldiers abroad and to talk to most communist leaders. There have been exceptions (we have refused to talk to Cuban, North Korean, and North Vietnamese leaders at times), but we have always dealt with the Soviet Union. Thus those who agree with U.S. policy would be liberal according to one question and conservative according to the other. It just does not make sense to treat these two questions as interchangeable.

The size of government questions are also about vastly different subjects. The 1950s question is about government intervention in electric power and housing (the question does not even specify whether the "government" is local, state, or national). The 1960s question is about the power of the government in Washington. The reference to "the individual person" probably suggested civil liberties to many respondents. Of course, many ideas would occur to different people—civil rights, racial integration, student protests, welfare, the whole range of Great Society programs, and many other things as well. How many people would think of electric power and housing? Probably not many. In short, the two questions are just not about the same subjects. So why should they be considered interchangeable?

Curiously, there was a 1964 question that was somewhat similar to the 1950s power and housing question. The 1964 question was

Some people think it's all right for the government to own some power plants while others think the production of electricity should be left to private business. Have you been interested enough in this to favor one side over the other? [If Yes] Which position is more like yours, having the government own power plants or leaving this to private business?

This question is obviously much closer to the 1950s question. The housing aspect was dropped—which is a serious comparability problem—but the rest of the question is a much better match. Presumably, Nie and his colleagues chose the power of government question instead of the more similar electric power question because the power of government question was repeated in 1968 and later surveys.[9]

Whatever the reason, the two questions were not interchangeable. As Bishop et al. reported (1978a, p. 257–58), the correlation between the two questions in 1964 was only −.24 (the sign is negative because the

9. Of course, this did little good because the size of government question was dropped from the analysis in 1972.

two questions are worded in opposite directions). Thus one need not rely only on common sense to see that the two questions are not interchangeable. The data show that the relationship is weak. The size of government question that Nie et al. chose is actually more closely related to most of the other issue questions used in the analysis than to the electric power question that most closely matches the 1950s question.

In addition, there are other minor, but potentially influential differences in the substance of the two different versions of the questions. The aid to education question was about Washington helping to build schools if local cities could not afford it. The revised version of the question was whether the government in Washington "should provide education for grade and high school children." Gone was the condition, if cities and towns need help. Moreover, the questions had changed from public school construction to general aid to education.

The question was probably changed because the issue had changed in the country, and the Michigan researchers wanted to ask about a current issue. Not only had the issue changed; the sides had changed as well. It would be a mistake to assume that the people who were liberal on school construction were also liberal on general aid and that conservatives on the first issue were conservatives on the second.

Indeed, the historical record suggests this is not the case. Aid to education passed in April, 1964, when aid proponents revised their plans, abandoning money for teachers' salaries and school construction aid (which would have gone only to public schools) and substituting government assistance in purchasing textbooks and equipment (which would go to both public and private schools) (Johnson 1971, pp. 206–12). When the proposed package extended aid to private schools, Catholic leaders reversed their opposition, and the bill passed. So the two issues were not interchangeable.

The employment question also changed somewhat. The original question was whether the government should see to it that everyone who wants to work can find a job. The revised question was whether the government should see to it that everyone has a job and a good standard of living. It is not easy to see what difference that would make, but it is clear that a new idea was introduced into the question, and it may have had some effect. As several critics have said, with such different questions used before and after 1964, why should one expect the results to be comparable? There is no reason to do so.

A final problem with the marginal distributions resulting from the change in question wording is that the filters changed (Bishop et al. 1978a). The 1956 filter reads, "Now would you have an opinion on this or not?" The 1964 filter is, "Have you been interested enough in this to favor one side over the other?" The 1964 filter makes it easier to decline to answer than the earlier filter. Thus between the 1950s and the 1960s, there was an increase in both the number responding "Don't know" and the number saying that they had either "no opinion" (1950s) or "no interest" (1960s). The differences were not enormous. The largest was with the aid to education question. The 1950s version yielded 9 percent don't knows and no opinions; the 1960s version yielded 18 percent—a 9 percent difference. The average difference was only 2 percent.

Still, those who were filtered out were presumably the most likely to give random responses or "non-attitudes." By filtering out these random responders, the 1960s questions should have slightly increased the consistency of the remaining sample. Thus the change in filters may have artificially biased the results in favor of the increased consistency hypothesis.

Comparing Correlations

The controversy over question wording is not, of course, over whether it is methodologically acceptable to ignore changes in question format when tracing time trends. Few political scientists have used the attitude items to follow trends in opinion over the 1960–1964 period.[10] Nie, Verba, Petrocik, and the other proponents of the changing American voter thesis certainly never analyzed any time trends with question wording changes in them.[11]

The controversy is over the extent to which correlations between the different types of items are comparable. That is, can one compare a correlation between 1956 agree/disagree questions to a similar correlation between 1964 balanced questions? Even though the distributions of the items cannot be compared over time, perhaps the correlations between them can. Indeed, some analysts (e.g., Davis 1971) maintain that although question wordings may ruin comparisons among marginal distri-

10. For a lamentable exception, see Maddox and Lilie (1984). In their analysis of opinion over time, they blithely ignored the change in question wording. They assumed that all observed change between 1960 and 1964 is real.

11. Nie et al. (1976, pp. 195–96) did analyze the behavior of subgroups relative to the rest of the population. As they explained, this sort of analysis is on firmer methodological footing.

butions over time, they do not affect the correlations between items. However, Schuman and Duncan (1974, p. 236) pointed out that although analysts may assume that correlations are unaffected, there are few demonstrations that this assumption is justified. They provided several real examples in which comparing correlations would be a serious mistake.

The logic of comparing correlations despite changes in question wording is initially appealing. Suppose a change in question wording merely shifted respondents along a scale while keeping the original ordering of respondents intact. For instance, suppose the wording change in the jobs questions just pushed everyone in the conservative direction. A hypothetical example of this is shown in Figure 12. The initial positions of four respondents (A, B, C, and D) are shown on the upper scale. Each respondent moves one unit to the right, and their final positions are shown on the lower scale. Uniform changes such as these have little or no effect on the resulting correlations. In the hypothetical example in Figure 12, there is no effect whatsoever. In real examples, there can be some small changes in the values of the correlations, but they are not likely to be large.

Uniform shifts have no effect on correlations because in an ordinal statistic such as gamma, the scale values play no part. Only the order of the respondents on the scale matters in the calculation of gamma. So if A is to the left of B, who is to the left of C, who is to the left of D, then so far as gamma is concerned, nothing at all has changed. Thus if changes in question wording cause only uniform shifts in respondents, gammas can be compared across differently worded questions.[12]

The fact that survey questions offer discrete scales, not continuous ones like the one in my hypothetical example, would make some difference, but not much. The problem with discrete scales (i.e., scales offering only a few possible responses) is that all respondents will not be pushed uniformly. That is, all "ones" will not become "twos," all "twos" will not become "threes," and so forth. In practice, even when a change in question wording gives people a uniform push along a scale, some—but not all—people are moved from one category to another. That is, all the liberals do not become moderates. Some liberals are pushed to the right; others are not. Insofar as the movement is not uniform, the correlation will be affected.

12. For those who prefer interval measures such as Pearson's r, the explanation is slightly more complicated, but the result is the same. Uniform shifts have no effect on correlations because correlations measure association in relative order.

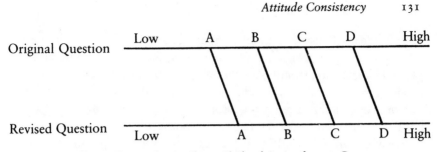

Figure 12. The Effects of a Uniform Shift of Attitudes on Gamma

Following this logic, Nie and his colleagues (Nie and Andersen 1974; Nie et al. 1976) assumed that correlations could be compared despite the change in question wordings.[13] The marginals might not be comparable, but the correlations would be. Thus given the assumption of the change in question wording having a uniform effect, their analysis of consistency would be acceptable.

Unfortunately for Nie and his colleagues, the assumption underlying the comparability argument is false. The key assumption is that the wording change does nothing except move respondents along a scale. The original ordering is assumed to be kept by the new question. Yet the very reason for the SRC change in wording is also the reason the original orderings were not kept: The questions were contaminated with response set bias.

The problem with response set bias is that it is not uniform. Some people have a strong tendency to agree, others a mild tendency; some have no bias at all; and some have a tendency to disagree. Thus response set bias is not a constant influence, but a source of variance unrelated to the substance of the question. Removing the response set variance does not uniformly push respondents along a scale. Some respondents will answer more conservatively, others more liberally; others will not be affected. The bottom line is that when the question wordings were changed, one systematic source of variance (response set bias) was removed, and a new source of variance was added (the effect of the counterarguments). Therefore the new questions do not keep the original order. And that is precisely why the new questions were asked.

13. Nie et al. (1976, pp. 195–96) did not explicitly discuss the statistical assumptions they made in comparing correlations. They stated that correlations could be compared even though marginal distributions could not, but they did not say why. Instead they dealt with a range of other matters in their explanation of why they decided that the change in question format was irrelevant (see Nie and Andersen 1974, pp. 550–51, n. 10). However, this logic necessarily underlies their position.

Thus the usual justification for comparing correlations when questions have been changed does not apply. In general, the justification never applies when changing from Likert format questions to balanced questions or vice versa. Minor wording changes may indeed preserve the original ordering, but adding or removing response set bias is virtually guaranteed not to preserve that ordering. Because response set bias is a substantive source of variance, it would almost be as if one were comparing substantively different questions. In sum, the statistical justification for comparing correlations across the 1960–1964 gap is bogus. The analysis should not have been done.

Further Problems

As Bishop et al. (1978a, pp. 260–65) first pointed out, in order to make comparisons across the 1960–1964 gap with its enormous change in marginal distributions, Nie and his colleagues collapsed the 1950s questions from their original five points to three—liberal, moderate, and conservative. They followed two guidelines in the recoding: (1) The proportions in the three categories were to be as equal as possible. (2) The recoding was not permitted to place respondents from agree and disagree categories in the original variable into the same category in the recoded variable.

In addition to sidestepping the problem of the enormous changes in marginal distributions, this recoding was required to make the correlation coefficients (gammas) comparable across the time gap. Gamma is sensitive to the number of cells in a table. Because the 1950s and 1960s versions of the questions had different numbers of response categories, they had to be recoded so that they would all be the same (Nie and Andersen 1974, pp. 546–47, n. 7).

Although the recoding scheme resolved one problem with using gamma, another problem remained. Gamma is unstable when it is calculated from tables with small cell frequencies (Blalock 1972; Mueller et al. 1970; Weissberg 1976). Small cell N's were a problem with the 1964 data.

The 1964 format questions were essentially dichotomous questions. Respondents could volunteer centrist opinions, but that type of response was not suggested. The result was that in 1964, relatively few respondents took the middle positions. This caused a problem with gamma: When the center cell in a 3 × 3 table has a small frequency, gamma is unstable and can easily be inflated. To see how this works, see Table 21, which shows the cross-tabulation of the size of government and black fair

TABLE 21. Percentage of the Total Sample Falling into
Each of Nine Cells in a 3×3 Cross-Tabulation of Issue Questions
About the Size of Government and Black Welfare in the 1956 and 1964
SRC Election Studies

1956

| | Size of Government | | |
Black Welfare	Liberal	Centrist	Conservative
Liberal	16.7	11.0	18.7
Centrist	8.7	9.5	10.4
Conservative	7.3	4.9	12.7

1964

| | Size of Government | | |
Black Welfare	Liberal	Centrist	Conservative
Liberal	36.7	1.8	10.5
Centrist	3.7	.7	3.6
Conservative	15.8	1.8	25.5

Source. Bishop et al. 1978a, t. 3, p. 261.

housing and jobs items in 1956 and 1964. The entries in each cell are the percentages of the entire sample for each year falling into that cell (sometimes called corner percentages). The important figures here are the two central cells. In 1956, 9.5 percent of the sample took centrist positions on both questions; in 1964, that number had fallen to only .7 percent. The fact that this number is very small makes gamma unstable and, in this case, inflated.[14]

To see why this is the case, consider the formula for calculating gamma:

$$Gamma = \frac{C - D}{C + D}$$

Where C = the number of concordant pairs
D = the number of discordant pairs

14. To say that a coefficient is "unstable" is to say that changes in a few cases will cause large changes in the value of the coefficient.

Concordant pairs are pairs of cases lying along the main diagonal of the table. For instance, if respondent A is liberal on both items, and respondent B is conservative on both items, then that pair of respondents is concordant (because respondent B has a higher score on both items than respondent A). One can thus count the concordant pairs of respondents by starting in the upper left-hand cell and multiplying its frequency by the frequency of every cell below and to the right of it. After adding up these products, one repeats the process with the cell to the immediate right of the upper left-hand cell and continues the process for every cell. Discordant pairs are pairs of cases lying along the minor diagonal (from upper right to lower left). The method of counting them is the same (Blalock 1972; Mueller et al. 1970). Tied pairs (i.e., pairs of cases in which respondents give the same answer on one or both items) are ignored in the calculation of gamma.

As Bishop et al. (1978a, p. 261) comment in discussing the problem with the small central cell frequency,

the dichotomous forced-choice items in the 1964 study, by pushing many more respondents into the only available end categories and leaving very few in the center category, creates a much larger multiplier for the upper-right or upper-left (and lower-left and lower-right) corners of the contingency table than the 1956 items, which spread the cases more evenly through the middle three categories of the five-point Likert item.

In other words, by forcing more cases into the corners, the 1964 format inflates the number of concordant and discordant pairs. The inflation results from the fact that for a given case in, say, the upper left-hand corner cell, there are four other cells that are concordant (below and to the right), but for a case in the center cell, only two cells are concordant. In effect, this is because gamma does not include tied pairs in its calculation. Pairs in the corner cells have four cells with which they can form concordant or discordant pairs, but pairs in the central cells have only two cells with which they can form pairs. Thus pushing cases into the corners makes gamma very unstable. In this case, the result is an inflated gamma.

Bishop et al. did not claim that this problem with the marginal distributions is the sole cause of the increase in consistency, but that it is a contributing cause, along with many others. Insofar as that goes, they are right. Yet this is probably only a minor problem.

The defenders of the changing American voter thesis (Nie and Rabjohn 1979; Petrocik 1978) did not respond to this argument about gammas, but they might well have done so. The problem with the argument is that it is limited to 1964 and 1968. In 1972, the question formats were changed once again. This time the questions remained the same, but the response categories were changed. Instead of being offered two choices, respondents were offered a seven point scale with the two endpoints labeled by the two positions offered in the questions. The new seven point scales did not force respondents into the corners. Instead, respondents were distributed over the full range, with a fair number always choosing the centrist option—number 4. Despite this change in format, the level of consistency did not change. Thus the forced choice questions in 1964 may have explained part of the 1964 jump, but they could not explain why attitude consistency remained high after 1964.

The most reasonable conclusion seems to be that the 1964 results were somewhat contaminated, but the contamination was only a minor contributing cause. Because attitude consistency remained high without the forced choice format, that cannot explain the jump in consistency. Of course, this problem was with the choices offered to the respondents. It has nothing to do with the basic—and extremely important—change from Likert questions to balanced questions.

The Experimental Evidence

The arguments discussed so far are all based on analysis of the statistical and theoretical properties of the questions and the historical data. There were, however, several experimental replications of the two question formats. Although these data are not without their problems, they offer another important basis for deciding what really happened during the first four years of the sixties.

Four question wording experiments are reported in the literature on the change in question format. Two involved students, one was based on samples from the Twin Cities, Minneapolis and St. Paul, Minnesota, and one was part of a national survey conducted by NORC.

Brunk (1978) examined six of the seven pairs of questions used by Nie et al. (excluding the foreign affairs questions).[15] He randomly administered one of two versions of the questionnaire (1950s or 1960s format) to 225 undergraduates at the University of Iowa.[16] Then, following the

15. Brunk did not use the foreign affairs questions because in 1968 and 1972 they dealt with the Vietnam War and were thus inappropriate after it was over. He did not explain why he did not use the 1964 cold war question about talking with communist leaders.

16. The only difference between the SRC version and Brunk's was that he sub-

TABLE 22.   Brunk's Iowa Student Experiment

1960 SRC Interview Format

	E	SA	BW	M	SI
Average N = 83					
Employment (E)	E	SA	BW	M	SI
School aid (SA)	−.07				
Black welfare (BW)	.03	.04			
Medicare (M)	.40	.21	.10		
School integration (SI)	.06	−.26	.24	−.06	
Size of government	−.07	−.26	.40	−.02	.08

1964 SRC Interview Format

	E	SA	BW	M	SI
Average N = 78					
Employment (E)	E	SA	BW	M	SI
School aid (SA)	.68				
Black welfare (BW)	.57	.28			
Medicare (M)	.86	.85	−.11		
School integration (SI)	.68	.45	.52	.30	
Size of government	.26	.70	.03	.80	.29

	Average Gammas of the Experimental Groups	
	1960 Format	1964 Format
All questions	.05	.48
Size of government question removed	.07	.51
Size of government question removed and social welfare question gammas averaged	.07	.40

Source. Brunk 1978, t. 2, 3, pp. 353, 354.

rules set down by Nie et al. for collapsing the 1950s format questions into three categories, he recoded the data.

Brunk's experiment yielded two important findings. First, four of the

---

stituted "blacks" for "negroes" and "colored persons" wherever either term appeared in both question formats. This seems to be both reasonable and advisable.

six questions produced significantly different distributions of responses. That is, the two types of questions were not interchangeable. Second, and more important, he found that the inter-item gammas produced by the 1964 format questions were substantially higher than those produced by the 1950s questions (see Table 22). The 1950s questions had an average gamma of .05; the balanced questions had an average gamma of .48. Although this dramatic difference cannot be generalized from a group of Iowa students to the U.S. population, it certainly puts in doubt the bland assurances that the items are interchangeable.

The other experimental examination of the question formats with college students was conducted by John Petrocik (1978). As he and his co-authors did in *The Changing American Voter*, Petrocik combined questions in five areas. This makes the findings exactly comparable with the Nie et al. work, but it does not allow one to break out the data on individual questions when two or more questions were used in an area. For instance, Petrocik reported the average correlation between "social welfare" and other items. Social welfare is the label for questions about guaranteed jobs, aid to education, and Medicare. All three are lumped together and thus are indistinguishable. Because Petrocik focused his analysis on the NORC experiment, he neglected to report any details on how the UCLA student experiment was performed (e.g., number of cases).

Petrocik's results, although not as stark as Brunk's, reveal a difference in the two question formats (see Table 23). The 1950s version had an average gamma of .34; the later version had an average gamma of .44. Excluding the size of government question on the grounds that its meaning had changed by the 1970s, causing Nie et al. to drop it from their analysis (a suggestion of Petrocik's [1978, p. 366, n. 2]), raises the average gamma of the 1960s format questions to .52. Thus the difference between the two formats is .18, a respectable difference, although not as large as the one Brunk found or as the jump in consistency between 1960 and 1964. Nevertheless, allowing for the different population and possible changes in how respondents would interpret the questions over the years, Petrocik should probably have found his results fairly disturbing.

Sullivan, Pierson, and Marcus (1978) conducted a larger experiment on the general population in the Twin Cities in 1976. They drew two samples, administering the old questions to 200 persons and the new questions to 198 persons. Like Brunk, they did not use the foreign affairs questions.

The results of the Twin Cities experiment were almost exactly what one would expect if the jump in consistency was caused by the question

TABLE 23.   Petrocik's UCLA Experiment

	Election Studies					
	1956 & 1960	1964	1950s Format	1964 Format	1950s Format	1964 Format
Social welfare/ black welfare	.38	.48	.48	.63	.27	.49
Social welfare/ school integration	.16	.26	.07	.52	.32	.53
Social welfare/size of government	.16	.52	.30	.28	.52	.35
Social welfare/ cold war	−.09	.26	.12	.06	.37	.38
Black welfare/ school integration	.50	.71	.25	.77	.61	.88
Black welfare/size of government	.08	.51	.16	.22	.33	.30
Black welfare/ cold war	−.14	.29	.02	.09	.10	.41
School integration/ size of government	.20	.46	.37	.25	.23	.34
School integration/ cold war	.00	.20	.14	.22	.37	.43
Size of government/ cold war	.03	.42	.25	.16	.32	.30

Source. Petrocik 1978, p. 363.

Note: Cell entries are gammas.

wording change (see Table 24). The 1950s format questions yielded gammas very similar to the same questions asked during the 1950s, and the 1960s format questions yielded gammas similar to the real 1964 data. The only exceptions, as previously explained by Nie et al., were the correlations between the size of government question and other items. As predicted, size of government had ceased to be correlated with other liberal-conservative policy items. Thus the evidence against the changing American voter thesis continues to mount.

The data from the 1973 NORC experiment were reported by both Bishop et al. (1978b) and Petrocik (1978) and were challenged by Nie and Rabjohn (1979) as being critically flawed so that they were of no use.

TABLE 24.   The Sullivan et al. Twin Cities Experiment

	Correlations (Gammas) for Old and New Questions	
	Old Wording	New Wording
Welfare/black welfare	.28	.43
Welfare/integration	.11	.30
Welfare/size of government	.09	.14
Black welfare/integration	.35	.58
Black welfare/size of government	.09	.06
Integration/size of government	.20	.26

Source. Sullivan et al. 1978, p. 241.

In the experiment, NORC administered three separate versions of the issue questions to three subsamples of about five hundred persons each. The first version asked the 1950 format questions, the second asked the 1964 format questions, and the third asked the 1964 questions revised so that they had seven point response scales.

The results of the NORC experiment are presented in Table 25 as they were by Bishop et al. (1978b, p. 85, t. 1) so that the difference between two groups of correlations stands out clearly. Group B consists of all pairs of issues that include either the size of government question or the cold war question. Group A consists of all pairs of issues that do not include either of those questions.

The difference between the groups is enormous. In group A, there is a substantial increase in gammas between the two question formats. A difference exists for every pair of correlations. The average difference is .30, the same as the size of the 1960–1964 jump (.28). In group B, there are almost no differences. The average gammas for both versions of the questions are .14. A more detailed look at the data shows some movement. The average gamma increased about .06 for pairs including the cold war item, and it fell for pairs including the size of government item. Still, on the whole, question wording made little difference for the cold war and size of government questions.

In order to compare these results with the Nie et al. results, we can do as Nie and his colleagues suggested: drop the size of government item, and look at the average of the remaining items. Without size of govern-

TABLE 25. The NORC Experiment

Group A

Issue Pair	Pre-1964	1964	1968–1976
Welfare/medical	.58	.79	.56
Welfare/school aid	.42	.50	.35
Welfare/black welfare	.36	.65	.44
Welfare/school integration	.02	.59	.44
School aid/medical	.56	.80	.24
School aid/black welfare	.52	.61	.34
School aid/school integration	−.10	.51	.37
Medical/black welfare	.45	.62	.28
Medical/school integration	.02	.43	.24
Black welfare/school integration	−.25	.77	.57
Average gamma	.33	.63	.38

Group B

Issue Pair	Pre-1964	1964	1968–1976
Welfare/government power	−.13	−.14	−.05
Welfare/cold war	−.04	−.02	.00
Medical/government power	−.22	.06	.03
Medical/cold war	−.08	−.11	−.13
School aid/government power	−.14	−.14	.01
School aid/cold war	.06	.12	.08
Black welfare/government power	−.16	−.22	−.10
Black welfare/cold war	.02	.08	−.01
School integration/government power	.39	−.25	−.16
School integration/cold war	.09	.20	−.11
Government power/cold war	.17	.17	−.04
Average gamma	.14	.14	.07

Source. Bishop et al. 1978, p. 85.

Note: Average gammas are based on the absolute values of the gammas.

TABLE 26.   Average Gammas by Differences
in Question Format and Time of Interview

	1950s Format	1960s Format
At election time (1956 or 1964)	.13	.41
In 1973 (NORC experiment)	.22	.32 with size of government .37 without size of government

Source. Petrocik 1978, t. 2, p. 364.

ment, the 1950s format average is .24; the 1960s format average is .46, a difference of .22. That difference is not as large as the 1960–1964 jump of .28, but it is close enough for discomfort.

A better way to compare the experimental results with the original data is to follow the Nie et al. procedure for averaging the data. The authors of *The Changing American Voter* did not use a simple average, but instead averaged correlations within each of five policy areas, and then computed the average of the averages for those five areas. The result of this procedure, shown in Table 26, is more ambiguous than the other experimental data. When the data are calculated this way, the 1960s format questions have an average gamma of .37 (the size of government item is again dropped) versus the real figure of .41 in 1964. So the experiment reproduces the 1960s figure fairly well. But the 1950s average gamma is .22, a fair amount higher than the original figure of .13. How should these findings be interpreted?

Petrocik's position is essentially that we should treat the NORC experiment as an exact replication. The original difference between 1960 and 1964 correlations was .28. The experimental difference between the two formats was .15, or about 54 percent of the original difference. Therefore, Petrocik argues, we cannot attribute more than half the original shift to question wording. The other half is real change.

The problem with this argument is that the question wording experiments are obviously not exact replications. When NORC asked two versions of the questions, it asked them of a sample of citizens in 1973. The issues had changed, and to some extent, the ways in which people interpreted the questions changed as well. The school integration question provides an excellent example of this. In the early 1960s, the issue was whether the federal government should force an end to *de jure* segregation in the South. By the 1970s, the issue had become busing in both the North and the South. The question does not explicitly ask about either. It asks whether the federal government should see to it that white and black children go to the same school. In the context of 1956 and 1960, that meant one thing. By 1973, it mean something entirely different. Other questions have similar problems. Indeed, the size of government question was dropped because of such a problem.

Obviously, no exact replication is possible. Nie and Rabjohn (1979, pp. 148–49) made the same point in their own defense. The results of the experiments must be viewed as no more than approximations.

It follows that Petrocik's position is not tenable. It runs afoul of the scientific practice of assuming that the null hypothesis is true unless the evidence to the contrary is overwhelming (the assumption behind the conventional 95 percent confidence interval). It does so because we know there was a large question wording effect. Two experiments found that the effect was somewhat smaller than the 1960–1964 consistency increase (Petrocik's UCLA students and the NORC experiment), one experiment found that the effect was about the same size as the increase in consistency (the Twin Cities experiment), and one found that the effect was even larger (Brunk's Iowa students). Because we know the effect was large, but not exactly how large, we cannot confidently say that we *know* (with 95 percent or more confidence) that it was smaller than the jump in consistency. Lacking this confidence, we must conclude that the null hypothesis holds true: There was no sudden increase in consistency between 1960 and 1964.

One last objection to the NORC experiment remains. Nie and Rabjohn claimed that the results were worthless because of the changes in public opinion on those issues over time. Their objection is only to the NORC experiment; it does not apply to the other three experiments (cf. Sullivan et al. 1979, p. 178). Those results remain unchallenged.

Nie and Rabjohn (1979, pp. 143–49) criticized the NORC experiment on the grounds that the marginal distributions in the 1950s format questions were severely skewed, so much so that they created statistical problems. The distributions of some of the original 1950s questions and of the NORC questions are shown in Table 27. (The distributions for the original questions are averages of the 1956, 1958, and 1960 data to ease comparison.) If one uses a 70-30 threshold as a rule of thumb, four of the five NORC items in the table are, as claimed, quite skewed.

TABLE 27. Marginal Distributions on Pre-1964 Items:
1956–1960 Average and 1974 Replication

	SRC/CPS 1956–1960 Average	NORC 1974
Medical care:		
Liberal	64%	91%
Moderate	12	2
Conservative	24	7
Job guarantee:		
Liberal	64	86
Moderate	8	3
Conservative	28	11
Black welfare:		
Liberal	71	79
Moderate	8	6
Conservative	21	15
School aid:		
Liberal	69	77
Moderate	14	5
Conservative	17	19
School integration:		
Liberal	46	30
Moderate	7	5
Conservative	47	66

Source. Nie and Rabjohn 1979, p. 146.

Note: The five original response categories are collapsed into three categories.

There are two problems with extreme distributions according to Nie and Rabjohn. First, some portion of responses in every category is presumably response error. That is, respondents will misunderstand questions, interviewers will record answers incorrectly, and so forth. Thus Nie and Rabjohn suggested that as much as 5 or even 10 percent of the responses in any category may be erroneous. This means that a large portion of the conservative responses to the jobs and medical care questions may be error; consequently, the correlations based on them are suspect.

Second, as a practical matter, shifts in marginal distributions affect the sizes of correlation coefficients. Because the 1973 marginals are not the same as the original marginals, comparing the correlations is a mistake.

There are several problems with this argument. First, as noted previously, it does not apply to the Twin Cities experiment because the marginals in that study match those of 1960 and 1964.[17] Second, of the seven questions in the NORC experiment, only two—the jobs and medical care questions—have really extremely skewed disributions and are much different from the distributions in the 1950s. That is, even though the black housing/jobs and school aid items are skewed past the 70-30 threshold, they are not very different from the distributions that those questions received in the 1950s. Skewness may be a problem, but if it is, then it was also a problem in the 1950s. The distributions of both items changed by only 8 percent. That small shift is not going to ruin the comparability of the items, even if they do pass the magical 70 percent threshold (which, after all, is only a rule of thumb). Third, as Weisberg (1974) has shown, gamma is relatively insensitive to shifts in marginals distributions, far less sensitive than almost any other measure of association. And fourth, skewness does not necessarily increase the correlation. Rather, it makes correlations unstable. As skewness increases, they are not biased upwards as Nie and Rabjohn suggest. Instead, they become less stable so that they can go in either direction.

In sum, Nie and Rabjohn's objections to the NORC experiment are not persuasive. Certainly it is true, as they maintained, that exact replications are not possible. Yet this is not something that should lead one to conclude that *The Changing American Voter* was right. Nie and Rabjohn come close to saying that because the 1960–1964 shift is not falsifiable, one must conclude that it really happened. That argument is completely wrong. There were huge question wording effects in the 1960s. The burden of proof that some part of those changes was real lies with those who claim it was real.

Finally, Nie and Rabjohn (1979, pp. 149–67) present evidence that attitude consistency increased among a different set of items whose question wordings did not change over the years. Specifically, they examined a set of items about tolerance for atheists, socialists, and communists that Samuel Stouffer (1955) first asked in 1954. He asked respondents whether they were willing to let a member of each of those three groups give a public speech, teach in a college, or have a book in a public library. Those same nine items were asked again in the NORC General Social Surveys of 1972, 1973, and 1974. Because the exact question wordings and ques-

17. It may or may not apply to the student experiments. Because those marginal distributions were not reported, we do not know. Obviously, the Twin Cities experiment is the other important experiment.

tion order were maintained, the results are comparable across time with none of the methodological problems that faced the SRC/CPS items.

The data reveal that there was, in fact, an increase in consistency over the almost twenty-year period from 1954 to the early 1970s. The average gamma among the items increased from .67 to .80, a gain of .13. In addition, the authors performed a principal component analysis that showed that the first component explained 40 percent of the variance in 1954, but 53 percent of the variance in the 1970s. This, they said, demonstrated that the civil liberties items were becoming unidimensional.

Nie and Rabjohn use the civil liberties data as a basis for their argument that there really was a surge in consistency between 1960 and 1964. Their reasoning is that the civil liberties data show that such increases can occur, and that in a related set of items, an increase occurred during the same general period.

There are several problems with this argument. First, it is not at all clear why one can generalize from a narrow group of items that were specifically written to form a scale (the civil liberties items) to a broad group of items that were selected to represent the full spectrum of political conflict in an election (Bishop et al. 1979, p. 189). The comparison is at best strained.

Second, Nie and Rabjohn's principal component analysis contained an a priori assumption that a single dimension was the primary cause of all nine items. Sullivan et al. reanalyzed the data using a more sophisticated LISREL model. The Nie-Rabjohn single factor model fits the data very poorly. A six factor model with three group specific factors and three act specific factors (one factor each for speaking, teaching, and putting a book in the library) fits the data far better. On the basis of their analysis, Sullivan et al. suggested that the explanation for the increase in consistency was that respondents did not distinguish among the three groups as easily as they did in the 1950s. As the three groups became less distinct, the public began to treat them more similarly, and the correlations increased as a consequence. Thus Nie and Rabjohn's claim that the tolerance items are becoming unidimensional is not supported.

Third, Nie and Rabjohn presented the correlations of a tolerance scale built from the nine items with four other selected items intended to measure the liberal-conservative continuum (legalization of marijuana, black civil rights, abortion, equal rights amendment). The correlations were high, and Nie and Rabjohn used them to argue that tolerance was closely related to the liberal-conservative dimension. Bishop et al. (1979, p. 191) countered that there were a number of other available items that could have been correlated with the tolerance scale. A liberal-conservative self-placement scale, for instance, correlated at the fairly low level of .23 with the tolerance scale (compared to .53 for the "selected items"). Other items that Bishop and his colleagues examined yielded similarly poor results. Thus tolerance is apparently not very closely related to the liberal-conservative continuum, as Nie and Rabjohn maintained.

There is no evidence of much change from 1960 to 1964 among the items used to measure attitude consistency, but between 1954 and the early 1970s, there was a great deal of change in tolerance for civil liberties (Erskine and Siegel 1975). Certainly it is reasonable to expect that when public opinion on a set of issues changes, the relationship between the opinions may also change. For that matter, when the marginal distributions of items change, the correlation between them can change even if the underlying causal relationships remain constant.

There was a substantial growth in tolerance from the 1950s to the 1970s, coupled with a modest change in the inter-item correlations. This is hardly surprising. Yet Nie and Rabjohn would have us believe that even though there is no evidence of any changes in opinion between 1960 and 1964, there was a huge jump in consistency. That just does not follow.

The final conclusion about Nie and Rabjohn's tolerance argument is that it fails. The data they presented are certainly interesting for those who study tolerance, but they are just not relevant to the attitude consistency problem.

In the end, what should one make of the question wording controversy? There is not the slightest shadow of a doubt that the now notorious change in question wordings caused a jump in the correlations between the attitude items. Even the defenders of the changing American voter thesis admit this. By the time the mistake was recognized, it was too late to find out what had really happened in the early 1960s. Given the overwhelming evidence that most and possibly all of the jump in consistency was caused by the question wording switch, one has no choice but to conclude that nothing happened. Consistency did not increase; instead, measurement methods improved. Therefore what appears is an unchanging American voter.

Conceptualizing Attitude Consistency

Although a great deal has been written about attitude consistency, little attention has been given to the theoretical foundations of the idea. In particular, remarkably little has been written about the problem of how to choose the attitude questions that will be used in the analysis. There have been some ad hoc decisions to include or exclude variables, but there has not been any rigorous thinking on general rules for item selection. With the exception of Converse, who helped write the SRC questions in the 1950s studies, attitude consistency researchers have largely been limited to using whatever items SRC decided to put in the survey each time. Usually they have followed the "use all available items" approach to item selection.[18] If the items in a consistency analysis make any difference—and obviously they do—there must be some theoretically justified basis for selecting them. I will now return to the foundations of consistency theory and try to see what that basis might be.

Since Fritz Heider (1944, 1946) first proposed balance theory, there has been a proliferation of closely related theories, which are collectively referred to as cognitive consistency theories. Because they are so similar, I focus on balance theory, emphasizing the elements of Heider's theory that are common to all consistency theories. More detailed reviews are available in Brown (1965), Kiesler et al. (1969), and McGuire (1966).

Balance theory deals with the relationships between a person and objects in the person's phenomenological world. Heider distinguished two basic types of relationships, which can be either positive or negative. The first type is that of liking or evaluating. Examples of such relationships include loving, approving, disliking, and hating. The second type is that of associating. Examples of associating include similarity, possession, causality, and proximity.

A balanced or consistent state is defined in terms of combinations of relations between a person and an object or among a person and two objects. In the case of a person and a single object, a balanced state exists when both evaluative and associative relations are either all positive or all negative. For instance, when one likes a public policy (positive evaluation) and it is enacted (positive association) or when one dislikes a policy and it is not enacted, one is in a balanced state. On the other hand, when one likes a policy that is not enacted or dislikes a policy that is, one is in an imbalanced state.

In the case of a person and two objects, a balanced state exists when all relations are positive or when two of the three relations are negative (see Figure 13). For instance, if one likes a presidential candidate, favors pro-environmental policies, and believes that the candidate also favors those

18. Alternatively, this might be called the Mt. Everest method. Why use an item? Because it is there!

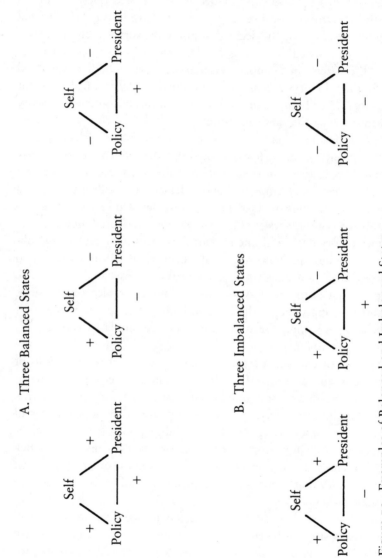

A. Three Balanced States

B. Three Imbalanced States

Figure 13. Examples of Balanced and Imbalanced States

Note: + means positive association (e.g., liking, preferring).
      − means negative association (e.g., disliking, opposing).

policies, one is balanced. Alternatively, if one opposes environmental policies, dislikes a candidate, and believes that the candidate favors those policies, one is again in balance. On the other hand, if one likes a candidate, opposes the environmental policies, but thinks that the candidate supports them, then an imbalanced state exists. In short, to be in a balanced or consistent state, one must like what one's friends like, dislike what one's friends dislike, like what one's enemies dislike, and so on.

According to Heider's model, balanced states are stable and resistant to change. Imbalanced states are unstable and are assumed to cause some sort of psychological tension that can be relieved only by changes among the relations toward a balanced state. Thus the psychological tension— referred to by other investigators as "stress," "discomfort," and "psychic pain"—is the dynamic force for attitude change.

The last central proposition of balance theory, which was pointed out by Osgood and Tannenbaum (1955) and Abelson and Rosenberg (1958), is what might be called the association condition: In order for an imbalanced set of attitudes to produce any tension, the individual must associate the various elements with one another. As long as the individual does not connect potentially conflicting ideas and perceptions with one another, there will be no conflict, and hence no tension and no attitude change. When an individual does bring conflicting ideas into association with one another, perhaps by simply thinking about them together, tension will be produced, and attitude change may result.

The association condition can be recognized as Converse's (1964, p. 208) dynamic case definition of constraint. When change in one attitude causes change in others, the attitudes are constrained. That, of course, is the association condition. So Converse's dynamic case definition is that attitudes are constrained when they are sufficiently closely associated with one another to make the attitude change dynamics of the consistency model relevant.

This also explains why consistency is a measure of political sophistication. People who know a good deal about politics, who think about the issues, and who understand the arguments that connect different issue positions—that is to say, people who are sophisticated—will be constrained. People who do not have the facts to connect the issues, or who do not think about politics so that they never get around to connecting the issues or who do not understand the arguments that connect the issues—that is to say, the unsophisticated—will not be constrained. Thus the theoretical foundations for Converse's work on attitude consistency stem from the work of Heider and others in cognitive consistency theory.

In his famous investigation of mass belief systems, Converse (1964) dealt with the nature of consistency, its sources, and a number of related characteristics. Although he established cognitive consistency theory as a basis for analyzing attitudes, his discussion was not very rigorous. He neither presented a set of theoretical propositions outlining his own version of consistency theory nor relied on any other published version of the theory. (In fact, Converse actually cited only a single consistency theory study [McGuire 1960], and he used it only to make a minor point about consistency stemming from logical relationships.) Instead, he presented a general discussion without treating any aspect of the underlying theory in detail. This vagueness caused many problems.

However, one can hardly blame Converse for not providing a detailed analysis. He did what he set out to do. He sought to assess the extent of ideological thinking in the mass public, not to forge a formal theory of belief systems. His analysis is a first attempt to extend consistency theory into the political sphere.[19] He left for later investigators the problem of developing a more formal model. The problem is that no one fully developed that model.

I now turn to Converse's typology of the sources of constraint to show how his work and consistency theory fit together. Converse identified three sources: (1) logical—in the sense of formal logic, (2) psychological—in the sense of the rationality of a strong argument, and (3) social—in the sense of social pressures to accept certain opinions. Let me consider how we might define consistency for these three sources.

The nature of logical constraints is simple. A set of attitudes is consistent if it is consistent according to the rules of formal logic. That is, a set of propositions is consistent if both a proposition and its negation cannot be derived from the set (Mates 1972). For instance, it would be inconsistent to believe that (1) all men are mortal, (2) Socrates was a man, and (3) Socrates was not mortal.

As Converse pointed out, few political issues are subject to logical constraints. There are, however, exceptions. For instance, principles of civil liberties such as freedom of speech can be logically related to specific, concrete applications. If one favors absolute freedom of speech, then one should favor it for communists, fascists, and so forth. Most consistency

19. This is a bit of an exaggeration. A few social psychologists examined political beliefs in their experiments. In addition, McPhee et al. (1962) examined attitude consistency a few years earlier. Their analysis is a more sophisticated, yet theoretically less useful analysis. So although Converse is not the first political scientist to examine attitude consistency, he is the first important one.

studies, of course, do not deal with examples of reasoning from the general to the specific, so logical constraints are rarely relevant.[20]

Psychological constraints are more common among political issues, but harder to define rigorously. Heider's basic idea of bringing a set of evaluations and associations into balance applies, but because the sets to be balanced are sometimes long chains of reasoning, the problem is difficult. For instance, what do the principles of liberalism imply for our foreign policy in Nicaragua? Many arguments are possible, and evaluating them with the simple calculus Heider and his fellow consistency theorists offered is no easy task.

Coherent, persuasive arguments are like obscenity. We cannot define them precisely, but we know them when we see them. Although formulating a clear definition is probably impossible, one cannot criticize Converse on this score. After all, this imprecision in defining consistency is a well-known problem of nearly all consistency theories. Zajonc (1960, p. 285) provided an anecdote that illustrates the problem nicely: "Festinger once inquired in a jocular mood if it followed from balance theory that since he likes chicken, and since chickens like chicken feed, he must also like chicken feed or else experience the tension of imbalance."

There have been several efforts to develop formal methods for assessing arguments, but they have all been fairly narrow. The most important of these are Abelson and Rosenberg's (Abelson and Rosenberg 1958; Rosenberg and Abelson 1960). Although their "symbolic psycho-logic" is interesting, it is far more limiting than common notions about what constitutes a good argument. For instance, their model deals only with dichotomous variables. Seven point attitude scales do not work in their model. Thus, such efforts are of little use here. We must accept the obscenity standard.

Social constraints, which Converse maintained were more common than either logical or psychological constraints, are fairly similar to psychological constraints. The difference is that whereas psychological sources involve bringing a set of opinions into balance, social sources involve bringing both opinions and evaluations of people into balance.[21]

20. For an excellent discussion of the differences between "vertical" constraint (connections between general propositions and specific ones) and "horizontal" constraint (connections between two or more general propositions), see Conover and Feldman (1980).

21. This is not what Converse said. I am restating his definitions in such a manner that they can be usefully related to cognitive consistency theory. The goal is to develop a basis for item selection within Converse's framework.

For instance, if an individual likes President Reagan, and the president advocates abolishing the Department of Education, then the individual should favor abolishing the department. As in the example, social constraints usually involve politicians or other influential public leaders.

Again, the definitions of balance and imbalance come directly from cognitive consistency theory (i.e., a set of three elements is balanced if all three relations are positive or if two are negative and the third is positive). Here, however, the chains of reasoning to be balanced are much shorter and easier to analyze. Why should a liberal oppose American involvement in Nicaragua? Because Ted Kennedy, Tip O'Neil, and other leading liberals oppose it.

In light of these definitions, I can now ask how one knows when a given pair of attitudes is consistent. Converse's answer is that to the extent that the attitudes are socially constrained, they will fall into a liberal-conservative ordering because that is how elites' beliefs are ordered. It follows that a pair of attitudes is consistent when both are liberal, both are moderate, or both are conservative.

In terms of balance theory, Converse's theory may be stated as follows: (1) Elites may be placed on the liberal-conservative dimension.[22] (2) Elites advocate issue positions associated with their ideological positions. (3) The mass public learns issue positions from elites. (4) To the extent that individuals learn from elites, they will be consistent. Figure 14 illustrates the theory for the case of attitudes toward abortion and welfare spending. Liberal elites favor both abortion and spending more money on welfare (indicated by the pluses in the figure). Conservative elites oppose abortion and prefer spending less money on welfare. So to be consistent, the individual must adopt either the liberal or the conservative package of opinions.

The reasons Converse gave for emphasizing the social sources of constraint become clear when one considers this example. First, there obviously are no direct logical relationships between this pair of issues. That is, all combinations of attitudes toward abortion and welfare spending are logically consistent. Second, although there may be several good arguments (psycho-logical relationships) that connect the two attitudes, they are certainly not going to be obvious to many people. Few survey

22. I am using the term "political elites" here in a broad sense. I refer to elected political officials, candidates, political columnists, and other political activists. In order to use this model as a basis for item selection, a researcher would have to develop a more precise definition. It is not important here.

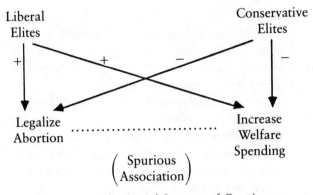

Figure 14. The Social Sources of Consistency

Note: + means positive association (e.g., preferring).
− means negative association (e.g., opposing).

respondents would be able to construct arguments connecting attitudes on those two issues. The social connections, however, are quite evident. Most liberals take one side, and most conservatives take the other on both issues.

Another way to think about this model is to consider the relationship between the two attitudes. The correlation between the attitudes is a spurious one. The attitude consistency model implies that correlations between attitudes are spuriously caused by outside forces—specifically, by political elites.

There are two important limitations on this model. First, it ignores other sources of consistency. Political elites are certainly the dominant sources of political messages, but they are not the only ones. There are psychological and occasionally logical sources of constraint. Moreover, there are other social sources of constraint. The Catholic church, for instance, currently opposes abortion and supports increased welfare spending. Devout Catholics who follow the church line would, therefore, be judged inconsistent.

The alternative sources of constraint provide alternative criteria with which to define and measure attitude consistency. For instance, one could investigate how consistently Catholics adhere to official church doctrine. Converse dismissed these alternative criteria in his discussion of idiosyncratic ideologies. Here I wish only to note that Converse's theory can be used to analyze many idiosyncratic ideologies just as well as it can be used to analyze mainstream ideologies.

A second limitation with the model is that it does not apply to all is-sues. All issues are not fought along liberal-conservative lines. An equally important point is that even among those issues that do have liberal and conservative positions, the strength with which the issue positions are as-sociated with liberalism or conservatism may vary.

Although most controversial issues have liberal and conservative sides, some do not. Regional and sectional cleavages dominate several policy areas such as energy, water, and agriculture. As a case in point, the cur-rent farm crisis pits most senators and representatives from farm states against those from nonfarm states. Thus what to do about the rising tide of bankrupt farmers has niether a clear liberal nor a clear conservative position. Liberals and conservatives take both sides.

Some issue positions are more closely associated with liberalism and conservatism than others. That is, the extent to which an issue can be thought of as fitting into a liberal-conservative framework is a matter of degree. There are two ways an issue can fail to fit into the framework. First, differing mixes of liberal and conservative leaders can take oppos-ing sides on the issues.[23] The two extremes are (1) all liberals in one camp, all conservatives in the other and (2) half the liberals and half the conser-vatives in one camp and the other liberals and conservatives in the other camp. Thus the first problem is one of mixed messages, or item ambigu-ity. When political elites tell the public what the positions are, how clear or mixed is the message? In this case, the message is ambiguous to the extent that the sources are mixed. The less ambiguous the message (i.e., the less mixed the sources), the more easily the public will learn it.

Second, political leaders can vary the attention they give to an issue. By talking about an issue more and saying that it is important, politicians can go a long way toward teaching the public what they think. However, even if politicians disagree about an issue, they do not have to talk about it much. This is frequently the fate of more technical issues, for instance, what position to take in the trade-off between inflation and unemploy-ment. Again, the clearer the message, the better the public will learn it. In this case, clarity is a function of how loud the message is, or how salient it is, rather than the extent to which it is mixed.

At this point, supporters (or former supporters) of *The Changing American Voter* should recognize that both of these variables—the ambi-

---

23. For simplicity, I am assuming there are only two sides to every issue here. That is obviously not so, but it eases the explanation.

guity and salience of the messages—are environmental. Nie and his colleagues argued that parties became more distinct (i.e., the messages became less ambiguous) and the political rhetoric heated up (i.e., politics became more salient) in the early sixties. They used this argument to explain the 1960–1964 surge in consistency. Although this across the board surge did not happen, it does not follow that other, lesser changes did not occur; nor does it follow that the environmental causes of change that Nie et al. identified are not real. Of course the environment influences the public. What political leaders say has an impact. The impact is not as large as Nie et al. suggested. However, it is important for the problem of item selection. Nie et al. demonstrated that point when they showed that the size of government item ceased working in the late 1960s and early 1970s.

Few issues are completely unrelated to the liberal-conservative dimension, but conversely, few fit it exactly. Thus the practical problem for those who wish to measure attitude consistency is what these points reveal about item selection.

Measuring Attitude Consistency

Within a given year, message ambiguity and salience are fixed. That is, during a single campaign, politicians choose what issues to emphasize and take fixed positions on them.[24] Across years, however, that is not true. The issues change over time, the politicians change over time as old politicians fade away and new ones rise to take their places, and the positions individual politicians take change over time.

Over the years, these changes can be dramatic. The problem of integration changed from being one of southern schools segregated by southern law (*de jure*) to being one of northern schools segregated by neighborhoods (*de facto*) and being integrated by busing. The politicians and their favored issues changed from Kennedy's focus on economic legislation, to Johnson's sweeping Great Society social legislation and Asian war, and then through the Watergate years to Carter's politics of trust and reconciliation, and finally to Reagan's years of building up the nation's defense and deficit. Even politicians' positions can change over

24. Within a year, there may be some changing of positions and some changing of which issues are emphasized, but not much. More to the point, the SRC/CPS data come from a brief period before and after the elections, and there is certainly not going to be much change within such a short period.

time. The middle-aged actor entering politics in the early 1960s who denounced Medicare as little more than thinly disguised communism had completely reversed himself, embracing it as an essential part of the safety net for the elderly, by the time he was elected president in 1980.

The implication of these observations is that although comparing the consistency of groups within a single year is acceptable, comparing consistency across years is not. In order to do that, one needs to know the characteristics of the messages each year. Without that knowledge, one cannot tell whether a change in consistency resulted from a change in the electorate's understanding of politics or from a change in the clarity of the message coming from the elites. With the knowledge of the messages, one can control for the message characteristics and figure out what changed.

To speak of "controlling" for message characteristics is perhaps getting a little beyond the present state of research on attitude consistency. For those using simple correlations to measure attitude consistency, the question is one of item selection. However, item selection is one way of controlling for message characteristics. One simply holds sources of variance (the message characteristics) constant.

So how does one select items? The most direct way of assessing item ambiguity is to take a sample of liberal and conservative elites and administer the possible attitude questions to them. For instance, one might use a sample of candidates for or members of Congress. One would then select items on which some minimum percentage (e.g., 80 percent) of liberals took one side and a similar percentage of conservatives took the other. Of course, this raises the problem of just who should be considered a liberal and who a conservative, but there are reasonable ways of making those distinctions; for instance, one might use the ratings of well-known national liberal and conservative organizations such as the Americans for Democratic Action and the Americans for Constitutional Action. In short, one could select items by using a criterion group. Item salience could be measured from content analyses of the news media. If an issue were mentioned often enough, it would be included.

The difficulty such suggestions raise is that in order to make comparisons across time, one needs samples of elites who are asked questions that exactly match questions asked of a mass sample at two or more time points. This is not such a difficulty for future studies of attitude consistency, but it is for studies of past attitude consistency. The problem is that no one has conducted the appropriate elite studies to match the CPS National Election Studies. In the best known elite-mass comparison of consistency (Converse 1964), the author compared a mass sample to a 1958 sample of candidates for the House of Representatives. The problem was that the questions did not match; indeed, they were fairly different. The sad fact is that there are no elite surveys with matching mass surveys appropriate for studying attitude consistency.[25] Therefore there are no matching elite and mass surveys with which to examine changes in attitude consistency over time.

Despite all this talk of the importance of the message characteristics and item selection, one might remain somewhat skeptical. So far I have only argued that these matters are important; I have yet to demonstrate it. Because no appropriate elite samples are available, there remains only one way to demonstrate the importance of item selection—show how the results of past studies might have differed had the authors selected different items.

The most obvious example of the difference that item selection can make is Nie and Andersen's ad hoc solution to the size of government problem. Had Nie and Andersen not reasoned their way clear to drop size of government from 1972 on, they would have been left with an embarrassing fall in attitude consistency to explain. Their consistency index for domestic items (average correlation) would have fallen from .51 in 1968 to .29 instead of from .51 to .49—the insignificant dip they reported.

Converse's original work on attitude consistency had its own questionable item selections. Converse (1964, p. 229) passed over the item selection problem by saying only that it was a "purposive" sampling of controversial issues. Yet it turned out that one of those issues was not very strongly related to any of the others—namely, the federal housing and power item. The average correlation among the four domestic items in 1956 was .23. Had the power and housing item been dropped, the average would have jumped to .36, a substantial increase. According to Bennett (1973, p. 558n), in 1960, the domestic items would have risen even higher, to .42. Although these average correlations are still lower

25. The 1972 convention delegate study contains only a few questions that match the 1972 national election study. A CBS News/New York Times survey (Bishop and Frankovic 1981) has several problems; chief among them are the facts that the elite and mass sample questions were worded differently, and the Democrats and Republicans in the elite sample seem to agree on almost all the issues. There are a few other elite-mass matching samples in the literature, but they do not deal with national samples, or they are not repeated over time, or the questions do not match. In short, there are no useable data sets.

than the .49 found by Nie and Andersen for 1964, they are far closer than the original level of .23. Indeed, it is hard not to believe that had Converse used a different set of items, the small jump from .42 to .49 would have been either dismissed by later investigators or interpreted quite differently.

Thus a little playing around with item selection can make most of the 1960–1964 leap in attitude consistency vanish before one's eyes. This is a serious problem, and *not* just for the changing American voter thesis. This is a problem for anyone who wishes to look at changes in consistency over time. As the housing and power example demonstrates, the results of one's consistency study will depend on the items one selects. One set of items will yield an increase in consistency; another set will yield a decrease; still another may yield no change at all. Converse's "purposive sampling" of issues may have been adequate to his task, but it is certainly not adequate to the task of examining changes in consistency over time. Without some rigorous basis for item selection, the entire undertaking is defeated at the outset.

Summary Comments

Like the levels of conceptualization indexes, the measures of attitude consistency are critically flawed for comparisons across time. The changes in question wordings render comparisons across the 1960–1964 gap useless. This has been debated in the literature and, I expect, proved to almost everyone's satisfaction.

What has not been debated in the literature is the argument that because of the failure to apply cognitive consistency theory to the problem of item selection, the entire effort to examine consistency across time is problematic at best and more likely a complete failure. Few investigators have given more than passing mention to how they went about choosing items for analyzing attitude consistency. On the few occasions when the matter was explicitly discussed, it was done on an ad hoc basis. The reasons given for using some items and not others were not rigorously tied to a theory of consistency. Indeed, the underlying theory was usually ignored.

Thus one of the critical flaws with the investigations of the levels of conceptualization was also a critical flaw in the investigations of attitude consistency. In both cases, political scientists gave little attention to the theories upon which the measures were based. In both cases, that was a mistake.

Four

Changes in the Public's Political Sophistication

Neither the level of conceptualization indexes nor the attitude consistency measures works. Neither is capable of measuring change over time in the public's political knowledge and sophistication. So what does work? How can one measure change in the way the public thinks about politics? And what do such measurements indicate about change in the public's knowledge and sophistication? These are the questions I address in this chapter.

Preliminary Considerations

There are few measures of political knowledge and sophistication that are available over any extended number of survey years, and all of the measures have problems. This unfortunate state of affairs is in some ways the result of progress in research. In the early years of survey research, there were a fair number of information questions. Indeed, one of the most important early findings of survey researchers was how little the public knew about politics (Erskine 1962, 1963a, 1963b, 1963c; Hero 1959; Hyman and Sheatsley 1947; Kriesberg 1949; Metzner 1949; Patchen 1964; Robinson 1967; Withey 1962). The public's lack of information was so well established that scholars lost interest in studying the subject. Because survey questions asked of national samples are scarce and valuable resources, fewer questions were asked to assess the public's knowledge, and more questions were asked about other, more interesting topics—many suggested by *The American Voter*.

Throughout the 1950s and 1960s, the number of political knowledge questions dwindled. The Gallup Poll, for instance, used to ask such questions as "How many senators are there from your state?" and "Can you tell me what is meant by the term 'Electoral College'?" By 1960, it had abandoned the practice (Gallup 1972). Erskine (1963a, p. 133) noted this decline in her comprehensive review of "all available questions" on political textbook knowledge. She found 110 questions over the 1947– 1962 period. In the first four years, 46 questions were asked; in the next four years, 42 questions appeared; in the next four, only 18 questions were used; and by the last four years, from 1959 to 1962, just 4 questions were asked. In other words, over that sixteen-year period, information questions virtually vanished.

Another reason for the scarcity of questions about political information is that they are hard to ask. Because people know so little about politics, factual questions with right or wrong answers are often embarrassing to respondents. They cause problems in the interview situation, and are therefore difficult to ask. As an example of this, consider the fate of the information questions asked in the CPS 1972 National Election Survey. There were only a few questions asking the most basic facts—how many times can a person be elected president, how long is a senator's term, which party had a majority in the House of Representatives before and after the election. Interviewers later objected to these questions because respondents had complained to them. The interviews were supposed to be about the respondents' opinions, not about their knowledge. Apparently, some respondents got upset. Consequently, most of the information questions were not repeated in later years.

The result is that few information questions were repeatedly asked across the years. As Converse (1975, p. 101) remarked, this lack of a record of the public's information level is "deplorable." The CPS National Election Surveys contain a few such questions, but none is very good. The NORC General Social Surveys do not have any political information questions. The Gallup and other private surveys have occasional information questions, but because those organizations focus on contemporary politics, few questions are repeated, and only one of them (recall of congressman's name) is repeated systematically over a long time span. In short, if one wants to examine changes in the public's knowledge over time with direct questions about factual information, one has to make do with a very small set of questions.

Aside from the lack of repeated information items, there is another more subtle difficulty in looking at the changes in people's knowledge.

Many items are not quite comparable over time. Circumstances that make some items more or less difficult to answer correctly change from year to year. At first this idea might seem to be the same as the thesis argued by *The Changing American Voter*, namely, changes in the environment cause changes in political sophistication. It may sound similar, but it is not. The claim is that changes in the environment cause changes in the difficulty of specific information items. The two ideas are quite different. To see the distinction, consider how we use information items to measure political knowledge. We select a small set of items, usually no more than three or four. Each item asks for a specific piece of information. However, we are not actually interested in those pieces of information, but rather in what we can infer beyond those three or four facts. We care not about the individual's knowledge of those specific facts, but about how much the individual knows about politics in general. We use the small set of items to infer how much the respondent knows about the realm of politics.

By way of example, consider the 1968 questions asking what type of government the People's Republic of China has and whether the PRC was a member of the United Nations. Knowing those facts is not what we care about. If two people know exactly as much as one another except that one person knows these two additional facts, we would think them equally sophisticated. We would not really care about the difference. Yet if one person knows both facts and the other does not, it is a good bet that the one who knows about China also knows a good deal more about a wide range of other political issues. In short, when we measure information, we have little reason to be interested in the content of the scale. Our interest lies in what we can use the scale to measure—general political information.

There are, of course, cases in which researchers are interested in specific facts. For instance, those who study congressional elections care about whether respondents know the candidates' names. In this and similar cases, the researcher's interest is not in general political knowledge. These examples of interest in specific items are irrelevant to this inquiry.

It follows that environmental changes that affect *only* the item in question and not the individual's overall information level are changes that must be ignored. That is, when circumstances change so that a specific fact becomes better or less well known, but nothing else changes, we want to be able to identify that change and adjust for it when making comparisons over time. For example, consider what might happen if a question about the government of South Africa had been repeatedly asked since the 1950s. Up until the recent surge of news about the movement for freedom and civil rights for South Africa's blacks, few Americans would be likely to know much about South Africa. Now that the anti-apartheid movement is getting lots of media attention, the number of people who know about the country has certainly risen. But does that mean that the public is becoming more sophisticated? It does not. Just as South Africa is gaining in recognition, Afghanistan, Biafra, Bangladesh, and other foreign media hot spots of the past are fading. Overall knowledge has not really changed. Instead, some facts are becoming more widespread, and others are becoming less so.

In sum, the political environment can change in ways that cause the relationship between an information item and the individual's total knowledge to change. Put more technically, the item's "difficulty" can change.[1] When these changes occur, the inferences one can draw from the item must also change. Although it is not easy to do, one must try to identify changes that affect only the item and to adjust our over time comparisons for those changes. That is, one must try to get past superficial changes in the method of measuring information so changes in general information over time can be measured.

The criteria for selecting information items were (1) an item had to be repeated at least two or more times, (2) at least one of those times had to be 1960 or earlier, and at least one had to be 1964 or later, and (3) the item had to be repeated in an identical or nearly identical format. That is, the time series had to include the 1960–1964 gap so that the great leap forward thesis could be tested. The condition that the items had to be identical is, of course, necessary for any sort of comparisons across time.

These conditions eliminated almost all available information items. Few of the SRC/CPS National Election Study items were repeated more than once, and even fewer included both sides of the 1960–1964 gap. For instance, the question about what sort of government the people of mainland China have was asked only in 1964 and 1968. Because it does not include the critical early 1960s, it was not included.

The problem of differently worded questions being asked at different times also eliminated some measures. The most important measure to be rejected because of changes in question wording is the party difference

1. In more formal terms, the relationship between a test item and the overall characteristic one wants to measure can be represented by an "item characteristic curve." For a discussion of this relationship, see Bejar (1983), Lord and Novick (1968), or Osterlind (1983).

scale used in Chapter 2. This scale counts the number of differences between the Democratic and Republican parties that each respondent sees on a series of issue questions (the same issue questions used to measure attitude consistency). The problem is the same as the one with attitude consistency. The wordings of the questions were changed between 1960 and 1964, with the result that the relationships between the party difference scale and all other measures sharply changed. As a consequence, the party difference scale is not comparable across the 1960–1964 gap. Although the scale seems to be an excellent measure for use in cross-sectional analyses, it cannot be used in a time series investigation.[2]

Measures of Political Knowledge

The best information measure available is the number of responses to the like/dislike questions. The assumption underlying this measure is that the more one knows, the more one will have to say when asked open-ended questions about the parties and candidates. The statistics presented in Chapter 2, as well as those presented by Kessel (1980, ch. 7 and ap. A) attest to the measure's validity and reliability. Because this measure is available over the entire time span of this study, it can be used to assess changes in the public's political thinking.

There are, of course, problems with the number of responses as a measure of political knowledge and sophistication. The first problem, noted earlier and also pointed out by Kessel (1980, p. 275), is that a more talkative person will receive a higher score irrespective of his or her knowledge of politics. Although I doubt that this is much of a problem, there is no way of estimating the bias introduced by talkativeness. However, there is no reason to expect talkativeness to change over time. Thus because our interest here is in using this measure for comparisons over time, this problem is not a cause for worry. A constant source of bias over time (talkativeness) will not affect over time comparisons.

A second problem, related to the first, is that the number of responses is not directly a measure of knowledge. No answers are graded right or wrong. This is in no sense a direct test of what the respondent knows. Thus talkativeness can intrude, and so can other influences. For instance, interest in politics can cause people to say more, irrespective of their nor-

2. I do, however, include it in my upcoming factor analysis of information items.

TABLE 28.   Mean Number of Responses by Year

	1956	1960	1964	1968	1972	1976
Party response	3.5	3.3	3.1	3.7	2.9	3.0
Candidate response	4.1	4.1	4.5	4.5	4.1	4.4
Total	7.6	7.4	7.6	8.2	7.0	7.0

Source. Data are from the CPS 1956–1976 American National Election Studies.

mal talkativeness or of their knowledge of politics. Still, although the number of responses has problems, they do not seem to be overwhelming.

The mean number of responses by each respondent to the party questions, the candidate questions, and the two combined from 1956 through 1976 are shown in Table 28. Although there is a little fluctuation up and down in each of the three time series, there is no overall trend in any of them. The average number of responses to the party questions moves around between 2.9 and 3.7. The average number of candidate responses varies more narrowly between 4.1 and 4.5. Neither measure shows the electorate becoming either more or less knowledgeable and sophisticated over time. In particular, there is little change in the number of responses between 1960 and 1964, the period of the great leap forward in sophistication according to *The Changing American Voter*. The number of party comments declines slightly from 3.3 to 3.1, and the number of candidate comments rises slightly from 4.1 to 4.5. The picture is one of an unchanging American voter.

Another measure of political knowledge is recall of the names of candidates in contested congressional elections. This measure has an advantage in that it asks for a specific piece of information, and one can identify right and wrong answers. Yet this measure has its own problems, the major one being that various political factors that influence how well representatives and their challengers are known have been changing over time. For instance, hotly contested, close elections make both contestants better known because of the campaign spending, media attention, and so forth. Yet the number of close elections for the House has declined sharply since the 1950s (Burnham 1975; Mayhew 1974). The result may be that fewer people know their representatives than would had the number of close elections remained the same over the years.

Another factor is the effort that members of the House put into building their reputations in their districts. As Fiorina (1977), Mayhew (1974), and others have shown, politicians are spending far more time and effort than they used to wooing their constituents (Jacobson 1987, ch. 3). They visit their districts more often. They send more mail home. They spend more staff money on casework and playing the ombudsman role. These factors may contaminate long-term trends in candidate recall. Thus although recall is a fairly good measure of information (and one of the few that was asked repeatedly), it is hardly a perfect measure. It may work reasonably well with cross-sectional data, but using it for comparisons in time series involves some risks.

Keeping these qualifications in mind, consider the data on recall to see if they reveal any trends. Three different sets of recall data are shown in Table 29, two from CPS data and one from Gallup data. The first set, collected by Ferejohn (1977) is based on voters in contested congressional districts. The second set, collected by Cover (1976), is based on both voters and nonvoters in all districts in which incumbents ran for reelection. The third set, from the Gallup Poll, is based on all respondents to the poll and thus includes both contested and uncontested seats.[3]

Scanning down each column of figures reveals a fair amount of fluctuation. Ferejohn's figures for recall of incumbents, for instance, vary from 50 to 64 percent. The one pre-1964 data point, 58 percent correct recall, is exactly the same as the average of the 1964 and later figures. That is, there is no difference between recall in the pre- and post-1964 periods. The other time series point to the same conclusion. None of the three data sets reveals any increase in recall over time. In fact, while the Ferejohn and Gallup data show no trends of any kind, the Cover data show an actual decline in recall starting in 1970. Mann (1978, p. 27) suggested that the decline is concentrated among nonvoters. Yet whatever the source of the decline, two data sets show no change over a thirty-year time span, and one data set shows a decline. There is certainly some fluctuation from one year to another. For instance, recall during presidential election years seems to be somewhat higher than during other years, but nothing here suggests any increase in knowledge over time. So again the finding is that the American voter is unchanging.

Another often used measure of political information is based on the respondents' knowledge of control of the House of Representatives. In

3. All three data sets are reported by Mann (1978). The Ferejohn data are supplemented by Crotty and Jacobson (1980). The Gallup data are supplemented by additional time points from Gallup (1972).

TABLE 29.   Recall of Candidates' Names
in Contested House Elections

Year	Ferejohn (1977) CPS Voters Only		Cover (1976) CPS All Respondents		Gallup (1972)
	Incumbents	Non-incumbents	Incumbents	Non-incumbents	Incumbents
1942					50%
1947					42
1957					35
1958	58%	38%	44%	28%	
1964	63	40	52	32	
1965					43
1966	56	38	40	23	46
1968	64	46	50	34	
1970	55	31	35	16	53
1972	50	31	36	19	
1974	57	32	34	16	
1978	61	38			

Source. Both the Ferejohn and Cover data are from the CPS 1956–1978 American National Election Studies. The Ferejohn data are calculated by Ferejohn (1977, p. 170) and Crotty (1984, p. 218). The Cover data are computed by Cover (1976, p. 58) and Mann (1978, p. 27). The Gallup data are from Gallup (1972).

Note: The Ferejohn data are based on voters in contested seats. The Cover data are based on all respondents in seats contested by incumbents. The Gallup data are based on all respondents irrespective of whether their congressional races are contested or not or whether incumbents are running.

every presidential election year since 1960, the CPS National Election Studies have included a pair of questions asking which party had a majority in the House before and after the election. This seems to be a much more useful measure of political information. It clearly measures knowledge that is needed to follow what is happening in Washington. Not knowing which party is running one of the houses of Congress makes it extremely difficult to blame or reward the party in power. Therefore this knowledge is required to vote rationally.

The problem with knowing which party controls the House is that voters apparently confuse control of the White House with control of Congress. Arseneau and Wolfinger (1973, p. 3) first suggested this when they were looking at data on which party controlled the House prior to the election. They found that although 69 percent of the sample knew the right answer in 1966, only 50 percent did in 1970. They interpreted the sharp drop as being caused by the change from unified control of government by the Democrats in 1966 to divided control in 1970. Indeed, as Arseneau and Wolfinger point out, the figure of 50 percent knowing the right answer in 1970 closely matches the 47 percent who knew the right answer in 1958 when the government was last under divided control (see Stokes and Miller 1962). In other words, Arseneau and Wolfinger were arguing that the 1966–1970 difference in knowledge was caused by the items becoming easier to answer. There was no overall change in knowledge; it was just easier to know the right answer in 1966.

Another variation on this problem of confusion is that voters may confuse control of the House with control of the Senate. In 1980, when the Republicans won control of the Senate for the first time since the 1950s, only 14 percent of the sample knew that the Democrats controlled the House both before and after the election (see Table 30). This startlingly low level of information certainly resulted from the Republicans' victory in the Senate and the enormous amount of media coverage it received. For my purposes, the implication is that one has to be careful using these items in comparisons across time.

The specific information index used is the same one used in Chapter 2, that is, the number of correct answers given to the questions about which party had a majority in the House before and after the election. The bottom row of Table 30 reveals that the percentage who knew both answers rose from 43 percent to 60 percent from 1960 to 1964, and then returned to the upper 40 percent range until the 1980 election reduced the people to utter confusion. Here is evidence that the public became more knowledgeable between 1960 and 1964. Is it reliable?

There are two reasons not to accept this evidence without corroboration. First, by 1968, the level of knowledge had returned to the 1960 level. That is, this index does not match the level of conceptualization indexes. According to the levels indexes, the public became more sophisticated between 1960 and 1964, and remained that way through the 1970s. According to the index of information about the control of the House, 1964 was an isolated year in which the people temporarily knew more. Although it shows a surge from 1960 to 1964, it does not support the thesis of *The Changing American Voter;* rather, it contradicts it by falling in 1968.

Second, Lyndon Johnson's 1964 landslide was accompanied by a huge

TABLE 30.   Knowledge of Control of the House

	1960	1964	1968	1972	1976	1980
Know neither	32%	17%	27%	29%	31%	28%
Know one	25	23	28	23	20	59
Know both	43	60	45	48	49	14
N	1,932	1,450	1,348	1,119	2,403	1,405

Source. Data are from the CPS 1960–1980 American National Election Studies.

Note: The questions were "Do you happen to know which party elected the most members to the House of Representatives in the elections (this/last) month? Which one?" and "Do you happen to know which party had the most members in the House of Representatives in Washington before the elections (this/last) month? Which one?" Both incorrect responses and "Don't know" responses were counted as incorrect.

increase in the margin by which the Democrats controlled the House (thirty-seven seats). The media response to the Democrats' newly dominant position may well have resulted in the surge of knowledge about the House majority. One might initially object that the same jump in knowledge did not occur eight years later, when Richard Nixon had a similar landslide. However, in that case there was relatively little change in Congress. The Republicans gained only twelve seats in the House, and they actually lost two seats in the Senate. So although the media presented it as a huge triumph for Nixon, it was obviously not a triumph that extended to Congress. Because the media were not talking about the huge gain in Congress, one should not expect to see a gain in information in 1972.

In sum, these items about control of the House do not provide a basis for saying that the public's knowledge and sophistication changed over the 1960s and 1970s. Even if one accepts the data at face value and ignores the obvious problems in making comparisons across time, one is still left with a one time surge in knowledge in 1964. *The Changing American Voter*'s thesis of a new level of sophistication following 1964 is just not supported.

A different way of measuring how much people know about politics is to find out whether they see any important differences between the Democratic and Republican parties. The assumption underlying this method is that there really are important differences between the parties. If one makes this assumption, one can take the percentage of people who say that there are important differences as a measure of the public's political knowledge.

There may be a problem with this measure as well. At some times, the differences between the parties, especially as they are represented by their presidential candidates, are larger than at other times. For instance, the differences between the parties (as represented by the candidates) in 1964 or in 1980 were far greater than the differences in 1960 or in 1968.

Whether this is a problem is not clear because it seems that this type of change may be closer to *The Changing American Voter*'s idea of environmental change than to the item-specific notion of change discussed previously. That is, if voters become aware of more differences between the parties, it seems reasonable to infer that they have gained a fair amount of information about the policy positions of the two parties. This is not a narrow increase in information that is specific to one item. Thus it seems that changes in this measure reflect real changes in the public's knowledge of politics. For this reason, one should probably conclude that this is one of the better information scales.

The public's perception of differences between the parties, shown in Table 31, does not change much over time. From 1952 through 1976, the percentage of those seeing differences ranges from 46 to 52 percent—a fairly narrow range presumably reflecting nothing more than sampling error. The only year that stands out is 1980, when the proportion of those seeing a gap jumps to 58 percent. Although it is easy to attribute the higher 1980 figure to Ronald Reagan, it is not so clear why a similarly high figure was not found in 1964. In any event, insofar as the perception of differences measures knowledge and is comparable over time, these data indicate that there was no change over time. In particular, there was no sudden surge to a new level of understanding in 1964. Again, the evidence leads to rejection of *The Changing American Voter*'s thesis.

The foregoing measures are all somewhat distant from the notion of "sophistication" as supposedly reflected in the level of conceptualization indexes. The names of the candidates for Congress, which party controls the House, whether there are differences between the parties, and so forth are not at all the same as whether one thinks in an ideological way. Two more direct measures of ideological thinking, or more precisely, knowledge of ideological terms, are available. The first is the question, which party is more conservative. Presumably, those who report that the Republicans are more conservative understand the meaning of the term better.

Here again the contrast between the particular candidates in each election might make the answer more or less obvious from one election to the next. For instance, one might expect the 1964 and 1972 elections—each with its own blatantly ideological candidate—would yield a higher num-

TABLE 31.   Perception of Important Differences Between the Parties

	1952	1960	1964	1968	1972	1976	1980
Percent seeing important differences	50	50	51	52	46	47	58

Source. Wattenberg, 1984, t. 4.1, p. 52. Data are from the CPS 1952–1980 American National Election Studies.

Note: In 1952, the question was "Do you think there are any important differences between what the Democratic and Republican parties stand for, or do you think they are about the same?" In 1960, 1964, and 1972–1980, it was "Do you think there are any important differences in what the Republicans and Democrats stand for?" In 1968, it was "Do you think there are any important differences between the Republican and Democratic parties?" Responses of both "No difference" and "Don't know" are combined as no difference.

TABLE 32.   Knowledge of Which Party Is More Conservative

	1960	1964	1968	1972	1976
Republicans	85%	81%	88%	79%	75%
Democrats/Don't know	15	19	12	21	24
N	1,308	1,045	958	800	1,996

Source. Data are from the CPS 1960–1976 American National Election Studies.

Note: The question was "Would you say that one of the parties is more conservative than the other at the national level?" (If yes) "Which party is more conservative?" (If no) "Do you think that people generally consider the Democrats or the Republicans more conservative, or wouldn't you want to guess about that?"

ber of correct answers. It might be easier to attach the ideological labels to the candidates. However, if voters learned more than just which labels went with which candidates, if they learned something about what those labels meant, this would be a good measure over time.

Table 32 shows the percentage of those identifying the Republican party as the more conservative of the two. There is again some fluctuation from one election to the next. Somewhat unexpectedly, there is a very slight downward trend. In the three elections in the 1960s, from 81 to 88 percent of the voters knew which party was more conservative; in the two elections in the 1970s, only 79 and 75 percent of the respondents gave the right answer. In addition, the 1964 and 1972 elections do not stand out. If anything, in both years, fewer people got the answers right than had done so four years previously. (The 1960–1964 difference, however, is a trivial 4 percent.) Once again, the data give little comfort to *The Changing American Voter* thesis.

The second more direct measure of knowledge of ideological terms (and thus possibly of ideological thinking) is the proportion of people who recognize and understand what the term "conservative" means. In 1960, respondents to the SRC/CPS National Election Study were asked to identify the more conservative party and then asked, "What do you have in mind when you say that the Republicans (Democrats) are more conservative than the Democrats (Republicans)?"

Converse (1964, p. 219) found that about half the population reasonably understood the liberal-conservative distinction. Using the same question from the 1964 study, Pierce (1970) replicated Converse's measure and came up with exactly the same result—half the population understood the term. Twenty years later, Luttbeg and Gant (1985) replicated the Converse-Pierce measure and again got the same result—half the population understood the liberal-conservative distinction.

A fourth replication of the strata of knowledge and understanding was conducted by Jennings and Niemi (1974, pp. 110–13). Using data from a national representative sample of high school students and their parents who were surveyed in the spring of 1965, Jennings and Niemi found that 45 percent of the parents fell in the top two levels of "reasonable" understanding. Because the Jennings and Niemi sample is of parents with high school students, it does not match the other representative national samples. Still, the 45 percent figure is in line with the other research.

In addition to the replications of the "strata of knowledge and understanding" measure, there is one other measure of how many people understand the liberal-conservative distinction. In June, 1940, the Gallup Poll asked people to explain what the terms "liberal," "conservative," and "radical" mean. The questions were of the form, "Please tell me in your own words what you consider a liberal in politics."[4] In scoring the answers, the Gallup Institute used the same general approach as did Converse and his colleagues twenty years later; they were "careful to give the voters the benefit of any reasonable doubt" (Benson 1940, p. 131). Unfortunately, Gallup did not report the results for each individual question; instead, they grouped the three questions together into a scale and

4. The terms "radical" and "conservative" were used in the other two questions. See Benson (1940).

reported the "average." Still, this scale of understanding of the liberal-conservative distinction is reasonably comparable with the scale later developed by the Michigan researchers.[5]

The results of this 1940 Gallup Poll are startlingly similar to those obtained by the strata of knowledge measure. Forty-eight percent of the 3,054 respondents gave "correct" responses, 14 percent gave answers that were deemed "doubtful," and 38 percent either did not answer or gave answers that were obviously incorrect. In short, the Gallup results match the CPS results.

Thus these are three replications of the strata of knowledge and understanding measure—1960, 1964, and 1980. And there is one earlier problematic time point—1940. So not only does this cover a forty-year time span, but it also covers the supposedly crucial 1960–1964 gap quite well. All four times the measure yielded the same answer. There was no change in the public's understanding of the liberal-conservative distinction.

Whether people are able to use ideological terms in their thinking and whether they do in fact use them are different. Nevertheless, it certainly seems odd that there was a huge increase in the number of those who thought in ideological terms while there was no corresponding increase in the number who could think in those terms. Like all the other measures discussed, this one provides no basis for saying that there was an increase in the public's sophistication during the 1960s.

Finally, there are a few scattered items that can be culled from the Gallup Poll. In examining the public's knowledge of foreign affairs, Smith (1972) sought to discover whether the public had become more knowledgeable over the years. He faced the same lack of information items. Nevertheless, from the few items he was able to find, Smith concluded that little had changed since the 1940s.

Smith's (1972, pp. 271–72) collection of information questions from the Gallup Poll consisted of recall of congressmen's and senators' names and the following items:

In 1950, a year of war in Asia for the United States, 66 per cent of the American public could correctly identify the U.S. Secretary of State. . . . (AIPO: Dec. 1950). Sixteen years later, in 1966, another war year in Asia for the United States, the figure was approximately the same—65 per

5. In addition to the fact that Gallup did not use the same coding procedures as CPS in analyzing their data, sampling procedures in 1940 were somewhat different from those in the 1956–1976 period. See Glenn (1970).

cent (AIPO: March, 1966). . . . A prominent writer on foreign affairs, Walter Lippman, was correctly identified in May, 1945, by 40 per cent of the public . . . (AIPO: May, 1945), and by 32 per cent in 1963 (AIPO: July, 1963). . . . In 1965, 20 per cent of the public had a reasonably correct idea of the magnitude of China's population; in 1952, using any figure between 300 million and 700 million as a reasonably correct estimate of its purported 500 million population at that time, a corresponding figure of 24 per cent was obtained (AIPO: Feb., 1952).

Beyond Smith's few items, there exists only one other Gallup Poll question that was asked with nearly identical language on both ends of the 1960–1964 gap: "Can you tell me what the term 'filibuster' in Congress means to you?"[6] In 1947, 48 percent of the respondents gave responses judged to be reasonably correct; in 1949, 54 percent were correct; and in 1964, the figure was the same—54 percent. These data may indicate a decline in knowledge because when the 1964 question was being asked, there was an important civil rights filibuster going on; yet when the two earlier questions were asked, there was no current filibuster, nor had there been one recently. Thus the finding is either no change or a decline in knowledge, depending on how one wishes to interpret the data.

Although these items hardly make up an impressive data set, they tell the same story that all the other data have told. Little or nothing has changed. So this is still more evidence that the political knowledge of the American voter did not grow. The alleged transformation of the American voter between 1960 and 1964 did not happen. None of these measures shows any trend of increasing knowledge and sophistication.

The Structure of the Information Items

My interest in measures of political information is not in the content of each specific information item. I do not care about whether respondents can recall the names of their representatives, but about what that recall implies about the respondents' general political knowledge. Thus I need to know whether the various items are, indeed, all measuring the same unobserved "knowledge."

In order to show that the information items and scales all measure a

6. The quoted question was reported in the April 5, 1947, Gallup Poll. In the February 11, 1949, version, the first word in the question was changed to "Will." In the March 25, 1964, version, the "in Congress" was dropped. None of these changes seems significant.

single latent variable, one can investigate the items with factor analysis. If a single factor underlies all the observed information measures, it will go a long way toward showing that they are all tapping the same phenomenon.

Even though a factor analysis yields but a single factor, it does not prove that a single variable causes all the observed variables. As Piazza (1980) argued, in addition to a factor analysis, one must also look at the relationship of the variables to other variables not included in the factor analysis. I do that in Chapter 5.

Seven items in the CPS National Election Studies were used for the factor analysis: the number of party responses, the number of candidate responses, which party was thought to be more conservative, the party difference index, the information index based on knowing which party controlled the House of Representatives before and after the presidential election, an index based on recall of candidates for the House, and a count of the number of "don't knows" in response to the issue items in the surveys.[7] The DK count is intended to measure the respondent's range of opinions—one of Converse's characteristics of a sophisticated person.

Only five of these items are used in the time series discussed in the rest of this chapter. The other items, the party difference index and the DK count, cannot be used in the time series because their construction changed radically between 1960 and 1964 and again between 1968 and 1972. The purpose for including them in the factor analysis is to validate the measures of political knowledge more thoroughly. None of the results changes much when either the party difference index or the DK count or both are dropped. In fact, dropping the difference index improves the performance of the factor analysis in 1960 and 1964.

The results of the maximum likelihood factor analyses for each year are shown in Table 33. The table shows only the factor loadings for the first factor in each year because all the solutions had only one factor. The eigenvalues at the bottom of Table 33 show the strength of the first factors. All the eigenvalues are 2.8 or greater. They indicate that the factors explain from 46 to 73 percent of the variance in the observed variables—an impressive standard.

---

7. The issue items were the ones used as the base for the party difference index. The questions were, of course, not the same. In the DK count, respondents were asked to place themselves. In the party difference index, respondents were asked to place the parties or asked which party was closest to them. The exact construction of both indexes varies by year. See Appendix 2.

TABLE 33. Maximum Likelihood Factor Analysis
of Information Items

	1956	1960	1964	1968	1972	1976
Number of party responses	.72	.65	.64	.67	.65	.73
Number of candidate responses	.75	.73	.60	.65	.63	.68
Conservative party question	—	.45	.51	.49	.48	.57
Information index	—	.51	.56	.48	.48	.59
Recall of candidates	—	—	.43	.39	.31	—
Difference index	.35	.35	.24	.54	.72	.67
DK count	.55	.53	.57	.62	.56	.58
Eigenvalue	2.91	3.04	2.84	3.36	3.63	4.32
Percent variance explained	73%	51%	46%	48%	52%	72%
Second eigenvalue	.13	.15	.34	.31	.31	.24
N	1,762	1,100	1,405	1,328	1,095	1,881

Source. Data are from the CPS/SRC 1956–1976 American National Election Studies.

The eigenvalues of the second factors are presented in Table 33 to show that they are all of trivial size. None even approaches 1.0, which is the conventional threshold for including factors (Harman 1976). The first factor clearly dominates in every year.[8]

The factor loadings are also all very strong. The only weak ones are for the party difference index from 1956 to 1964 and the candidate recall index. The change in the party difference index loadings is easy to explain. The index, based on the issue scales, changed whenever the issue scales were changed. In 1972 and 1976, it was constructed from the seven point issue scales (see Appendix 2), and this accounts for its rise from low loadings to very strong ones.

8. Examination of the scree plots supports this conclusion. The other factors are all trivial and all similar to the second factor. The plots look like classic examples of clean first factors.

The candidate recall indexes do not work particularly well. In two of the three years in which they are available, their loadings fall under the .40 rule-of-thumb threshold for including variables in factor analyses. As shown in Chapter 5, the recall questions behave differently from the other indexes in a couple of important respects. Thus a fair conclusion seems to be that recall of candidates' names is the weakest of all the information items and is the least closely related to general political information.

Despite the weakness in the recall questions and in the party difference index in the early years (an index I am not using in the time series), the overall picture provides strong support for the position that the information items are all measuring the same phenomenon. Thus there is a good set of information items available on the CPS National Election Surveys—a valuable and untapped resource.

The Causes and Correlates
of Sophistication

We will now begin to look at a series of variables that are supposedly related to political knowledge and sophistication. These are some of the criterion variables from Chapter 3. These variables are all hypothetically causes of knowledge.

This section is called "Causes and Correlates" for two reasons. First, only in the case of one variable, education, is the causal direction unambiguous. In all the other cases, it is reasonable to assume that the variables—interest in politics, attention to politics in the media, and so forth—are both causes and consequences of knowledge. That is, there is a set of feedback loops. For instance, greater interest in politics undoubtedly causes a certain amount of learning about politics. Greater knowledge, in turn, causes interest in politics (Hyman and Sheatsley 1947; Star and Hughes 1950).

Second, some of these variables may be only correlates of information rather than causes. For instance, it seems certain that interest in politics causes people to acquire knowledge about politics. Yet it is far less certain that, for instance, strength of party identification causes knowledge. Perhaps being a strong identifier gives one an incentive to learn more, but perhaps other causes of both strength of identification and knowledge have induced a spurious relationship.

Still, no matter how one interprets the relationships between these variables and political knowledge, it is reasonable to conclude that if

TABLE 34.   The Change in Education

	1956	1960	1964	1968	1972	1976	1980
0–8 years	31%	30%	25%	23%	20%	17%	12%
9–11 years	18	19	20	18	18	15	15
High school graduate	22	29	31	32	33	35	36
Some college	20	12	13	14	16	18	21
College graduate	8	10	11	13	13	15	16
N	1,754	1,949	1,562	1,553	2,702	2,857	1,610

Source. Data are from the CPS 1956–1980 American National Election Studies.

these variables change, there are corresponding changes in the public's knowledge. Because these variables may tap aspects of political knowledge and sophistication that were missed by the direct measures of information in "The Structure of the Information Items," these hypothetical causes and correlates are important.

The first and most obvious cause of political sophistication is education (Converse 1975; Kraus and Davis 1976, ch. 4; McCombs and Mullins 1973; Schramm and Wade 1967). It is one of the two variables chosen by the authors of *The American Voter* to validate the levels index (Campbell et al. 1960, pp. 250–53). The American public's educational level advanced throughout the 1960s and 1970s (see Table 34). Between 1956 and 1980, the number of college graduates doubled from 8 to 16 percent, and the number of those who had dropped out before completing eight years of schooling had fallen from 31 percent to only 12 percent. Thus it would seem only reasonable to conclude that political sophistication must have advanced as well.

The advance in education was, of course, a fairly steady one. On the basis of this, Campbell et al. (1960, p. 255) predicted "a slow upgrading in the level of conceptualization." Their prediction was wrong. Instead, there was a sudden jump in the levels between 1960 and 1964. As Nie et al. (1976, pp. 119–21) demonstrated, level of conceptualization jumped within educational categories. The steady advance in education contributed little to the surge in the levels index.

Nevertheless, the levels indexes do not work. So the prediction of Campbell and his colleagues must be judged by other standards. The findings in "Measures of Political Knowledge" show that the prediction was wrong, but why should this be? Why should education have little or no effect on sophistication? The answer may well lie in the changing nature of politics in American society. Other changes in the public seem to have counterbalanced the growth of education. In particular, while education has risen, the interest in politics of each educational group has fallen. The result is that, depending on how one measures interest in politics, there has been either a slight decline in political interest or no change at all. In short, the effect of the rise in education seems to have been canceled out by the decline of interest in politics within each educational level. I will puruse this problem further in the next chapter. For now, let us turn to measures of interest in politics.

Three different measures of interest in politics are presented in Tables 35 and 36. The first measure, shown in Table 35, is the question, "Generally speaking, would you say that you personally care a good deal which party wins the presidential election this fall, or that you don't care very much which party wins?" This measure reveals a slight decline in concern over the outcomes of presidential elections during the last two decades. In the first three surveys, from 65 to 69 percent of the respondents express concern; in the last four surveys, from 57 to 62 percent say they care a good deal. Thus while education rose, concern over the outcomes of the presidential races fell.

The second and third measures of interest, shown in Table 36, are directed at how much people follow campaigns. The CPS question is, "Some people don't pay much attention to the political campaigns. How about you, would you say that you have been very much interested, somewhat interested, or not much interested in following the political campaigns so far this year?" The Gallup question is, "How much thought have you given to the coming elections?" Although the responses to the questions fluctuate somewhat, neither one reveals any overall trend. Thus again, despite the increase in education and the fact that education and interest are related, there is no evidence for any rise in interest in politics.

These findings about the unchanging level of interest in politics are important. In the first place, *The American Voter* identified these two variables as being theoretically critical. Combining the two into a scale of "psychological involvement in politics," Campbell et al. used them to validate the levels index and to explain turnout and other types of behavior.[9]

9. For some unexplained reason, Campbell et al. used different versions of their "involvement" scale. The two questions presented in Tables 35 and 36 were used to validate the levels index, and therefore they are used here. Elsewhere in *The Ameri-*

TABLE 35. Care About the Presidential Election Outcome

	1956	1960	1964	1968	1972	1976	1980
Care a good deal	65%	67%	69%	60%	62%	58%	57%
Don't care very much	35	33	31	40	38	42	43
N	1,682	1,831	1,491	1,457	2,602	2,769	1,515

Source. Data from the CPS 1956–1980 American National Election Studies.

Note: The question was "Generally speaking, would you say that you personally care a good deal which party wins the presidential election this fall, or that you don't care very much which party wins?"

TABLE 36. Interest in Political Campaigns

	CPS				Gallup	
Year	Very Much	Somewhat	Not Much	(N)	A Lot/ Some	Little/ None
1954					40%	60%
1956	30%	40%	31%	(1,753)		
1958					41	59
1960	38	37	25	(1,919)		
1964	38	37	25	(1,564)		
1968	39	40	21	(1,546)		
1970					43	57
1972	32	41	27	(2,699)		
1976	36	42	21	(2,856)		
1980	30	44	26	(1,565)		

Source. CPS data are from the CPS 1956–1980 American National Election Studies. Gallup data are from Gallup 1972, 1978.

Note: The CPS question was "Some people don't pay much attention to the political campaigns. How about you, would you say that you have been very much interested, somewhat interested, or not much interested in following the political campaigns so far this year?" The Gallup question was "How much thought have you given to the coming elections?" [Oct. 15, 1954; Oct. 8, 1958; Sept. 20, 1970]

In the second place, further research over the ensuing years demonstrated that interest in politics, rather than education, is the key variable in explaining sophistication (Converse 1975, 1980). Interest in politics and attention to politics in the media seem to be intervening variables between education and political knowledge. That is, education causes interest and attention, which in turn cause knowledge and sophistication. Education itself has little direct effect. On this point, McCombs and Mullins (1973) argued that the simple political knowledge gained from education is only a small part of education's effect. Its principal effect is that education teaches the habit of scanning the media for political information, and that habit leads to knowledge about politics.

Because of this connection, the failure of interest in politics to rise as a result of rising education may partly explain the findings of the earlier part of this chapter, that there has been no general increase in political knowledge since the 1950s. Why the increase in education failed to produce an increase in interest is not clear.

Another aspect of general interest in politics is attention to politics in the mass media. This is closely related to interest in politics because media attention questions focus on specific behavior that stems from interest in politics. In effect, the interest questions ask, "Do you follow politics?" The media attention questions ask, "How do you follow politics?"

The mix of media that people chose to use changed sharply during the 1950s with the introduction of television and continued to change throughout the 1960s and 1970s. During the 1950s, television developed from a new medium to the dominant form of mass communication in our society. The use of radio to follow politics declined as the use of television grew. Both of these trends leveled off by the 1960s. Thus one must be careful in interpreting these data on media use. Because of the rapid changes in the 1950s, one should probably not use media attention to measure sophistication before 1960 because doing so might be confusing the spread of television with changes in how much attention people gave to politics.

Tables 37 and 38 present several ways of looking at the changes in media attention. The upper half of Table 37 shows the results of the media questions asked in the CPS National Election Studies, specifically, whether

---

can Voter, other questions on political efficacy and sense of citizen duty were included in an "involvement" scale. The efficacy questions are also used in this study, but they are treated separately. See Campbell et al. (1960, pp. 107n, 252n).

TABLE 37.   Frequency of Media Use

CPS: Media Usage

Medium	1952	1956	1960	1964	1968	1972	1976
Newspapers	79%	68%	80%	78%	75%	57%	73%
Radio	70	45	42	49	41	43	45
Magazines	40	31	41	39	36	33	48
Television	51	74	87	89	89	88	89

Roper: Most Important News Source

Medium	1959	1961	1963	1964	1967	1968	1971	1972	1974
Newspapers	57%	57%	53%	56%	55%	49%	48%	50%	47%
Television	51	52	55	58	64	59	60	64	65
Radio	34	34	29	26	28	25	23	21	21
Magazines	8	9	6	8	7	7	5	6	4
People	4	5	4	5	4	5	4	4	4
Don't know	1	3	3	3	2	3	1	1	*

Sources. CPS data are from the CPS 1952–1976 American National Election Studies. Roper data are from the Roper Organization, "Trends in Public Attitudes Toward Television and Other Mass Media, 1959–1974." New York: Television Information Office. Quoted in Janowitz 1981.

Note: The CPS question was "We're interested in this interview in finding out whether people paid much attention to the election campaign this year. Take newspapers for instance, did you read much about the campaign this year in any newspaper? How about radio—did you listen to any speeches or discussions about the campaign on radio? How about magazines—did you read about the campaign in any magazines? How about television—did you watch any programs about the campaign on television?" The Roper question was "First, I'd like to ask you where you usually get most of your news about what's going on in the world today—from the newspapers or radio or television or magazines or talking to other people or where?" (Respondents were allowed to name more than one source.)

the respondent had followed the current campaign in each of the four media—television, radio, newspapers, and magazines. The spread of television stands out clearly. In the 1952 survey, only 51 percent of the respondents said they had watched programs about the campaign on television. Four years later, the number had increased to 74 percent. By 1960, it had reached 87 percent, a level it maintained through 1976.

As television spread in the early 1950s, radio use declined. In 1952, 70 percent of the respondents said they had listened to something about the

TABLE 38. Evaluations of Media

Which of the Media:	Television			Newspapers			Magazines			Radio		
	1960	1970	1980	1960	1970	1980	1960	1970	1980	1960	1970	1980
Gives the most complete news coverage?	19%	41%	51%	13%	9%	5%	3%	4%	5%	18%	14%	10%
Gives you the clearest understanding of the candidates and issues in national elections?	42	59	56	36	21	21	10	8	11	5	3	3
Presents the fairest, most unbiased news?	15	13	17	31	23	20	9	9	9	22	19	18
Is the most educational?	32	46	49	31	26	22	31	20	22	3	4	2
Presents things most intelligently?	27	38	44	27	18	19	27	18	19	8	9	6

Source. Data reported in Bower 1985, t. 2.4, p. 17.

campaign on the radio. By 1956, that percentage had dropped to 45 percent, near which it stayed throughout the remainder of the survey years. Newspaper use also declined slightly according to the CPS survey, but the overall decline was accompanied by a good deal of fluctuation. In the first three survey years, from 68 to 80 percent of the respondents said they read about the campaign. In the last three years, by contrast, from 57 to 75 percent said they read about the campaign in newspapers. Magazine usage does not seem to drop off. Although there is a fair amount of fluctuation from year to year, the overall level remains constant.

The Roper questions presented in the lower half of Table 37 approach media attention differently. Those questions ask people from which source they get most of their news. Here there is evidence that the influence of television continued to spread after 1960. Whereas in 1959 about half the respondents said that their main source of news was television, by 1974, that number was up to 65 percent. As television rose in importance, the other three media fell. Radio fell the most, dropping from 34 percent to 21 percent. Newspapers declined from 57 percent to 47 percent, and magazines edged down slightly from 8 to 4 percent.

Table 38 presents another set of survey results that help assess media use over the last two decades. In 1960, 1970, and 1980, NORC and Roper conducted three major surveys of television use (Bower 1973, 1985; Steiner 1963). Because the latter two surveys were largely replications of the first, they provide a time series of evaluations of the media. The data presented in Table 38 are comparative evaluations in which respondents were asked which medium gave the most complete news coverage, gave the clearest understanding of the candidates and issues in the national elections, presented the fairest news, was the most educational, and presented things most intelligently.

The results of these questions all point in the same direction. In each case, the public thought television became more useful and newspapers became less so. The results for radio and magazines were mixed, with the two falling in some cases and remaining steady in others. The key result, of course, is the shift from newspapers to television because these are the primary sources of news and information about politics.

The most important evaluations are the first two—which medium gave the most complete news and which gave the clearest understanding of elections. In the first category, television moved from 19 percent to just over half the respondents saying that it provided the best news, while newspapers declined from 13 to just 5 percent. In the second category, the proportion saying that television gave them the best understanding rose from 42 to 56 percent, while the number saying that newspapers helped them most dropped from 36 to 21 percent.

The decline of reading is also apparent in newspaper circulation figures. Table 39 presents the number of daily newspapers in the United States, their total circulations, and the circulations as a proportion of the civilian population. From 1956 through 1980, the number of daily newspapers and their total circulation remained about the same, but the population changed. The result of the growing population was a steadily declining proportion of the population that read a daily newspaper. In 1956, paid circulation was about 34 percent of the population; by 1980, it had fallen to a little over 27 percent.

The implication of these figures is that the CPS questions underestimate the growing influence of television. Although the proportion of people who saw programs about campaigns on television may have remained constant in the 87–89 percent range during the 1960s and 1970s, the influence of television was still growing. More people came to depend on television as their primary source of political news. Television became more trusted and highly valued as a news source. On the other side, newspapers—the principal alternative to television—declined. The number of people who read newspapers, the number who said that newspapers were their most important source of news, and the number who rated newspapers most highly all declined (Bogart 1984).

A final way of looking at media attention is by using the CPS questions from Table 37 and counting the number of media in which people said they followed politics. Those data are presented in Table 40. Although there is some fluctuation over time, the only trend that appears is the decline in the number of people who do not follow politics in any media. In 1956 and 1960, 8 and 11 percent of the respondents said they did not read or hear or see anything about the campaign. From 1964 through 1976, that number had dropped to 3 to 6 percent. Most of these people presumably became television watchers by the middle 1960s. Aside from that group, there is no trend toward following politics in a growing number of media. Moreover, there is clearly no sudden jump in media attention between 1960 and 1964. Given these figures together with the data on media previously discussed, one can conclude that the growth of television use offset the small declines in the other media.

In sum, total media use did not change. It did not rise with education, as some might have predicted. Instead, there was a change in the mix of

TABLE 39.   Declining U.S. Newspaper Circulation

Year	Number of Daily Papers	Total Paid Circulation	Circulation as % of Population
1956	1,772	57,317,086	34.1%
1960	1,763	58,881,746	32.9
1964	1,763	60,412,266	31.6
1968	1,752	62,535,394	31.4
1972	1,761	62,510,242	29.9
1976	1,762	60,977,011	28.0
1980	1,745	62,201,840	27.4

Sources. Number of daily newspapers and total daily paid circulation are from *Editor & Publisher International Yearbook* (New York: Editor & Publisher, various issues). Civilian population data are from U.S. Bureau of the Census, *Statistical Abstract of the United States, 1986.*

TABLE 40.   Number of Media Used to Follow Politics

Number	1956	1960	1964	1968	1972	1976
None	8%	11%	3%	4%	6%	6%
One	19	12	12	16	21	15
Two	32	27	30	32	33	23
Three	28	34	36	34	27	34
Four	13	17	19	14	13	23
N	1,762	1,741	1,449	1,348	1,119	2,403

Source. Data are from the CPS 1956–1976 American National Election Studies.

Note: The questions are the same as in t. 37.

media that people used to follow politics. The question now is, what differences did that make in the sophistication of the American public?

Even though overall media attention levels have not changed, the decline in newspaper and magazine readership may have caused a decline in the level of public knowledge. As anyone who has compared the newspaper and television coverage of the same event can attest, the newspaper coverage is far more thorough. Television news usually consists of a series of short reports on unrelated subjects—usually chosen for their action, drama, and splashy pictures (Kraus et al. 1974; McClure and Patterson 1973; Wamsley and Pride 1974). Many observers argue that television's need for exciting pictures leads television journalists to ignore the important political issues and concentrate on trivial aspects of politics such as campaign rallies, crowds, and the candidates' embarrassing statements (Carey 1976; Hofstetter and Zukin 1979; Roberts and Maccoby 1985; Robinson 1975). Indeed, even television news coverage of presidential debates—which might seem to be nothing but information about issues—usually focuses on the trivial (e.g., Reagan's dismissal of his age as an issue with his comment about Mondale: "I am not going to exploit, for political purposes, my opponent's youth and inexperience" [Polsby and Wildavsky 1988, p. 216]).

The result is that television presents a chaotic clutter of bits of information that the viewer is unlikely to piece together for any real information gain. McClure and Patterson's (1973) study nicely illustrates this point. They found that immediately after watching network news broadcasts, most viewers were unable to recall any of what they had just seen. Other scholars have examined television news recall and have come up with similar findings (Booth 1970–1971; Neuman 1976). The "montage" of television news was entertaining, but not very informative.

It should be small wonder, then, that television watching seems to have little impact on how much people know about politics. In fact, the studies that have examined how much people learn from television and newspapers indicate that reading about politics has a substantial effect, but watching television has either very little or no effect on learning (Becker et al. 1979; Becker and Whitney 1980; Clarke and Fredin 1978; Patterson 1980; Patterson and McClure 1976; Quarles 1979; Roberts and Maccoby 1985; Robinson 1972a, 1972b; Schramm and Wade 1967; Tan and Vaughn 1976; Wade and Schramm 1969).

The implication of these studies is that the rising use of television and the slightly declining use of magazines and newspapers should be slightly decreasing the overall level of public knowledge. Of course, that the measures of knowledge show no change might lead one to speculate that the rise of television and decline of the print media are offset by the rise in education. That is, increasing education may be making up for the damage done by the decline of reading. The available data, unfortunately, do not allow us to find out whether this is the case.

A step beyond expressing interest and following politics in the media is actual political participation. As Converse (1964, p. 229) noted, any group that takes an active interest in politics should be more politically sophisticated than those who are not interested in politics. It follows that a growth in participation in campaigns should produce a corresponding growth in knowledge and sophistication.

One qualification should be kept in mind. The campaign reform act of 1974 that limited donations and expenditures for the 1976 presidential campaigns may have influenced two types of activity. First, by limiting the sizes of donations and establishing a system of federal matching funds for small donations to presidential candidates, the reform act created a set of incentives for candidates to increase the number of donors. Second, by limiting expenditures in the presidential campaigns, the reform act caused the candidates to reduce the amount they spent on campaign buttons and bumper stickers. Both of these limitations apply only to 1976.

The data, shown in Table 41, tell the same story as all previous data. Aside from the drop in the use of campaign bumper stickers and buttons, nothing changed. There was no trend toward either more or less participation, and there was no sudden jump in participation between 1960 and 1964. In particular elections, some people became active and others ceased to be active (Beck and Jennings 1979), but on balance, there was no change. Thus once again there are no signs of growing political sophistication.

Another possible cause of political sophistication is external political efficacy.[10] In general, political efficacy is the sense of political effectiveness—that is, "the feeling that individual political action does have, or can have, an impact upon the political process" (Campbell et al. 1954, p. 187). A measure of efficacy was first introduced by Campbell et al. (1954). Shortly thereafter, Lane (1959) suggested that political efficacy should properly be thought of as having two aspects: the sense that one is effective and the sense that the government is responsive. Although Lane's analysis was filled with insight, it was not filled with hard data to back up his insights. Some fifteen years later, Balch (1974) provided the data to support Lane's distinction between internal efficacy—the sense the one is effective—and external efficacy—the sense that the government is responsive (cf. Craig 1979).

My interest is in external political efficacy. This is usually measured by two statements with which respondents are asked to agree or disagree:

10. My discussion of the changes in political efficacy is necessarily brief. For a more thorough discussion and analysis, see Abramson (1983, ch. 8–10).

TABLE 41. Participation in Campaign Related Political Activities

Activity	1956	1960	1964	1968	1972	1976
Contribute money	10%	12%	11%	9%	10%	9%
Bumper sticker/button	16	21	16	15	14	8
Work for candidate	3	6	5	5	4	5
Attend rally/meeting	10	8	8	9	9	7
Express opinions	29	33	31	29	31	37

Source. Data are from the CPS 1956–1976 American National Election Studies.

Note: The questions were "Did you give any money to a political party this year?" "Did you wear a campaign button or put a campaign sticker on your car?" "Did you do any work for one of the parties or candidates?" "Did you go to any political meetings, rallies, dinners, or things like that?" "During the campaign, did you talk to any people and try to show them why they should vote for one of the parties or candidates?" All questions were coded yes, no, dk, or na.

(1) "People like me don't have any say about what the government does." (2) "I don't think public officials care much what people like me think." The efficacious responses, supposedly given by people who think the government is responsive to them, are to disagree with each statement.

Political efficacy is usually associated with political participation rather than political knowledge. Indeed, the concept of efficacy was originally developed to explain why people vote and participate in other ways. However, it seems reasonable to hypothesize that efficacy and knowledge are related as well. It is easy to see why efficacy should cause political knowledge. A heightened sense of efficacy gives one a reason to become politically informed. If the government is, in fact, responsive to citizens, then political knowledge should be useful because it should make political activity more effective. On the other side, political knowledge may also lead to efficacy. Perhaps the more one knows about the political system, the more one realizes that he or she can make a difference through political activity.

In sum, external political efficacy and political knowledge are related. Each may cause the other, but efficacy is probably a stronger cause of knowledge than knowledge is of efficacy.

The data on efficacy, as previously suggested, do not provide any basis for the conclusion that political knowledge has increased in the last couple of decades. The percentages of respondents agreeing and disagreeing with the two efficacy statements are presented in Table 42. Scanning

TABLE 42.   External Political Efficacy

Question		1956	1960	1964	1968	1972	1976
No say:	Agree	28%	27%	30%	41%	36%	42%
	Disagree	72	73	70	59	64	58
No care:	Agree	27%	25	37	44	51	54
	Disagree	73	75	63	56	49	46

Source. Data are from the CPS 1956–1976 American National Election Studies.

Note: Both questions were statements that the respondent was asked to agree or disagree with. The efficacious responses for both questions are "disagree."
No say: "People like me don't have any say about what the government does."
No care: "I don't think public officials care much what people like me think."

the "Disagree" rows of Table 42 (disagreeing with the statements is the efficacious way of responding) shows that external political efficacy fell from 1956 through 1976. The first statement, "People like me don't have any say," remained roughly constant at about 72 percent disagreement from 1956 through 1964; then it fell to the 60 percent range from 1968 on. The second statement started to drop off between 1960 and 1964, when disagreement fell from 75 percent to 63 percent. It continued to fall through 1976, when disagreement bottomed out at 46 percent. Because the number of people giving efficacious responses fell through the 1960s, one must conclude that if anything, political knowledge fell as well. There is certainly nothing here to sustain the claim that knowledge increased during the 1960s, especially not during the crucial 1960–1964 period.

Another possible cause of political sophistication is strength of party identification. Various aspects of party identification have received a great deal of attention in recent years. Strong party identifiers have more information than weaker identifiers, and pure independents have less information than any identifiers (Kamieniecki 1985, pp. 90–93; Keith et al. 1977). Therefore if strength of party identification causes knowledge, the well-known decline in party identification might account for a decline in political knowledge.

The data on strength of party identification are shown in Table 43. Although there is certainly a decline in party strength over the six elections, the decline does not come at the right time to influence the 1960–1964 changes in sophistication. That is, the changes in party strength occur between 1964 and 1972. From 1956 to 1964 and from 1972 to 1980, party

TABLE 43.   Strength of Party Identification

Strength	1956	1960	1964	1968	1972	1976	1980
Strong	36%	35%	37%	30%	25%	24%	26%
Weak	37	38	38	39	38	39	37
Independent-Leaner	15	15	15	19	22	22	21
Independent	8	8	8	11	13	14	13
Apolitical/DK	3	4	2	1	2	1	2

Source. Data are from the CPS 1956–1980 American National Election Studies.

identification is stable. Thus once again there is no explanation for the 1960–1964 gap.

To summarize, education increased, and that should have led to a rise in sophistication. However, interest in politics and use of newspapers and magazines to follow politics fell slightly, and external political efficacy and strength of party identification fell quite a bit. Those findings should lead us to expect a decline in sophistication, although perhaps only a slight one.

On balance, one should not be surprised to find no change at all. That is, the findings in this section are consistent with those about the direct measures of knowledge and sophistication discussed in the first section of this chapter—namely, the political knowledge and sophistication of the American electorate remained unchanged between the late 1950s and the late 1970s. When we abandon the more complicated and methodologically flawed measures discussed in the earlier chapters, the levels of conceptualization and attitude consistency, there is no evidence at all of a changing American voter. To the contrary, what we find is the unchanging American voter.

FIVE

Explaining Changes
in the Public's Knowledge

The public's level of knowledge has not changed since 1956. This seems paradoxical because one of the principal causes of knowledge, education, rose substantially since the 1950s. Indeed, looking at the steady rise of education in this country, Converse (1964) predicted that attitude consistency and level of conceptualization would both increase slowly over the years. If education causes knowledge of politics, and if education increased, why did knowledge not rise?

Beyond the public's curious failure to gain a greater understanding of politics, one might reasonably wonder about the causes of political knowledge. A number of hypothetical causes of knowledge were identified, but no specific model explaining knowledge was proposed. That is, I have yet to specify and test a model of political knowledge.

Both gaps can be filled at the same time. In this chapter, I will present and test a simple model of political information. Using that model, I attempt to find out why education increased but information did not and to identify the circumstances under which the public's political knowledge will increase. Finally, I make some predictions about the future growth of knowledge and understanding.

Modeling Political Sophistication

Some readers may regard simultaneous equation models as inherently better. Yet for modeling sophistication, both simultaneous equation models and simple recursive models suffer serious drawbacks, and neither can be considered preferable on statistical grounds. I have therefore chosen to present a simple recursive model of political sophistication. I begin by stating the problem and my reasons for choosing a recursive model.

Building a model to explain political information presents a serious difficulty. Several key variables cause one another. As mentioned in Chapter 4, interest in politics, attention to politics in the print media, political efficacy, political activity, and political sophistication might all reasonably be expected to cause one another.

For instance, interest in politics presumably causes people to pay more attention to politics and thus to learn more about politics. Moreover, the interested will be more likely than the uninterested to understand and remember what they hear or read about politics. So interest causes both media attention and sophistication. But knowing a good deal about politics is likely to make people more interested in it and, similarly, to make people pay more attention to politics in the media. Thus interest, media attention, and knowledge may all cause one another.

Similarly, people who become politically active (e.g., perhaps because asked to work by friends) will learn about and become interested in politics. But people who learn about politics (e.g., perhaps as a result of a required political science course) may become more interested in politics and more likely to become actively involved.

Finally, people who believe that the system will respond to them (i.e., the efficacious) have an incentive to learn about politics. In addition, those who know a good deal about politics should know that they have some influence if they choose to try. In sum, all these variables may cause one another.

In general, this is a problem of simultaneity—variables are simultaneously causing one another. The statistical problem that stems from this is that the measured association between any two of the variables reflects a mix of the effects of the variables on each other. Thus if one were to estimate a simple recursive regression equation such as the one shown in Figure 15A to explain one of the variables, the results would be biased.[1] The equation would treat all the association between the two variables as if it were caused by one of them.

There are several standard statistical solutions to this problem—two-stage least squares, three-stage least squares, and so forth. In order to use one of these methods, one specifies a simultaneous equation model. That

---

1. This is "simultaneous equation bias." For a discussion of this bias and simultaneous equations in general, see Kelejian and Oates (1981), Pindyck and Rubinfeld (1981), or any standard econometrics textbook.

Figure 15A. A Recursive Model (One-Way Causation)

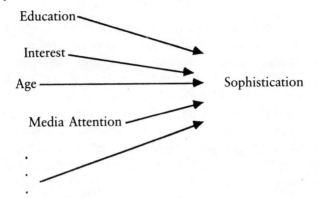

Figure 15B. A Simultaneous Equation Model (Two-Way Causation)

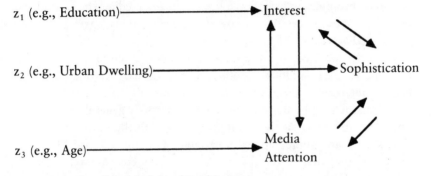

Figure 15. Possible Models of Sophistication

is, one writes a set of equations explaining each of the interdependent variables. For my purposes, I would have to write one equation for sophistication as the dependent variable, one for interest as the dependent variable, one for media attention, one for activity, and one for efficacy (see Figure 15B).

In order to identify the model (i.e., in order to be able to solve the equations and estimate coefficients), each dependent variable must have one or more unique causes.[2] That is, there must be variables that cause, say, sophistication, but cause no other dependent variable (interest, me-

2. Exactly how many unique causes or, more properly, "predetermined" variables depends on the details of the model. We need not concern ourselves with these details here. See discussions of simultaneous equation identification in any econometrics textbook. The model shown in Figure 15B is only for purposes of illustration; it is not identified.

dia attention, etc.). In Figure 15B, these unique causes are denoted by Z's (Z_1, Z_2, Z_3).

This turns out to be an extremely difficult problem. One must ask, what causes sophistication that does not also cause interest or media attention or political activity or political efficacy (but is included in the SRC questionnaire)? Similarly, what causes interest, but nothing else? What causes activism, but nothing else? What about efficacy?

Adding to the difficulty of answering these questions is the ambiguous nature of the interest question: "Some people don't pay much attention to the political campaigns. How about you, would you say that you have been very much interested, somewhat interested or not much interested in following the political campaigns so far this year?" The question mixes two theoretically distinct concepts—interest in politics and media attention. The first sentence of the question is about paying attention to the elections, presumably by following them in the media. The second sentence asks about interest "in following" the campaigns, again a reference to the media.

Does the question measure interest or media attention? It is hard to tell. The two are muddled together.[3] Survey researchers may be in the habit of referring to the question as an interest question, but to many respondents, it may be not about interest but about general media attention. The ambiguity of the question makes it all the harder to identify causes that are unique to each variable. Finding a cause of the interest question that is not also a cause of the media questions may be impossible.

Reviewing the variables available in the CPS questionnaire shows that no variables uniquely cause only one of the key variables. There are no a priori theoretical grounds for identifying a simultaneous equation model.

I could arbitrarily identify the model with a series of false assumptions. For instance, I could claim that education causes interest in politics, but nothing else; age causes media attention, but nothing else; urban dwelling causes sophistication and nothing else; and so on (shown in parentheses in Figure 15B). But making such false assumptions would just be biasing and distorting the results. I could identify the model, but I

3. This statement is backed by some statistical evidence as well as by the face validity argument. Factor analyses of the four media questions and the interest question yield a single dominant factor in each year. There is not a trace of a second factor. Although this finding does not prove that the interest question is just a general media attention question, it is indicative of the muddle.

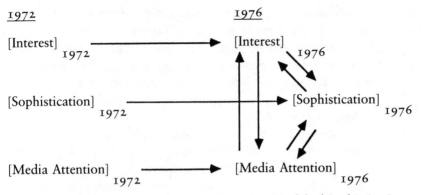

Figure 16. A Dynamic Simultaneous Equation Model of Sophistication

would not necessarily get any closer to the truth. To the contrary, arbitrarily identifying the model might hopelessly confuse matters.

An alternative approach to identifying models is to use lagged versions of the dependent variables as independent variables. That is, I might use the CPS 1972–1976 panel study to build a dynamic model. This approach requires the assumption that each of the key variables (interest, media attention, sophistication) caused only itself over time as shown in Figure 16. For instance, one would have to assume that interest in 1972 caused interest in 1976, but it did not cause sophistication, political activity, or anything else. In effect, the assumption is that there is no intermingling of cause and effect over the four years between the two waves of the panel.

That assumption is just not believable. Surely if interest causes people to acquire knowledge during the course of a campaign, then interest must cause people to acquire knowledge between campaigns as well. If the assumption is not true, then the model will not work. It, too, will produce biased results.

A second problem with using the lagged dependent variables to identify the model is that it would not reveal much of interest. Although it would help sort out the mixture of cause and effect in 1976 (assuming no intermingling of effects over time), it would not reveal much about other, exogenous causes.

The problem is that the exogenous variables (education, age, urbanization, etc.) are all relatively constant over time for individuals. If they cause media attention, interest, and sophistication, then they must cause them in 1972 as well as in 1976. For instance, if education has an influence on sophistication, then that would enter the model in the first wave—1972. Education would have no additional effect in 1976. Thus by including the first wave of lagged dependent variables, I would eliminate the effects of the exogenous variables, such as age. This would restrict the focus to short-term influences on interest, media attention, sophistication, and so forth. The long-term effects would be buried in the lagged endogenous variables.

Upon considering the differences between simple recursive models and simultaneous equation models, there does not seem to be much of a basis for choosing one over the other. The recursive model will give biased answers, but using the simultaneous equation model requires making false assumptions, which would yield biased answers. In short, there is no way to win.

I have chosen to use a single equation recursive model because it seems to me that the simpler model will yield more easily interpretable results. Explaining a simultaneous equation model would be more complicated, and because such a model could make no claim on being more accurate or more realistic, the added complication would be pointless.

The reader should, however, keep in mind the limitations on the conclusions to follow. The key assumption here is that interest, media attention, political activism, and political efficacy all cause knowledge. To the extent that that is not true, the results are biased.

A Simple Recursive Model of Political Knowledge

The variables to be explained here are those discussed in Chapter 4: the number of party responses, the number of candidate responses, the knowledge that the Republican party is the more conservative party, the information index based on knowledge of which party held a majority in the House before and after the election, and the recall index based on knowledge of the two candidates for the local House seat.

These variables could, of course, be combined into a single overall index of political knowledge. The factor analysis in Chapter 4 provides a basis for doing that. I do not combine the variables because I want to find out how each of them relates to the independent variables in my analysis. As Piazza (1980) has demonstrated, even though a factor analysis shows that a single factor underlies a set of observed variables, it is possible that those variables relate in different ways to other variables.

For instance, the data to follow show that whereas people who live in big cities are likely to know more according to most measures of information, they are likely to be less able to recall the names of their congressional candidates. Thus all types of information are not the same. As Jennings and Niemi (1974, pp. 94–96) have noted, different types of information are caused by different factors. In my data, most of these differences are fairly small; yet some are large enough to merit serious attention.

The independent variables will also be the same ones discussed in Chapter 4, but with three additions: The independent variables will be education, political activity, external political efficacy, political involvement (care about the outcome of the presidential race and political interest), attention to politics in the print media (newspapers and magazines), on television, and on radio, strength of party identification, degree of urbanization, age, and income. Because all these variables but the last three and the revised print media variable were discussed in Chapter 4, I limit my comments to these four.

The variable print is simply the sum of the newspaper and magazine variables from before. Respondents are scored 0 if they followed politics in neither medium, 1 if they followed politics in one of the two, and 2 if they followed politics in both. The reason for combining the two is that in several of the equations, they suffered from a multicollinearity problem (Kelejian and Oates 1981). That is, the two are correlated with each other at a sufficient level so that one or the other or both were often not statistically significant. Thus the crucial characteristic being measured is not whether people read newspapers or read magazines, but that they read something. When the two were combined into a single index, they were almost always significant.[4]

The degree of urbanization variable is a four point scale based on the CPS urbanization measures.[5] The idea behind the variable is that people living in urban areas (the high end of the scale) have more opportunities to acquire information than rural dwellers because there are more media, and the newspapers tend to be of better quality in urban areas.

An important exception to this is that rural newspapers give more coverage to congressional candidates than do urban newspapers (Manheim

4. Combining attention to politics on television and on radio into an electronic media variable did not work. Reading newspapers and reading magazines are related and partly interchangeable types of behavior. Watching television and listening to radio are not particularly related. Radio and television are not significant because they have no effect, not because of multicollinearity.

5. For details on the construction of this and other variables, see Appendix 2.

1974). Thus recall of the names of congressional candidates may not have the same relationship to urbanization as do other measures of information. However, on the whole, it seems very likely that urbanization causes information and thus should be included in the model.

Age, scored in decades,[6] was included for two reasons. First, it is a well-known cause of participation. Its relationship to voting is well known (Squire et al. 1987; Wolfinger and Rosenstone 1980; Wolfinger et al. 1981). It is also related to other types of participation (Milbrath and Goel 1977; Verba and Nie 1972). The connection with participation suggests that it might also be related to knowledge.

Second, as Jennings and Niemi (1974, ch. 3) showed in their examination of high school students and their parents, each group scored higher on different types of knowledge. The high school students had a greater knowledge of the mechanics of governmental structure; their parents had a greater knowledge of political history and possibly of foreign affairs. The knowledge of government structure was presumably the result of recent high school civics classes. Moreover, none of the information items in my study tests knowledge of government structure—for instance, the length of the president's term. So the most reasonable hypothesis here is that information is positively related to age.

In their analysis of the second wave of their panel study, Jennings and Niemi (1981) found that the knowledge of the young had increased since the first wave. They concluded, "Knowledge of partisan politics is still being learned as individuals enter the adult world" (p. 41). Thus there is a solid basis for expecting knowledge to increase with age.

The final new variable is family income. For this variable, respondents were scored according to their percentile in the population. Thus income is scored to show relative position in the population, not real income. For example, a person whose income fell at the fiftieth percentile of the income distribution in a given year was scored 50.

Income was originally included based on the hypothesis that political information would be caused by socioeconomic status. It was thought that higher status persons would be socialized to have greater interest in politics and consequently greater information about politics. Moreover, the individual components of socioeconomic status—education, occupation, and income—were each expected to have impacts on information.

6. More precisely, age was scored in decades without rounding off. That is, a person who is, say, twenty-six years old is given a score of 2.6. In 1956, the SRC National Election Study asked age only within categories. See Appendix 2 for full details on variable coding.

The connection of education is obvious. It might also be hypothesized that higher incomes and better occupations would give people greater stakes in the system and would thereby result in greater information.

It turned out that occupation had no effect. That is, when occupation was included either with or without income in the equation, it had no statistically significant effect. Consequently, occupation was dropped from further consideration. However, income did indeed have an effect on some types of information.

Urbanization, age, and income were not included in the Chapter 4 discussion of changes over time because they do not change much over time. The urbanization and age distributions have changed slightly over time, but not nearly enough to have any significant impact on information levels. Income certainly has changed over time, but here it is coded by percentiles, not by real or inflated dollars. The result is that income, as measured here, did not change over time either.

The Results of the Models

The results of the six regression models are presented in Table 44 through 49. Rather than discuss each table individually, I discuss each variable in turn to highlight the effects of variables and focus on how they differ from one dependent variable to the next. Before turning to the tables, I have three summary comments.

First, the effects of the independent variables are all moderate to small. Judging either by the objective standards of the unstandardized regression coefficients or by the relative standards of the standardized coefficients (betas), no one variable has a large effect on any dependent variable. The largest betas in these tables, for instance, are generally only a little over .20.

Second, the independent variables do a good job of explaining all six knowledge measures. With the exception of two of the early party difference indexes, the equations explain from 12 to 32 percent of the variance. In the realm of survey research, that is a fairly respectable job.

Finally, the party difference index is really three different indexes because its construction changed twice (1960–1964 and 1968–1972).[7] This will complicate the discussion because the different versions must be distinguished. The last version, used in 1972 and 1976, is clearly the best.

---

7. These were major format changes. There were also minor changes in the filters and, of course, changes in the questions that were asked from year to year.

TABLE 44. Number of Party Responses

	1956	1960	1964	1968	1972	1976
Education	.19	−.04**	.32	.31	.36	.48
	(.10)	(−.02)	(.18)	(.16)	(.17)	(.19)
Activity	.20	.05**	.26	.24	.47	.30
	(.06)	(.01)	(.07)	(.06)	(.12)	(.07)
Efficacy	.09**	.21*	.01**	.07**	.02**	.00**
	(.03)	(.06)	(.00)	(.02)	(.01)	(.00)
Involvement	−.33	−.39	−.30	−.36	—	—
	(−.27)	(−.24)	(−.20)	(−.21)		
Care	—	—	—	—	−.26	−.30
					(−.09)	(−.10)
Interest	—	—	—	—	−.26	−.34
					(−.14)	(−.17)
Print	.37	.36	.31	.52	.16**	.49
	(.12)	(.11)	(.10)	(.14)	(.04)	(.13)
Radio	−.17*	.04**	.12**	.10**	.04**	.23**
	(−.04)	(.01)	(.03)	(.02)	(.01)	(.04)
Television	.28	.54	.10**	.10**	.20**	.19**
	(.05)	(.07)	(.01)	(.01)	(.02)	(.02)
Urbanization	.14	.17	.26	.17	.32	.35
	(.07)	(.08)	(.12)	(.07)	(.11)	(.10)
Age	.18	.11	.19	.20	.22	.26
	(.11)	(.07)	(.13)	(.13)	(.14)	(.16)
Income	.006	.004**	.001**	.005*	.003**	.005
	(.07)	(.05)	(.01)	(.06)	(.03)	(.05)
Strength of party identification	.27	.24	.35	.20	.20	.21
	(.11)	(.10)	(.14)	(.07)	(.07)	(.07)
Intercept	1.70	1.93	0.29	1.20	0.26	−.59
Adjusted R^2	.28	.14	.21	.21	.19	.29
N	1,664	849	1,246	1,227	994	1,490

Source. Data are from the CPS/SRC 1956–1976 American National Election Studies.

Note: Standardized coefficients are in parentheses. *p < .10, borderline significance **p > .10, not significant

TABLE 45. Number of Candidate Responses

	1956	1960	1964	1968	1972	1976
Education	.32	.19	.33	.26	.27	.48
	(.18)	(.12)	(.20)	(.15)	(.14)	(.21)
Activity	.16	−.13**	.11**	.21	.43	.13**
	(.05)	(−.03)	(.03)	(.06)	(.12)	(.03)
Efficacy	.16	.32	.05**	.05**	−.05**	.08**
	(.06)	(.10)	(.02)	(.01)	(−.02)	(.03)
Involvement	−.28	−.34	−.28	−.30	—	—
	(−.24)	(−.22)	(−.20)	(−.20)		
Care	—	—	—	—	−.05**	−.06**
					(−.02)	(−.02)
Interest	—	—	—	—	−.32	−.39
					(−.19)	(−.22)
Print	.42	.49	.35	.45	.26	.55
	(.14)	(.15)	(.12)	(.14)	(.08)	(.16)
Radio	−.04**	.24*	.05**	.18**	.20**	.31
	(−.01)	(.06)	(.01)	(.04)	(.04)	(.06)
Television	.20*	.30**	.28**	.15**	.45*	.56
	(.04)	(.04)	(.04)	(.02)	(.06)	(.06)
Urbanization	.14	.05**	.27	.15	.19	.12*
	(.07)	(.03)	(.13)	(.07)	(.07)	(.04)
Age	.08	−.05**	−.02**	−.03**	−.03**	.01**
	(.05)	(−.03)	(−.01)	(−.02)	(−.02)	(.00)
Income	.010	.003**	.001**	.005	.009	.004**
	(.12)	(.04)	(.02)	(.06)	(.11)	(.04)
Strength of party identification	.08**	.07**	−.13*	.09**	.06**	−.04**
	(.04)	(.03)	(−.05)	(.04)	(.02)	(−.01)
Intercept	2.21	3.44	3.48	3.34	2.66	2.21
Adjusted R²	.32	.18	.20	.19	.21	.27
N	1,664	849	1,246	1,227	994	1,490

Source. Data are from the CPS/SRC 1956–1976 American National Election Studies.

Note: Standardized coefficients are in parentheses. *.05 < p < .10, borderline significance **p > .10, not significant

TABLE 46. Which Party More Conservative

	1960	1964	1968	1972	1976
Education	.03	.03	.06	.06	.10
	(.08)	(.09)	(.17)	(.15)	(.24)
Activity	.02**	.04	.06	.03**	.08
	(.02)	(.06)	(.08)	(.05)	(.11)
Efficacy	.02**	.01**	.01**	.01**	.02**
	(.02)	(.01)	(.01)	(.02)	(.04)
Involvement	−.04	−.03	−.03	—	—
	(−.12)	(−.11)	(−.11)		
Care	—	—	—	−.03**	.00**
				(−.05)	(.01)
Interest	—	—	—	−.01**	−.03
				(−.04)	(−.08)
Print	.13	.14	.09	.09	.05
	(.19)	(.21)	(.13)	(.13)	(.08)
Radio	−.03**	.03**	.00**	.03**	.03**
	(−.03)	(.03)	(.00)	(.03)	(.03)
Television	.08**	−.00**	.07**	.09*	.03**
	(.04)	(−.00)	(.04)	(.06)	(.02)
Urbanization	.02**	−.01**	−.00**	.04	.02**
	(.05)	(−.01)	(−.01)	(.08)	(.03)
Age	.02*	.03	.04	.01*	.02
	(.06)	(.11)	(.15)	(.05)	(.09)
Income	.002	.002	.002	.001*	.001
	(.10)	(.12)	(.13)	(.06)	(.07)
Strength of party identification	−.01**	−.00**	.02*	.01**	.01**
	(−.03)	(−.01)	(.05)	(.01)	(.03)
Intercept	.24	.14	−.01	.07	−.13
Adjusted R²	.13	.15	.17	.12	.19
N	849	1,246	1,227	1,000	1,490

Source. Data are from the CPS/SRC 1960–1976 American National Election Studies.

Note: Standardized coefficients are in parentheses. *.05 < p < .10, borderline significance **p > .10, not significant

TABLE 47. Information Index (Which Party Controls the House)

	1960	1964	1968	1972	1976
Education	.07	.09	.10	.09	.12
	(.12)	(.16)	(.17)	(.13)	(.16)
Activity	.04**	.13	.06*	.13	.17
	(.02)	(.12)	(.05)	(.10)	(.13)
Efficacy	.12	.03**	.01**	.04**	.05
	(.11)	(.03)	(.01)	(.04)	(.05)
Involvement	−.05	−.06	−.09	—	—
	(−.09)	(−.13)	(−.17)		
Care	—	—	—	−.06	−.01**
				(−.07)	(−.02)
Interest	—	—	—	−.08	−.08
				(−.14)	(−.13)
Print	.16	.13	.11	.15	.24
	(.14)	(.12)	(.09)	(.14)	(.21)
Radio	.02**	.10	.04**	−.05**	.06**
	(.01)	(.07)	(.03)	(−.03)	(.04)
Television	.16*	.13	.08**	.12**	.05**
	(.06)	(.05)	(.03)	(.04)	(.02)
Urbanization	−.02**	−.06	−.05	.04**	−.01**
	(−.02)	(−.08)	(−.06)	(.05)	(−.01)
Age	.02**	.04	.00**	.05	.05
	(.03)	(.09)	(.01)	(.10)	(.11)
Income	.003	.003	.002	.002	.003
	(.11)	(.12)	(.07)	(.10)	(.10)
Strength of party identification	.02**	.01**	.02**	.04**	.03**
	(.02)	(.02)	(.02)	(.04)	(.03)
Intercept	.44	.64	.85	.38	.09
Adjusted R²	.14	.20	.14	.20	.30
N	849	1,246	1,227	994	1,490

Source. Data are from the CPS/SRC 1956–1976 American National Election Studies.

Note: Standardized coefficients are in parentheses. *.05 < p < .10, borderline significance **p > .10, not significant

TABLE 48. Recall of House Candidates' Names Index

	1964	1968	1972
Education	.05	.05	.08
	(.08)	(.08)	(.13)
Activity	.26	.24	.19
	(.20)	(.18)	(.17)
Efficacy	−.03**	.03**	−.01**
	(−.03)	(.03)	(−.01)
Involvement	−.04	−.06	—
	(−.08)	(−.10)	
Care	—	—	−.05
			(.06)
Interest	—	—	−.01**
			(−.02)
Print	.15	.13	.11
	(.12)	(.10)	(.11)
Radio	.04**	−.04**	.04**
	(.02)	(−.02)	(.03)
Television	.14*	.05**	.13*
	(.05)	(.02)	(.05)
Urbanization	−.20	−.16	−.12
	(−.24)	(−.18)	(−.14)
Age	.01**	.05	.05
	(.01)	(.09)	(.12)
Income	.003	.003	.002*
	(.09)	(.10)	(.06)
Strength of party identification	.05*	−.01	−.04*
	(.05)	(−.01)	(−.05)
Intercept	.43	.38	.02
Adjusted R²	.18	.16	.13
N	1,246	1,227	994

Source. Data are from the CPS/SRC 1964–1976 American National Election Studies.

Note: Standardized coefficients are in parentheses. *.05 < p < .10, borderline significance **p > .10, not significant

TABLE 49. Party Difference Index

	1956	1960	1964	1968	1972	1976
Education	.22 (.07)	.02** (.01)	.09 (.08)	.01** (.00)	.22 (.10)	.52 (.18)
Activity	.16** (.03)	.29 (.07)	.18 (.08)	.17** (.04)	.25* (.06)	.36 (.07)
Efficacy	.48 (.10)	.18* (.06)	−.12 (−.07)	.12** (.03)	.01** (.00)	.02** (.00)
Involvement	−.34 (−.17)	−.11 (−.08)	−.03** (−.03)	−.40 (−.22)	—	—
Care	—	—	—	—	−.24 (−.08)	−.23 (−.07)
Interest	—	—	—	—	−.34 (−.18)	−.35 (−.15)
Print	.37 (.07)	.13 (.04)	.13 (.07)	.39 (.10)	.51 (.14)	.48 (.11)
Radio	.11** (.01)	.16** (.04)	.05** (.02)	.23** (.04)	.18** (.03)	.54 (.08)
Television	.12** (.01)	.12** (.02)	−.01** (−.00)	−.17** (−.02)	.88 (.10)	−.08** (−.01)
Urbanization	−.13** (−.04)	.04** (.02)	−.12 (−.09)	.31 (.12)	.43 (.14)	.44 (.11)
Age	.16 (.06)	.12 (.09)	.03** (.03)	−.12 (−.07)	−.19 (−.12)	−.05** (−.03)
Income	.020 (.13)	.001** (.02)	.001** (.02)	−.004** (−.04)	.000** (.00)	.003** (.03)
Strength of party identification	−.03** (−.01)	.06** (.03)	.06** (.04)	.57 (.20)	.28 (.09)	.47 (.14)
Intercept	.85	.13	.34	4.24	2.88	.97
Adjusted R²	.14	.03	.03	.17	.24	.24
N	1,664	849	1,246	1,227	994	1,490

Source. Data are from the CPS/SRC 1964–1976 American National Election Studies.

Note: Standardized coefficients are in parentheses. *.05 < p < .10, borderline significance **p > .10, not significant

Education, involvement (interest), and attention to politics in the print media are the three most influential variables. Education is positive and significant in all equations except the 1960 equation for number of party responses and the 1960 and 1968 versions of the party difference index. The coefficients in general are of moderate size. This can be seen by looking at the standardized regression coefficients (shown in parentheses). Ignoring the nonsignificant coefficients for the moment, betas range from .08 to .24, with most falling in the .10 to .20 range. These are certainly big enough to warrant attention, but they are hardly big coefficients.

Looking at the unstandardized coefficients and considering the difference between the most and least educated also provides a measure of the size of the coefficients. For instance, in Table 44, a one-step increase in education was associated with a .19 increase in the number of party responses. Because education is measured on a five point scale, the difference between the most and least educated is .76 (= 4 × .19). Given that the average number of responses is 3.5, this might seem a substantial increase. Yet compared to the number of possible responses (0–20) or the normal range of variation from 1956 to 1976 (.81—see Table 50), the difference caused by education is not very big at all.

The effect of education is fairly similar across all the variables. Of the five information variables, education has the least effect on recall of candidates' names.

Political activity presents a much different picture. Activity seems to have some positive impact, but a fairly small one, on the information measures other than recall. Seventeen of the thirty-one coefficients are statistically significant at the .05 level, but most have betas under .10. The unstandardized coefficients tell the same story.

The effect of activity on recall of candidate names, however, is another matter. Here there is a moderate impact. Along with urbanization, political activity is one of the two variables with the largest impact on recall. The betas are all of reasonable size (.17 to .20), and the unstandardized coefficients indicate that the difference between being completely inactive and being at least somewhat active can be up to recalling one-half more name. Thus on activity, recall stands out from the pattern shown by the other measures of information.

The effects of political efficacy on information are easy to summarize: They do not exist. Efficacy is significant in only six of the thirty-one equations; moreover, two of the coefficients are very small, and one has the wrong sign. In two years, efficacy has an impact on the number of candidate responses; in two years, it has an impact on the information index; and in two years, it has an impact on the party difference index. On the whole, this seems to be a disconfirmed hypothesis.

Political involvement is another one of the three most influential variables. Unfortunately, it is a little difficult to assess in 1972 and 1976 because the response categories for the questions were changed, and thus the two questions rather than *The American Voter*'s involvement scale were used in the analysis.[8] The result is that the impact of the two questions is somewhat obscured by multicollinearity.[9] However, the net effect of the two variables in 1972 and 1976 is approximately the same as the effect of the single involvement scale in the earlier years. In general, the more interested and psychologically involved one is, the more one knows about politics. (Note that the negative coefficients are the result of using the CPS coding system. The larger the score, the less involved the respondent).

On the number of party and candidate responses, involvement has the largest impact. That is, interest in the election makes people have more to say about the parties and candidates. Although involvement has one of the larger effects on the other variables, its impact on those is only moderate to small, as indicated by betas of around .10. Other variables, however, generally have even smaller effects.

The variable print, measuring attention to politics in newspapers and magazines, is the third of the most influential variables. It is significant in all but one of the equations. As expected, the more one reads, the more one knows about politics. Again, although print is one of the three variables with the largest overall impacts, its impact is only moderate.

Using radio and television to follow politics did not have any impact. Radio was only significant in three of the thirty-one equations, and the coefficients were substantively trivial. A case that television had some influence (however small) can be made by noting that television was significant at the .05 level in five of the equations and was of borderline significance ($p < .10$) in four other equations. Moreover, a couple of those

---

8. This procedure was followed in the earlier chapters as well.

9. Some of the coefficients are not significant. In 1972 in the "Which party is more conservative" question, neither variable is significant. An F-test of the significance of the joint effect of the two variables shows that although individually they are not significant, as a pair they are. This is a reflection of the multicollinearity problem (see Kelejian and Oates 1981; Pindyck and Rubinfeld 1981, pp. 116–20).

coefficients were of moderate size (i.e., number of party responses in 1960, number of candidate responses in 1976). Still, the findings here match those of other studies (see Chapter 4), indicating that watching television has either a very small effect or no effect on political knowledge.

Strength of party identification has a moderate to small effect on the number of party responses and similar effects on the party difference index from 1968 through 1976. It is significant in all six equations in Table 44 and in the last three difference index equations. Other than that, it attains borderline significance in some other equations, but the coefficients are all trivial. Thus strong party identifiers tend to know more about the parties, and independents tend to know less—a hardly surprising finding. Because strength of party identification is associated only with measures of party knowledge, it seems reasonable to conclude that it is not a cause of general political knowledge.

It follows from the first point that the relationship between strength of party identification and information that others have found (e.g., Kamieniecki 1985; Keith et al. 1977) is accounted for by other variables. That is, being a strong identifier does not make one learn more about politics. Other variables account for the relationship.

Urbanization has different relationships with different dependent variables. In Tables 44, 45, and 49 (1968–1976 only)—covering the number of party and candidate responses and the party difference index—there are small, positive coefficients, indicating that people who live in larger cities are more likely to have more political knowledge than those living in rural areas.

Tables 46 and 47 show weak or nonexistent relationships. Urbanization is significantly related to knowledge of which party is more conservative in only one year, 1972, when it has a small, positive effect. The relationship of urbanization to information about control of the House of Representatives is unexpectedly negative in two years, 1964 and 1968. Still, the coefficients are quite small, and the other three years do not have significant relationships. Thus overall the data indicate no relationships with these two variables.

In the case of recall of the names of the candidates for the House, the relationship is entirely different. This is one of the strongest relationships in these equations with rural dwellers being more knowledgeable than urban dwellers. As suggested previously, the most likely explanation is that a member of Congress is a much more important figure in a rural area than in a big city. At the extremes, some cities have many representatives (e.g., New York City has fourteen), while rural areas have only one (e.g., the state of Wyoming). Thus there are many urban representatives in a single media market, and they must compete for news coverage. However, there is often a single representative in a rural media market, and that representative finds it much easier to get coverage (Manheim 1974). The result is that urbanization is negatively related to recall.

The effects of age on knowledge are much less complicated than those of urbanization. Age has a small, positive effect on all measures of knowledge except the number of candidate responses and the party difference index in 1968 and 1972. In general, as Jennings and Niemi (1981) found with their panel study, the older people are, the more they know.

The failure of age to affect number of candidate responses and party differences may be related to the weaker party association of the young (Abramson 1974, 1983; Campbell et al. 1960; Converse 1976; Kamieniecki 1985). However, because party identification itself does not cause knowledge, exactly what that relationship might be (if it exists) is unclear. Still, whatever the reason for age not causing number of candidate responses, the general pattern of age causing knowledge—albeit weakly—comes out clearly in the other tables.

Turning finally to income, there are small, positive relationships with all the variables but the party difference index (which has only one significant coefficient among the six). The weakest effects are on the two number of response variables. Only five of those twelve coefficients are significant at the .05 level. The effects are more consistent on the other dependent variables, with eleven of the thirteen coefficients being significant and the two exceptions being of borderline significance ($p < .10$). On the whole, income has a weak, positive effect on knowledge.

Let me briefly summarize the results of Tables 44 through 49. The three variables with the largest effects are education, involvement, and print attention. The three variables with either no effects or extremely small ones are external political efficacy, radio attention, and television attention. Because strength of party identification affects only the number of party responses and knowledge of party differences, it should probably be regarded as having no effect on general political knowledge. Activity, urbanization, age, and income have generally small, positive effects. Finally, recall stands out in that political activity has a moderate positive effect, and urbanization has a similar negative effect.

Changes in the Public's Knowledge of Politics

Together with the trends among the independent variables discussed in Chapter 4, these findings can tell us a good deal about change in the public's political knowledge and understanding. Education, which has a positive effect on knowledge, has been increasing in the last thirty years. The trend should have resulted in some increase in the public's knowledge. That, of course, was the expectation of the authors of *The American Voter*. However, that expectation was not borne out.

Some might have thought external political efficacy and strength of party identification to be two likely candidates to offset the rise of education. Both have declined a good deal since the early 1960s, but neither has any effect on political knowledge.

Attention to politics in the print media has a substantial influence on knowledge; yet it has declined only slightly.[10] Although that drop in reading may have caused some small decline in the public's knowledge, the effect is clearly quite small. The other media, television and radio, could not have contributed anything one way or the other because television has either a very small effect or none at all, and radio attention clearly has no influence.

The other independent variables have changed little or not at all over the years. Moreover, with the exception of involvement, they all have small effects on knowledge. Thus they, too, could not have contributed more than trivial changes to the public's knowledge since the fifties. Thus we are left with the curious combination of a rise in the level of education but no corresponding rise in public knowledge about politics. How could this happen?

Isolating the Effects of Education

In order to investigate this problem further, one needs to find out exactly what the effects of education were. If everything else had stayed the same,

10. The CPS National Election Study data, the top portion of Table 37, show a small overall decline in newspaper and magazine use (although year-by-year fluctuations are fairly large). Newspaper circulation data, Table 39, show about a 6 percent decline from 1956 to 1976. The data that indicate the greatest decline are from Bower (1985), shown in Table 38. Unfortunately, these data are not part of the CPS data sets.

would the rising level of education have produced a large increase in knowledge or just a small one? We know the trend and the sizes of the effects, but we do not know their impact.

One way to assess the effect of education is to find out what would have happened if education had increased but everything else had remained constant. That is, the equations in Tables 44 through 48 can be used to simulate the effects that the rise in education would have had if nothing else had changed. For example, if all the independent variables except for education had been exactly the same in 1976 as they were in 1956, how much would education have increased the public's knowledge?

The simplest way to simulate the effects of education is to focus on changes in the means of the dependent variables (i.e., the knowledge measures) caused by the actual changes in education.[11] The first step is to select an equation explaining one of the knowledge measures, say, the 1956 equation explaining the number of party responses. The second step is to calculate for that sample what would have happened if the education distribution had been the same as the distribution in a different year, say, 1976. That is, of interest is what the number of party responses would have been in 1956 if the people had had the same educations as the 1976 sample, but everything else had remained the same. The results of those calculations are shown in Tables 50 through 54.[12]

That fact that each equation can be used to calculate a predicted value for each survey year makes the simulation tables a little complicated. Look at Table 50 to sort out the information. The top row of Table 50 has the actual observed values for the mean number of party responses in each year. That is, in 1956, the average number of responses was 3.55, in 1960, it was 3.68, and so on.[13] Each row after the top consists of the pre-

---

11. One could, of course, simulate the entire distributions of each measure of knowledge. However, that approach would flood one in data without adding any useful information. If one were particularly interested in what percentage of the population would have passed some threshold as a result of the changes in education, the entire distribution would be of interest. Because none of the measures of information has any threshold (e.g., above which one might label respondents "ideologues"), there is little of value in the distributions.

12. The exact method for calculating the effects is described in Appendix 1.

13. The observed values here may differ slightly from the values shown in the tables in Chapter 4 because of the way the sample was selected. The data in Chapter 4 are based on all respondents. The data in Tables 50 through 54 are based on the respondents who were included in the regression equations shown in Tables 44 through 49. The regression equations were estimated using "listwise" deletion of missing data. In other words, respondents who did not answer questions were

TABLE 50.   Predicted Changes in Number of Party Responses

	Observed or Predicted Value for						
	1956	1960	1964	1968	1972	1976	High–Low
Observed value	3.55	3.68	3.29	3.87	3.06	3.17	.81
Predicting equation from							
1956	**3.55**	3.58	3.57	3.60	3.61	3.68	.13
1960	3.69	**3.68**	3.68	3.68	3.67	3.66	.03
1964	3.25	3.30	**3.29**	3.33	3.36	3.48	.23
1968	3.80	3.84	3.83	**3.87**	3.90	4.02	.22
1972	2.94	2.99	2.98	3.03	**3.06**	3.20	.26
1976	2.83	2.90	2.88	2.94	2.99	**3.17**	.34

Source. Data are from the 1956–1976 SRC/CPS American National Election Studies.
Note: Figures in boldface type are observed values.

dictions of mean number of party responses based on an equation for a different year. The second row, for instance, shows the predicted number of responses based on the 1956 equation. The first entry in that row is in boldface to indicate that it is the observed value for that year. The second entry in that row, 3.58, is the predicted mean number of responses in 1960 based on the 1956 equation. That is, if education increased from 1956 to 1960, but everything else stayed unchanged, the 1956 equation predicts that the average would be 3.58 responses—an increase of .03 responses.

The last column of Table 50 shows the difference between the largest and smallest value in each row. In the row of observed means, this is a measure of how much fluctuation there was in the real data. In the case of party responses, for instance, the range of variation was from 3.06 to

---

excluded from the analysis. People who do not answer questions tend to be less educated, lower income, less interested in politics, and so forth (Bartels 1986; Converse 1976–1977; Ferber 1966; Francis and Busch 1975; Schuman and Presser 1981). The result is that the listwise deletion procedure eliminates a disproportionate number of those low on information. Thus the data in Tables 50 through 54 generally show a somewhat higher level of information than the corresponding tables in Chapter 4. Aside from slightly exaggerating the level of public information, this should not have any effect on the analysis.

3.87, a .81 difference. The ranges of predictions are much smaller. The predictions based on the 1956 equation, for instance, range from 3.55 to 3.68, a difference of .13.

The range of predicted values provides a way to understand how much of an impact education had. In the case of the 1956 equation, the changes in education allow one to predict a .13 increase in the mean number of party responses. The equations from other years predict larger impacts, but the largest is only an increase of .34 responses. Although this is a statistically significant change in the number of responses, it is substantively small. Changes of .03 up through .34 are simply lost in the much larger range of natural fluctuation in the number of responses, .81.

Here recall an earlier point about the sizes of the regression coefficients. Although the coefficients for education were among the largest in the equations from Tables 44 through 49, they were of only small to moderate size. Moreover, the trend in education is a slow one. Over the twenty-year period from 1956 through 1976, the number of those with only elementary school educations decreased 14 percent, and the number of college graduates increased only 7 percent. Thus it is not surprising that education has such a small impact. It could hardly be otherwise.

The small impact of education is repeated in Tables 51–54. In Table 51, the different equations estimate the impact of education on number of candidate responses to be anywhere from .14 to .35 responses. Again, an average increase of under one-third of a response is a very small shift.

In Table 52, the effect of education on knowing which party is more conservative is estimated to be anywhere from 2 to 6 percent over the twenty-year span. Even taking the upper limit as the correct estimate, a 6 percent increase in the number of people getting the right answer is trivial.

In Table 53, education accounts for a change of .05 to .07 (2.5 to 3.5 percent) in people's scores on the information index. Finally, in Table 54, over the eight years from 1964 to 1972, education has an impact of .01 to .02 (1–2 percent) on recall, again, a trivial change.[14]

To summarize, the point of these simulations is to show how much impact education had had on the level of political knowledge over the twenty years from 1956 to 1976. When one sees a trend of rising education and an equation in which education has one of the larger influences

---

14. The party difference index is not used here because there were so many changes in how it was constructed over the years. No comparisons of this index over time can be made.

TABLE 51. Predicted Changes in Number of Candidate Responses

	Observed or Predicted Value for						
	1956	1960	1964	1968	1972	1976	High–Low
Observed value	4.18	4.55	4.69	4.69	4.40	4.63	.51
Predicting equation from							
1956	**4.18**	4.22	4.22	4.26	4.29	4.41	.23
1960	4.52	**4.55**	4.54	4.57	4.59	4.66	.14
1964	4.65	4.70	**4.69**	4.73	4.76	4.89	.24
1968	4.62	4.66	4.65	**4.69**	4.72	4.83	.21
1972	4.31	4.35	4.34	4.38	**4.40**	4.50	.19
1976	4.28	4.35	4.34	4.40	4.44	**4.63**	.35

Source. Data are from the 1956–1976 SRC/CPS American National Election Studies.
Note: Figures in boldface type are observed values.

TABLE 52. Predicted Changes in Knowing More Conservative Party

	Observed or Predicted Value for					
	1960	1964	1968	1972	1976	High–Low
Observed value	.68	.61	.64	.58	.59	.10
Predicting equation from						
1960	**.68**	.68	.68	.69	.70	.02
1964	.61	**.61**	.61	.62	.63	.02
1968	.63	.63	**.64**	.65	.67	.04
1972	.57	.57	.57	**.58**	.60	.03
1976	.53	.53	.54	.55	**.59**	.06

Source. Data are from the 1956–1976 SRC/CPS American National Election Studies.
Note: Figures in boldface type are observed values.

on knowledge, it is easy to jump to the conclusion that the result will surely be a rising level of knowledge. Yet such a conclusion would be wrong.

Rather than relying on intuition, one can put the information from the trends and the equations together and isolate the effects of education. Those effects are very small, and all of them were lost in each measure's

TABLE 53.   Predicted Changes in Information Index

	Observed or Predicted Value for					
	1960	1964	1968	1972	1976	High–Low
Observed value	1.37	1.48	1.21	1.23	1.27	.27
Predicting equation from						
1960	**1.37**	1.37	1.38	1.38	1.41	.10
1964	1.48	**1.48**	1.49	1.50	1.53	.05
1968	1.20	1.20	**1.21**	1.22	1.26	.06
1972	1.21	1.21	1.22	**1.23**	1.26	.05
1976	1.20	1.20	1.21	1.22	**1.27**	.07

Source. Data are from the 1956–1976 SRC/CPS American National Election Studies.
Note: Figures in boldface type are observed values.

TABLE 54.   Predicted Changes in Recall of Candidates

	Observed or Predicted Value for		
	1964	1968	1972	High–Low
Observed value	.87	.84	.55	.32
Predicting equation from				
1964	**.87**	.88	.88	.01
1968	.83	**.84**	.85	.02
1972	.53	.54	**.55**	.02

Source. Data are from the 1956–1976 SRC/CPS American National Election Studies.
Note: Figures in boldface type are observed values.

natural range of variation. Thus these data indicate that if one is looking for possible causes of growth in the public's knowledge and political sophistication, one had better look elsewhere.

Another Look at Education

The surprising finding that education does not seem to have a large impact on knowledge and sophistication indicates that the subject merits further investigation. I use the Jennings and Niemi Youth Socialization Panel Study to take another look at the effects of education. This is a national representative cross-section of high school seniors in 1965 who were reinterviewed in 1973 and 1982.[15]

Although the Jennings and Niemi data do not have the measures of sophistication used in the earlier analyses, they do offer one advantage—education changes for many of the respondents during the panel. Consequently, I can examine the effect of increases in education on respondents.[16]

Jennings and Niemi (1981, ch. 8) also investigated the effects of education on knowledge using Converse's "strata of knowledge and understanding" measure (discussed in Chapter 4) and a knowledge index. The index was the number of correct answers given to six questions—the length of a U.S. senator's term, the nation in which Marshall Tito was the ruler, the number of members of the U.S. Supreme Court, the name of the governor of the respondent's state, the location of the concentration camps in World War II, and whether F.D.R. was a Democrat or a Republican.

Jennings and Niemi presented two important findings. First, they found that understanding of the terms "liberal" and "conservative" increased over the 1965–1973 period, but that the factual knowledge index increased only slightly. Indeed, they observed that, "only slight shifts to adjacent categories took place," and they concluded, "On balance, factual inventories are relatively invariant" (p. 40).

Second, Jennings and Niemi (1981, ch. 8) discovered that a large portion of what might seem to be caused by education was actually the result of a selection process. Those who received advanced degrees were far more knowledgeable than those who merely graduated from high school. However, the difference in knowledge was only partly attributable to education. The additional years of school caused an increase in knowledge, but those who eventually received advanced degrees were more knowledgeable than those with lesser educations when they were all still in high school in 1965. That is, those who went on to higher education were more knowledgeable in the beginning.

15. There was also a matching sample of parents. Because the parents' educations remained largely constant, I use only the youth sample.

16. The CPS panel studies also allow us to look at change in education; however, education changes only for a small handful of respondents in either of the two CPS panel studies. Most of the respondents in the CPS studies, or for that matter, in any national representative survey, have already left school.

TABLE 55. The Effects of Education on Knowledge

Independent Variable	Knowledge Index	Strata of Knowledge and Understanding
Knowledge 1965	.57*	.23*
	(.03)	(.03)
Education	.13*	.23*
	(.03)	(.03)
In school	.41*	.33**
	(.14)	(.18)
Urbanization	.013	.04*
	(.015)	(.02)
Income	.0028**	.005*
	(.0016)	(.002)
Intercept	1.62*	1.92*
	(.17)	(.16)
N	615	615
R^2	.50	.23

Source. Data are from the Jennings and Niemi Youth Socialization Panel Study, 1965–1973–1982.

Note: Standard errors are in parentheses. *$p < .05$ **$.05 < p < .10$

The model presented here is a simplified version of the model presented earlier in this chapter. It was simplified by dropping all the variables that are not obviously causally prior to political knowledge and sophistication. That is, the attitudinal variables and media attention variables that may have caused simultaneous equation bias have been omitted. Omitting these variables should eliminate the bias. Therefore although we cannot examine the effects of efficacy, media attention, and so forth, we can focus on the effect of education.

The simplified regression model is designed to measure the effect of change in education on change in knowledge. To do this, the lagged value of the dependent variable is included as an independent variable. Thus for the knowledge index, the dependent variable is the knowledge index in 1973, and the independent variables are the knowledge index in 1965, education, urban residence, and family income in 1973. Education, urban residence, and income were the variables in Tables 44 through 49. Age is not included because it is constant for all respondents. Everyone in the sample was a high school senior in 1965, and they are all eight years older in 1973. The effect of age therefore is picked up in the equation's intercept term. Finally, a dummy variable was included to distinguish those who were currently in school when they responded to the 1973 questionnaire. This was done because colleges and universities often have a fair amount of political activity. Thus students are probably more likely than nonstudents to be exposed to political information.

The results of the analysis are shown in Table 55. Both models work reasonably well. In the first equation, with the strata of recognition as the dependent variable, all the variables except whether the respondent was a student in 1973 were statistically significant at .05, and that variable just misses (p < .07). In the second model, explaining the knowledge index, urban residence had no effect, and income was of only borderline significance (p < .09). In both equations, education was highly significant.

Education is measured as the number of years of college, from zero to seven.[17] Respondents who did not go to school after graduating from high school are scored 0, college graduates are scored 4, and those with postgraduate educations are scored from 5 to 7 (with more than seven years scored as 7). Thus we have an eight point scale.

To find the expected difference in knowledge between a high school graduate and a Ph.D., one multiplies the difference in education scores by the education coefficient. For the strata of recognition, the difference is 1.63; for the knowledge index, the difference is .90. Considering the enormous jump in learning between a high school graduate and a Ph.D., these are not very large differences.

Getting an advanced degree certainly increases one's likelihood of understanding the terms "liberal" and "conservative," but it hardly guarantees that one will know what they mean. Moreover, education has a smaller impact on factual knowledge. The added learning from high school to an advanced degree is expected to increase one's knowledge by less than one right answer in six questions.

To put the effect of education in the context used previously, consider the growth of education over recent decades. In 1960, the average adult[18] had completed 10.6 years of school; by 1980, the average person had completed 12.5 years, an increase of 1.9 years. Multiplying this increase by the education coefficients from Table 55 yields an increase of .44 on

17. Note that this is not the same coding as was used in the previous analyses.
18. These Census Bureau figures are for the median years of school completed by persons age twenty-five or over.

the strata of understanding measure and .24 on the knowledge index. Neither of these increases is very large.

When reviewing the findings based on the Jennings and Niemi survey, one must remember that the data are from a representative sample of high school seniors, not of the entire population. Nevertheless, the results are essentially the same as those based on the CPS data. Formal education has an effect on political knowledge and sophistication, but a small one. The growth of education in the United States over the past three decades may have done many things, but it did not contribute much to the public's understanding of politics. In sum, education is not the key to the public's understanding of politics.

Can the Public's Sophistication Change?

If education is not likely to cause any growth in the level of the public's understanding of politics, what might? That is an important question, but one which the data here do not answer. The data here indicate that the variables that change have little or no effect. Education does not have enough influence to cause more than minor change over decades. External political efficacy and party identification changed a good deal, and thus might change back at some time; but they have no effect on knowledge. Television grew enormously in the 1950s, but television has such a negligible impact that it caused no more than trivial change. Although predicting future developments in technology is a risky business, at the very least, this should give one pause before making any bold predictions about the effects of any new communications technologies.

The other variables remained basically constant over the twenty-year span of the study. Urbanization, age, and income are changing slightly, but hardly enough to have any important influence on the public's political knowledge. Moreover, these variables have small coefficients. Thus they cannot change enough to have any major impact on public knowledge.

The last two variables are political activity and involvement. Political activity remained basically constant over time. Involvement did fluctuate somewhat, and in a way that might suggest some hope for future change. The number of people who said they were very interested in politics fluctuated over a 9 percent range (see Table 36). Surprisingly, the years of highest interest, 1960–1968, do not correspond to the years of greatest turbulence, 1964–1972. This was one of the problems with the argument of *The Changing American Voter*. Still, one can argue that public events cause interest in politics, and this might seem to be a basis for looking for future growth in knowledge.

The problem here is that a little arithmetic shows that there would have to be staggering increases in interest before any important change in knowledge would occur. Even though interest in politics has one of the larger effects of any of the variables investigated, its effect are no more than moderate at best. To see the potential impact of interest, return to Tables 44 through 49 and examine the effect of changes in the involvement scale. As before, I simulate changes in the mean involvement score. This scale was used only from 1956 to 1968, but that period includes both high and low interest years. Because I want to find out how much change an increase in interest might cause, a rough idea of how much involvement might change is all that is necessary.

I start by using the range over which involvement varied to get an idea of its potential range. The lowest mean was 2.90 in 1960; the highest was 3.70 in 1956 (remember that low values of involvement indicate high levels of interest and vice versa). The difference in means is .80. To determine the effects of a .80 increase in involvement on the measures of knowledge, one needs the coefficients that show how much each knowledge scale changes in response to changes in involvement. Rather than using each coefficient from each year and calculating several different estimates, I use only the largest coefficient from any year. By using the largest coefficients, I exaggerate the amount of change potentially caused by increases in involvement. That is, the method of projecting the possible effects of an increase in involvement will be to find the maximum possible knowledge gain justifiable with the data.

Even with inflated estimates, the results are not encouraging. A .80 increase in involvement would result in increases of .31 and .27, respectively, in the number of party and candidate responses. These are very small increases.

Shifts in other measures are easier to assess intuitively. A .80 increase in interest would result in a 3 percent increase in knowing which party is more conservative. The results for the information and recall indexes are similar. They would increase by .07 and .05, respectively. Because these are both two point scales (0–2), this means that the increase in interest would yield increases of 3.5 and 2.5 percent along the scales (i.e., a .07 change on a two point scale is .07/2 = .035, or 3.5 percent, of the total scale). So there are 2.5 to 3.5 percent gains in knowledge—in other words, gains that are substantively trivial.

Even if interest increased by three times the amount previously recorded, there are still knowledge gains of only about 10 percent. Thus it seems difficult to believe that one should look here for any hope of future growth in knowledge.

The Limitations of Behavioral Research

The conclusion being approached is apparently that the American voter is and will be unchanging. I have identified a set of variables that explain political knowledge. Yet the variables that have any effects are fairly stable over time, and none of their effects is very big. Together, these facts provide no basis for predicting anything but trivial change in the level of public knowledge in the coming years. Before leaping to that conclusion, however, consider the limitations of the data, a set of surveys from the presidential election years from 1956 to 1976. There are two possible shortcomings of those data.

First, it is possible that some key variables are missing from the surveys or that I failed to recognize some key variables. These could be either independent variables or measures of knowledge. Considering independent variables first, there could be variables that have large effects that were not included in the analysis. Although the models explain fairly high percentages of the variances of the information measures, it is certainly possible that the models were misspecified, and that proper specifications would show that change is possible.

The other variables that might be missing are measures of knowledge and understanding. The measures used here cover a fair range, but they certainly do not cover all possible aspects of knowledge. It is possible, after all, that different types of knowledge may change independently of one another. If one could devise measures that reflect other types of knowledge—possibly more sophisticated types of thinking—one might find that some of them changed during the twenty years of this study. Although nothing in this study suggests the existence of other types of knowledge, neither does anything disprove the existence of other types or other measures of knowledge.

Second, it is possible that events or conditions that might cause major changes in knowledge did not happen during the 1956–1976 period. There was, of course, a fairly wide range of events during the twenty years covered by this study. The year 1956 was, relative to what followed, fairly quiet. In the following years, our nation was rocked by the civil rights movement, the Vietnam War, the Great Society programs, and a variety of social and political transformations. Huntington (1981) describes the sixties and early seventies as one of the great reform periods in our nation's history—a period not matched since the Progressive Era. By 1976, the nation was once again relatively tranquil.

Still, many people may have regarded these events as remote. They may have dominated television news more than they affected people's everyday lives. One can easily suggest two events that probably had more effect on people—the Civil War and the Great Depression. Alternatively, a change in our system of government might do the trick. For instance, if we were to develop "responsible" parties, the voters might respond by becoming more political. Somewhat more realistically, if we were to adopt a system of universal voter registration, the public might become more knowledgeable. If registration barriers are the principle reason people do not vote, then perhaps universal registration would cause more people to vote, and the former nonvoters would learn a little more about politics. Such gains would almost certainly be modest, but they might exceed what any of my simulations indicate.

I do not mean to suggest that gains in public knowledge require anything so drastic as another civil war or depression or a major change in our system of government. My point is that there are certainly events outside the range of the data that might cause great increases in knowledge and understanding of politics. What those events might be is obviously unknown.

Therefore although I can say that nothing here provides any basis for predicting any increases in political sophistication, it would be unwise to proclaim that there will never be any changes.

Concluding Comments

This book has presented an extended examination of various ways to measure political sophistication. An extended summary is not needed. There are, however, two subjects upon which I have some final comments and observations.

On the Influence of the Changing Political Environment

The traditional measures of sophistication—the level of conceptualization and attitude consistency indexes—have been shown not to work for comparisons over time. The other measures examined in Chapters 4 and 5 reveal no change over the twenty-year period of this study. Moreover, the data provide no basis for predicting any more than trivial changes in sophistication in the future.

The conclusion that follows from these findings is that the upheavals of the sixties had virtually no impact on the public's political knowledge and understanding. Although many of the public's beliefs and attitudes changed during the sixties (party identification declined, trust in the government declined, the feeling that the government was responsive to the people declined), knowledge and sophistication remained constant.

This does not mean that the sophistication of the American voter is immutable. It would be a mistake to conclude that what we now know about the political knowledge of the American voter will be true for all time or for that matter, even for the next decade. Events may yet cause some significant change. Still, a record of two decades without change provides little cause to expect any future changes.

On the Definition and Measurement of
Political Sophistication

The definition of sophistication that most political scientists use stems from Converse's work (see the "Introduction"). Sophistication supposedly has four components: range of opinions, amount of information, attitude consistency, and level of conceptualization. The latter two components have serious measurement problems. Attitude consistency has not yet been measured in a way such that it can be compared over time. Moreover, as it is traditionally measured (with correlation coefficients), it is a characteristic of a group or a population, not of an individual.[1] As for the other component, the levels of conceptualization simply do not exist.

Thus we are left with measures of range of opinions and amount of information. Are these sufficient to our needs? To answer this question, we must consider the difference between a high level of factual information and a high level of conceptual sophistication.

By conceptual sophistication, here, I mean how one organizes and processes information. That is, I am referring to the construct that the authors of *The American Voter* originally intended to measure with the level of conceptualization index—the use of capping abstractions to organize and process cognitions and attitudes about politics. Although the levels per se may not exist, it certainly does not follow that there are not more and less conceptually sophisticated ways of dealing with information. The question we want to ask, then, is, do we need a measure of conceptual sophistication or are our measures of information sufficient?

Consider the problem with the help of a hypothetical scale of information. Suppose we were able to construct an index of political information from a battery of questions that adequately covered the domain of politics.[2] This battery would include some questions on foreign affairs, some on domestic affairs, and so forth. In addition, it would contain a range of items from the very easy to the very difficult. Some might be simple recall questions (e.g., Name the nine members of the U.S. Supreme Court.).

---

1. Other methods for measuring consistency as an individual characteristic have been proposed. See Barton and Parsons (1977) and Smith (1982).

2. Assume we could agree on what makes up the domain of politics. I realize that there is disagreement on exactly what is politics, but that is irrelevant to the argument I want to make. In addition, some argue that information may be "domain specific." That is, a single information scale will not do; we need scales to measure each area of information. This argument, too, is irrelevant.

Others might call for more conceptually sophisticated factual information (e.g., What do you mean by the term "conservative"?).

Given such a scale, one can ask if there is a difference between a very high level of information and a high level of conceptual sophistication. Are having a great deal of information (including facts that are conceptually sophisticated) on the one hand and organizing and processing information in a conceptually sophisticated way on the other hand different from each other?

Pierce (1970) provides an example of this distinction. He developed two measures of sophistication—one of "informational ideologues" and the other of "conceptual ideologues." The first was based on understanding of the liberal-conservative distinction; the second was the level of conceptualization index. Even though the levels index is not valid, Pierce's distinction may be a valid one. There may well be a difference between merely knowing many facts, including what conceptually sophisticated words mean, and actually thinking in a conceptually sophisticated manner.[3]

Arguments on the both sides can be posed. In favor of the distinction, one can turn to virtually any psychology textbook to see that learning and memory (the basis for knowing many facts) are independent of intelligence (which is related to the idea of sophisticated thinking).[4] Moreover, one can cite examples of people with photographic memories, some of whom clearly have little understanding of the enormous number of facts they know (Krech et al. 1970, pp. 104–105). Thus memory for facts and conceptual sophistication are certainly not identical.

Against the distinction, one can cite a great deal of psychological work (including some by political scientists) that maintains that high levels of conceptual sophistication nearly always accompany high levels of information. Knowledge and conceptual sophistication are closely related. The reason, many investigators argue, is that conceptual sophistication is required in order to retain large amounts of information; thus the two come together.

3. Luskin (1987) rejected Pierce's distinction, arguing that the distinctions are only in our operational attempts to measure the underlying characteristic.

4. I use the term "intelligence" loosely. I wish to avoid the debate about what intelligence is and how to measure it. I should point out, however, that one of the standard criticisms of intelligence tests is that they measure only learned knowledge and thus are not tests of real intelligence (Jensen 1980). This is another example of the distinction between factual knowledge and conceptual sophistication in processing facts.

For instance, Campbell et al. (1960, p. 193)[5] declared, "Any cognitive structure that subsumes content of wide scope and high diversity must be capped by concepts of a higher order of abstractness." Luskin (1987, p. 862) wrote,

> The grouping and regrouping of information into increasingly abstract categories is among the commonest and most effective means of cognitive organization. . . . Thus the more highly organized the [political belief system], the more abstract the most abstract of its relatively central elements should be, and the more central such high-order abstractions as "liberal" and "conservative" should be to it.

That is, high level abstractions are used to organize large amounts of information.

The sources for most of these arguments by political scientists are psychologists who believe that information is stored in the form of concepts and relationships among concepts. As people acquire information, they develop hierarchical structures, or schemas, in which to store the information. The greater the amount of information, the larger the hierarchical structure, and the more abstract the unifying themes at the top (Anderson and Bower 1973; Bower et al. 1969; Crowder 1976; Reardon 1981; Schroder et al. 1967).

Of course, knowledge and conceptual sophistication are, as noted, not the same. No one claims that they are identical, only that they are closely associated. This leads to the practical question that political scientists must answer: Does it make any difference?

Granted that the two are distinct, they may be so closely related to each other that the distinction makes no difference for any question of interest to political scientists. What difference would the distinction make, for instance, for decisions about whether or not to vote, about vote choice, about whether to participate? There may be no difference. There may well be differences of importance to psychologists, but if we limit ourselves to questions of political interest, the differences may be trivial.

Whether or not there is a practical difference between factual knowledge and conceptual sophistication is, of course, not known. Nor will we know until someone develops a better measure of conceptual sophistication. Is this a useful research task?

On the whole, it seems to me that we would be far better off spending our time and effort using the existing measures of knowledge than seek-

5. Also quoted in Luskin (1987).

ing to develop new measures of conceptual sophistication. Few, if any, political science theories distinguish between knowledge and conceptual sophistication. Moreover, because the two are closely related, we may never be able to distinguish between them reliably with survey instruments. In sum, although this is an interesting topic, and certainly one worth pursuing, it does not seem to be one that should receive the highest priority.

Appendix One

The Simulation Method

The method for predicting what effect a change in an independent variable (e.g., education) would have on the mean of the dependent variable is straightforward. Four pieces of information are required: (1) a regression equation relating the independent variable to the dependent variable, (2) the mean of the independent variable from the equation, (3) the mean of the dependent variable from the year of the equation, and (4) the mean of the independent variable for the year in which one wishes to predict the dependent variable.

Given this information, one can use the fact that the regression solution (the line, plane, or whatever) always passes through the means of all the variables. The specific equation showing this is

$$\bar{Y} = b_0 + b_1\bar{X}_1 + b_2\bar{X}_2 + \ldots + b_k\bar{X}_k \tag{1}$$

This is sometimes referred to as the first "normal" equation of the instrumental variables solution to ordinary least squares regression (Kelejian and Oates 1981, pp. 47, 132–33).

It follows from equation (1) that if one wants to find out how the mean of the dependent variable will change when one of the independent variables changes, one need only concern oneself with the mean of that particular independent variable. Because the other variables are held constant, they can be ignored. Moreover, one need not pay any attention to the entire distribution of the independent variable in question because only its mean can affect the mean of the dependent variable.

Suppose then that one has the equation, knows the three means, and for simplicity, wishes to manipulate the independent variable X_1 (that is, one wants to find out what the mean of Y would be if X_1 were changed from its real value to the value of some other year one wishes to simulate).

Let $\bar{X}_1$ = independent variable mean from the equation year
$\bar{Y}$ = dependent variable mean from the equation year

$\bar{X}_p$ = independent variable mean (X_1) from the year to be predicted
$\bar{Y}_p$ = dependent variable mean from the year to be predicted
    (i.e., the unknown)

$$\bar{Y}_p = b_0 + b_1\bar{X}_p + b_2\bar{X}_2 + \ldots + b_k\bar{X}_k \tag{2}$$

If we subtract (1) from (2) and solve for $\bar{Y}_p$, we have:

$$\bar{Y}_p = \bar{Y} + b_1(\bar{X}_p - \bar{X}_1) \tag{3}$$

That is, in order to find the predicted value of the dependent variable, one simply finds the difference between the mean of X_1 in the year to be predicted and X_1 in the year of the equation. That difference is multiplied by the regression coefficient to find the change between the real value of the mean of the dependent variable and the simulated value. Then the change is added to the real value.

Appendix Two

Coding the Data

The Center for Political Studies' American National Election Studies were coded as indicated. For variable numbers, see the individual CPS codebooks.

Education: 0–8 years = 1; 9–11 years = 2; high school graduate, including technical school training = 3; some college = 4; college graduate = 5

Activity: nonvoter = 0; voted, but not otherwise active = 1; voted and performed one or more activities = 2. The activities are as follows: worked for a candidate or party, had button or bumper sticker, donated money, attended meeting or rally.

Media attention: the number of media (television, radio, newspapers, and magazines), from 0 to 4, in which the respondent has read or heard stories about the current campaign

Print: the number of print media, from 0 to 2, in which the respondent read stories about the campaign

External efficacy: based on two efficacy items: "People like me don't have any say about what government does" and "I don't think public officials care much what people like me think." Disagree with both statements = 2; agree with one and disagree with the other = 1; agree with both = 0.

Involvement: the American Voter's Involvement Scale, scored from 1 to 8. The scale is built from the care who wins and interest in outcome questions. See CPS codebooks for details.

Information: knowledge of which party controlled the House of Representatives before and after the election. Know both = 2; know one = 1; know neither = 0

Party Difference Scale: the proportion of issue items on which the respondent sees differences between the Democratic and Republican parties. The number of items and the wordings and formats of the items differ from year to year. The number of differences is rescaled to the 0–10 interval each year. In general, the items are those used for most attitude consistency studies plus all other available issue items with the same format. The variables used in each year are as follows:

1956: tax cut, guaranteed jobs, isolationism, government medical care, foreign economic aid, black housing and jobs, business influence on government, reciprocate USSR toughness, aid to education, foreign military aid, government utilities and housing, labor influence on government, befriending nations, dismissing communists, aid to noncommunist countries, school integration

1960: government utilities and housing, guaranteed jobs, isolationism, aid to education, economic foreign aid, black housing and jobs, foreign military aid, government medical care, school integration, avoiding war

1964: aid to education, government power, government medical care, guaranteed jobs, school prayer, foreign aid, talk with communists, fair employment, school integration, avoiding war, government utilities, trade with communists, public accommodations for blacks

1968: aid to education, size of government, government medical care, guaranteed jobs, fair employment, school integration, black accommodations, foreign aid, talk with communists, trade with communists, Vietnam, keep U.S. out of war

1972: guaranteed jobs, rights of the accused, busing, minority aid, health insurance, urban unrest, marijuana, tax rates, women's equality, Vietnam, inflation

1976: guaranteed jobs, rights of the accused, busing, minority aid, health insurance, urban unrest, marijuana, tax rates, women's equality

Urbanization: rural areas under 9,999 = 1; non-self-representing PSU's with 10,000 or more = 2; urban fringe of SMSA's under 49,999 = 3; central cities and urban fringe with 50,000 or more = 4

Family income: the percentile in the population of the given income category, from 0 to 100

Age: actual age in decades, except for 1956. The categories in 1956 are 18–21 = 0; 21–24 = 1; 25–34 = 2; 35–44 = 3; 45–54 = 4; 55–64 = 5; 65 or older = 6

Strength of party identification: strong identifiers = 3; weak identifiers = 2; leaning independents = 1; pure independents and apoliticals = 0; minor parties and NA = missing

The Jennings and Niemi Youth Socialization Panel Study was coded as follows:

Education: years of college from 0 (high school graduate only) to 7 (7 years or more). College graduates were scored 4.

In school: not attending college = 0; attending college = 1

Urbanization: rural, under 2,500 = 1; 2,500–9,999 = 2; 10,000–29,999 = 3; 30,000–49,999 = 4; 50,000–99,999 = 5; 100,000–149,999 = 6; 150,000–349,999 = 7; 350,000–499,999 = 8; 500,000–999,999 = 9; 1,000,000 and over = 10

Family income: the percentile in the population of the given income category, from 0 to 100

References

Abelson, Robert P., and Milton J. Rosenberg
  1958   "Symbolic Psycho-Logic: A Model of Attitudinal Cogni-
          tion." *Behavioral Science* 3 : 1 – 13.
Aberbach, Joel D., and Jack L. Walker
  1973   *Race in the City.* Boston: Little, Brown.
Abramson, Paul R.
  1974   "Generational Change in the American Electorate." *Ameri-
          can Political Science Review* 68 : 93 – 105.
  1983   *Political Attitudes in America: Formation and Change.* San
          Francisco: W. H. Freeman.
Achen, Christopher H.
  1975   "Mass Political Attitudes and the Survey Response." *Ameri-
          can Political Science Review* 69 : 1218 – 31.
Adorno, T. W., Else Frenkel-Brunswik, Daniel J. Levinson, and R. Nevitt
  Sanford
  1950   *The Authoritarian Personality.* New York: W. W. Norton.
Allen, Michael P.
  1976   "Conventional and Optimal Interval Scores for Ordinal
          Variables." *Sociological Methods and Research* 4 : 475 – 94.
Anderson, J. R., and G. H. Bower
  1973   *Human Associative Memory.* Washington, D.C.: Winston
          & Sons.
Arseneau, Robert B., and Raymond E. Wolfinger
  1973   "Voting Behavior in Congressional Elections." Paper deliv-
          ered at the 1973 annual meeting of the American Political
          Science Association, New Orleans, Louisiana.
Axelrod, Robert
  1967   "The Structure of Public Opinion on Policy Issues." *Public
          Opinion Quarterly* 31 : 51 – 60.

1973   "Schema Theory: An Information Processing Model of
           Perception and Cognition." *American Political Science Re-
           view* 67:1248–66.

Balch, George I.
1974   "Multiple Indicators in Survey Research: The Concept of
           'Sense of Political Efficacy.'" *Political Methodology* 1:1–43.

Bartels, Larry M.
1986   "Issue Voting Under Uncertainty: An Empirical Test."
           American Journal of Political Science 30:709–28.

Bartlett, F. C.
1932   *Remembering*. London: Cambridge University Press.

Barton, Allen H., and R. Wayne Parsons
1977   "Measuring Belief System Structure." *Public Opinion
           Quarterly* 41:159–80.

Bass, B. M.
1955   "Authoritarianism or Acquiescence?" *Journal of Abnormal
           and Social Psychology* 51:616–23.
1956   "Development and Evaluation of a Scale for Measuring So-
           cial Acquiescence." *Journal of Abnormal and Social Psy-
           chology* 53:296–99.

Beck, Paul, and M. Kent Jennings
1979   "Politial Periods and Political Participation." *American Po-
           litical Science Review* 73:737–50.

Becker, L. B., D. H. Weaver, Doris A. Graber, and Maxwell E. Combs
1979   "Influence on Public Agendas." In Sidney Kraus (ed.), *The
           Great Debates: Carter vs. Ford, 1976*. Bloomington: Indi-
           ana University Press.

Becker, L. B., and D. C. Whitney
1980   "Effects of Media Dependencies: Audience Assessment of
           Government." *Communication Research* 7:95–120.

Behr, Roy L., and Shanto Iyengar
1985   "Television News, Real World Cues, and Changes in the
           Public Agenda." *Public Opinion Quarterly* 49:38–57.

Bejar, Issac I.
1983   *Achievement Testing: Recent Advances*. Beverly Hills, Calif.:
           Sage Publications.

Bem, David J.
1965   "An Experimental Analysis of Self-Persuasion." *Journal of
           Experimental Social Psychology* 1:199–218.
1967   "Self-Perception: An Alternative Interpretation of Cog-
           nitive Dissonance Phenomena." *Psychological Review* 74:
           183–200.

1968   "Attitudes as Self-Descriptions: Another Look at the Attitude-Behavior Link." In Anthony G. Greenwold, Timothy C. Brock, and Thomas M. Ostrom (eds.), *Psychological Foundations of Attitudes.* New York: Academic Press.

1970   *Beliefs, Attitudes and Human Affairs.* Monterey, Calif.: Brooks/Cole.

Bem, David J., and H. K. McConnell

1970   "Testing the Self-Perception Explanation of Dissonance Phenomena: On the Salience of Premanipulation Attitudes." *Journal of Personality and Social Psychology* 14: 23–31.

Bennett, Stephen

1973   "Consistency Among the Public's Social Welfare Policy Attitudes in the 1960's." *American Journal of Political Science* 17:544–70.

1974   "Attitude Structures and Foreign Policy Options." *Social Science Quarterly* 55:732–42.

Benson, Edward G.

1940   "Three Words." *Public Opinion Quarterly* 4:130–34.

Berelson, Bernard R., Paul F. Lazarsfeld, and William N. McPhee

1954   *Voting.* Chicago: University of Chicago Press.

Berlyne, D. W.

1960   *Conflict, Arousal and Curiosity.* New York: McGraw-Hill.

Bishop, George F., and Kathleen A. Frankovic

1981   "Ideological Consensus and Constraint Among Party Leaders and Followers in the 1978 Election." *Micropolitics* 1: 87–111.

Bishop, George F., Robert W. Oldendick, and Alfred J. Tuchfarber

1978a   "Change in the Structure of American Political Attitudes: The Nagging Question of Question Wording." *American Journal of Political Science* 22:250–69.

1978b   "Effects of Question Wording and Format on Political Attitude Consistency." *Public Opinion Quarterly* 38:81–92.

1980   "Experiments in Filtering Opinions." *Political Behavior* 2:339–70.

Bishop, George F., Alfred J. Tuchfarber, Robert W. Oldendick, and Stephen E. Bennett

1979   "Questions About Question Wording: A Rejoinder to Revisiting Mass Belief Systems Revisited." *American Journal of Political Science* 23:187–92.

Blalock, Hubert M.

1972   *Social Statistics.* New York: McGraw-Hill.

Bobrow, D. G., and Donald A. Norman
1975   "Some Principles of Memory Schemata." In D. G. Bobrow and A. M. Collins (eds.), *Representation and Understanding: Studies in Cognitive Science*. New York: Academic Press.

Bogart, Leo
1984   "The Public's Use and Perception of Newspapers." *Public Opinion Quarterly* 48:709–19.

Booth, Alan
1970–   "Recall of News Items." *Public Opinion Quarterly* 34:
1971   604–10.

Borgatta, Edgar F., and George W. Bohrnstedt
1981   "Level of Measurement Once Over Again." In E. Borgatta and G. W. Bohrnstedt (eds.), *Social Measurement: Current Issues*. Beverly Hills, Calif.: Sage Publications.

Bower, Gordon H., Michael C. Clark, Alan M. Lesgold, and David Winzenz
1969   "Hierarchical Retrieval Schemes in Recall of Categorized Word Lists." *Journal of Verbal Learning and Verbal Behavior* 8:323–43.

Bower, Robert T.
1973   *Television and the Public*. New York: Holt, Rinehart and Winston.
1985   *The Changing Television Audience in America*. New York: Columbia University Press.

Bowers, K. S.
1981   "Knowing More Than We Can Say Leads to Saying More Than We Can Know: On Being Implicitly Informed." In P. Magnusson (ed.), *Toward a Psychology of Situations: An Interactional Perspective*. Hillsdale, N.J.: Erlbaum.

Boyle, Richard P.
1970   "Path Analysis and Ordinal Data." *American Journal of Sociology* 75:461–80.

Brown, Roger
1965   *Social Psychology*. New York: Free Press.

Brown, Stephen
1970   "Consistency and the Persistency of Ideology." *Public Opinion Quarterly* 34:60–68.

Bruner, J. S., J. J. Goodnow, and G. A. Austin
1956   *A Study of Thinking*. New York: Wiley.

Brunk, Gregory G.
1978   "The 1964 Attitude Consistency Leap Reconsidered." *Political Methodology* 5:347–59.

Burnham, Walter Dean

1965   "The Changing Shape of the American Political Universe."
        American Political Science Review 59:7–28.

1970   *Critical Elections and the Mainsprings of American Poli-
        tics.* New York: W. W. Norton.

1974   "Theory and Voting Research: Some Reflections on Con-
        verse's 'Change in the American Electorate.'" *American Po-
        litical Science Review* 68:1002–27.

1975   "Insulation and Responsiveness in Congressional Elec-
        tions." *Political Science Quarterly* 90:411–35.

Campbell, Angus, Philip E. Converse, Warren E. Miller, and Donald E.
Stokes

1960   *The American Voter.* New York: J. Wiley.

Campbell, Angus, Gerald Gurin, and Warren E. Miller

1954   *The Voter Decides.* Evanston, Ill.: Row, Peterson.

Campbell, Angus, and Robert L. Kahn

1952   *The People Elect a President.* Ann Arbor: University of
        Michigan, Survey Research Center.

Campbell, Donald T., and D. W. Fiske

1959   "Convergent and Discriminant Validation by the Multitrait-
        Multimethod Matrix." *Psychological Bulletin* 56:81–
        105.

Cantril, Hadley

1944   *Gauging Public Opinion.* Princeton, N.J.: Princeton Uni-
        versity Press.

Carey, J. W.

1976   "How Media Shape Campaigns." *Journal of Communica-
        tions* 26:50–57.

Carmines, Edward G., and Richard A. Zeller

1979   *Reliability and Validity Assessment.* Beverly Hills, Calif.:
        Sage Publications.

Cassel, Carol A.

1982   "Issues in Measurement: The 'Levels of Conceptualization'
        Index of Ideological Sophistication." *American Journal of
        Political Science* 28:418–29.

Cattell, R. B.

1962   "The Relational Simplex Theory of Equal Interval and Ab-
        solute Scaling." *Acta Psychologica* 20:139–58.

Chong, Dennis, Herbert McClosky, and John Zaller

1984   "Social Learning and the Acquisition of Political Norms."
        In Herbert McClosky and John Zaller, *The American Ethos:
        Public Attitudes Toward Capitalism and Democracy.* Cam-
        bridge, Mass.: Harvard University Press.

Clarke, P., and E. Fredin
    1978   "Newspapers, Television and Political Reasoning." *Public Opinion Quarterly* 42:143–60.
Conover, Pamela Johnston, and Stanley Feldman
    1980   "Belief System Organization in the American Electorate: An Alternative Approach." In John C. Pierce and John L. Sullivan (eds.), *The Electorate Reconsidered*. Beverly Hills, Calif.: Sage Publications.
    1984   "How People Organize the Political World: A Schematic Model." *American Journal of Political Science* 28:95–126.
Converse, Jean
    1976–   "Predicting No Opinion in the Polls." *Public Opinion Quar-*
    1977   *terly* 40:515–30.
Converse, Philip E.
    1964   "The Nature of Belief Systems in Mass Publics." In David Apter (ed.), *Ideology and Discontent*. New York: Free Press.
    1970   "Attitudes and Nonattitudes: The Continuation of a Dialogue." In Edward Tufte (ed.), *The Quantitative Analysis of Social Problems*. Reading, Mass.: Addison-Wesley.
    1972   "Change in the American Electorate." In Angus Campbell and Philip Converse (eds.), *The Human Meaning of Social Change*. New York: Russell Sage Foundation.
    1975   "Public Opinion and Voting Behavior." In Fred I. Greenstein and Nelson W. Polsby (eds.), *Handbook of Political Science*, vol. 4. Reading, Mass.: Addison-Wesley.
    1976   *The Dynamics of Party Support*. Beverly Hills, Calif.: Sage Publications.
    1979   "Comment" [Rejoinder to Wray 1979]. *Journal of Politics* 41:1182–84.
    1980   "Comment: Rejoinder to Judd and Milburn." *American Sociological Review* 45:644–46.
Converse, Philip E., and Gregory B. Markus
    1979   "Plus Ça Change . . . The New CPS Election Panel Study." *American Political Science Review* 73:32–49.
Costner, Herbert L.
    1969   "Theory, Deduction and Rules of Correspondence." *American Journal of Sociology* 75:245–63.
Couch, Arthur, and Kenneth Keniston
    1960   "Yeasayers and Naysayers: Agreeing Response Set as a Personality Variable." *Journal of Abnormal and Social Psychology* 60:151–74.

Cover, Albert D.
1976 "The Advantage of Incumbency in Congressional Elections." Unpublished Ph.D. dissertation, Yale University.

Craig, Stephen C.
1979 "Efficacy, Trust and Political Behavior: An Attempt to Resolve a Lingering Conceptual Dilemma." *American Politics Quarterly* 7:225–39.

Cronbach, L. J.
1946 "Response Sets and Test Validity." *Educational and Psychological Measurement* 6:616–23.
1949 *Essentials of Psychological Testing.* New York: Harper.
1950 "Further Evidence on Response Sets and Test Design." *Educational Psychological Measurement* 10:3–31.
1958 "Proposals Leading to Analytic Treatment of Social Perception Scores." In R. Tagiuri and T. Petrullo (eds.), *Person Perception and Interpersonal Behavior.* Stanford, Calif.: Stanford University Press.

Crotty, William J.
1984 *American Parties in Decline,* 2nd ed. Boston: Little, Brown.

Crotty, William J., and Gary C. Jacobson
1980 *American Parties in Decline.* Boston: Little, Brown.

Crowder, R. G.
1976 *Principles of Learning and Memory.* Hillsdale, N.J.: Erlbaum.

Davis, James A.
Elementary Survey Analysis. Englewood Cliffs, N.J.: Prentice-Hall.

DiPalma, Giuseppe, and Herbert McClosky
1970 "Personality and Conformity: The Learning of Political Attitudes." *American Political Science Review* 64:1054–73.

Downs, Anthony
1957 *An Economic Theory of Democracy.* New York: Harper and Row.

Duncan, Otis Dudley
1975 "Some Linear Models for Two-Wave, Two-Variable Panel Analysis, with One-Way Causation and Measurement Error." In Hubert M. Blalock (ed.), *Quantitative Sociology: International Perspectives on Mathematical and Statistical Modeling.* New York: Academic Press.

Eitzen, D. Stanley
1972– "Status Consistency and Consistency of Political Beliefs."
1973 *Public Opinion Quarterly* 36:541–48.

Enelow, James M., and Melvin J. Hinich

1984   *Spatial Analysis of Elections.* New York: Cambridge University Press.

Ericcson, K. A., and Herbert A. Simon

1980   "Verbal Reports as Data." *Psychological Review* 87: 215–51.

Erskine, Hazel G.

1962   "The Polls: The Informed Public." *Public Opinion Quarterly* 26:669–77.

1963a   "The Polls: Textbook Knowledge." *Public Opinion Quarterly* 27:133–41.

1963b   "The Polls: Exposure to Domestic Information." *Public Opinion Quarterly* 27:491–500.

1963c   "The Polls: Exposure to International Information." *Public Opinion Quarterly* 27:658–62.

1971   "The Polls: Red China and the U.N." *Public Opinion Quarterly* 35:123–35.

1972   "The Polls: Gun Control." *Public Opinion Quarterly* 36: 455–69.

Erskine, Hazel, and Richard L. Siegel

1975   "Civil Liberties and the American Public." *Journal of Social Issues* 31:13–29.

Ferber, Robert

1966   "Item Nonresponse in a Consumer Survey." *Public Opinion Quarterly* 30:399–415.

Ferejohn, John A.

1977   "On the Decline of Competition in Congressional Elections." *American Political Science Review* 71:166–76.

Field, John O., and Ronald Anderson

1969   "Ideology in the Public's Conceptualization of the 1964 Election." *Public Opinion Quarterly* 33:380–98.

Fiorina, Morris P.

1976   "Partisan Loyalty and the Six Component Model." *Political Methodology* 3:7–18.

1977   *Congress: Keystone of the Washington Establishment.* New Haven, Conn.: Yale University Press.

1981   *Retrospective Voting in American National Elections.* New Haven, Conn.: Yale University Press.

1986   "Information and Rationality in Elections." Paper prepared for John Ferejohn and James Kuklinski (eds.), *Information and Democratic Processes.* Champaign, Ill.: University of Illinois Press, forthcoming.

Fiske, Susan T., and Shelley E. Taylor
  1984   *Social Cognition*. New York: Random House.
Flavell, John H.
  1963   *The Developmental Psychology of Jean Piaget*. Princeton,
          N.J.: Van Nostrand.
Francis, Joe, and Lawrence Busch
  1975   "What We Don't Know About 'I Don't Knows.'" *Public
          Opinion Quarterly* 39:207–18.
Fuchs, Ester R., and Robert Y. Shapiro
  1983   "Government Performance as a Basis for Machine Sup-
          port." *Urban Affairs Quarterly* 18:537–50.
Gagne, Robert M.
  1970   *The Conditions of Learning*. New York: Holt, Rinehart and
          Winston.
Gaito, J.
  1980   "Measurement Scales and Statistics: Resurgence of an Old
          Idea." *Psychological Bulletin* 87:564–67.
Gallup, George H.
  1972   *The Gallup Poll: Public Opinion 1935–1971*. New York:
          Random House.
  1978   *The Gallup Poll: Public Opinion 1972–1978*. Wilmington,
          Del.: Scholarly Resources.
Gamson, William A., and Andre Modigliani
  1966   "Knowledge and Foreign Policy Opinions: Some Models
          for Consideration." *Public Opinion Quarterly* 30:187–99.
Gergen, Kenneth J., and Mary M. Gergen
  1980   "Causal Attribution in the Context of Social Explanation."
          In Dietmar Gorlitz (ed.), *Perspectives on Attribution Re-
          search and Theory*. Cambridge, Mass.: Ballinger.
Glass, David P.
  1985   "Evaluating Presidential Candidates: Who Focuses on Their
          Personal Attributes." *Public Opinion Quarterly* 49:517–34.
Glenn, Norval D.
  1970   "Problems of Comparability in Trend Studies with Opinion
          Poll Data." *Public Opinion Quarterly* 34:82–91.
Goodman, L. A., and W. H. Kruskal
  1954   "Measures of Association for Cross Classifications." *Jour-
          nal of the American Statistical Association* 49:732–64.
Graber, Doris A.
  1984a   *Mass Media and American Politics*, 2nd ed. Washington,
          D.C.: Congressional Quarterly Press.

1984b   *Processing the News: How People Tame the Information Tide.* New York: Longman.

Guilford, J. P.
1967   *The Nature of Human Intelligence.* New York: McGraw-Hill.

Hagner, Paul R., and John C. Pierce
1982   "Correlative Characteristics of Levels of Conceptualization in the American Public: 1956–1976." *Journal of Politics* 44:779–807.
1983   "Levels of Conceptualization and Political Belief Consistency." *Micropolitics* 2:311–48.
1984   "Racial Differences in Political Conceptualization." *Western Political Quarterly* 37:212–35.

Hagner, Paul R., John C. Pierce, and Kay G. Wolsborn
1983   "Ideological Conceptualization and the Opinion Bases of Partisan Choice." Paper delivered at the 1983 annual convention of the Midwest Political Science Association. Chicago, Ill.

Harman, H. H.
1976   *Modern Factor Analysis.* Chicago: University of Chicago Press.

Heider, Fritz
1944   "Social Perception and Phenomenal Causality." *Psychological Review* 51:358–74.
1946   "Attitudes and Cognitive Organization." *Journal of Psychology* 21:107–12.

Hero, A. O.
1959   *Americans in World Affairs,* vol. 1: *Studies in Citizen Participation in International Relations.* Boston: World Peace Foundation.

Higgins, E. Tory, and Gillian King
1981   "Category Accessibility and Information-Processing: Consequences of Individual and Contextual Variability." In Nancy A. Cantor and John F. Kihlstrom (eds.), *Personality, Cognition and Social Interaction.* Hillsdale, N.J.: Erlbaum.

Hill, David B., and Norman R. Luttbeg
1983   *Trends in American Electoral Behavior.* 2nd ed. Itasca, Ill.: F. E. Peacock.

Hofstetter, C. R., and C. Zukin
1979   "TV Network Political News and Advertising in the Nixon

and McGovern Campaigns." *Journalism Quarterly* 58: 472–79.

Huntington, Samuel P.
1981 *American Politics: The Promise of Disharmony.* Cambridge, Mass.: Harvard University Press.

Hyman, Herbert H., and Paul B. Sheatsley
1947 "Some Reasons Why Information Campaigns Fail." *Public Opinion Quarterly* 11:412–23.

Inglehart, Ronald
1979 "Political Action: The Impact of Values, Cognitive Level, and Social Background." In Samuel H. Barnes and Max Kaase (eds.), *Political Action: Mass Participation in Five Western Democracies.* Beverly Hills, Calif.: Sage Publications.
1985 "Aggregate Stability and Individual Level Flux in Mass Belief Systems: The Level of Analysis Paradox." *American Political Science Review* 79:97–116.

Iyengar, Shanto, and Donald R. Kinder
1987 *News That Matters.* Chicago: University of Chicago Press.

Iyengar, Shanto, Donald R. Kinder, John A. Krosnick, and Mark D. Peters
1984 "The Evening News and Presidential Evaluations." *Journal of Personality and Social Psychology* 46:778–87.

Iyengar, Shanto, Mark D. Peters, and Donald R. Kinder
1982 "Experimental Demonstrations of the 'Not-So-Minimal' Consequences of Television News Programs." *American Political Science Review* 76:848–58.

Jackson, D. N., and S. J. Messick
1958 "Content and Style in Personality Assessment." *Psychological Bulletin* 55:243–52.

Jackson, John E.
1983 "The Systematic Beliefs of the Mass Public: Estimating Policy Preferences with Survey Data." *Journal of Politics* 45:840–58.

Jacobson, Gary C.
1987 *The Politics of Congressional Elections,* 2nd ed. Boston: Little, Brown.

Jacoby, William G.
1986 "Level of Conceptualization and Reliance on the Liberal-Conservative Continuum." *Journal of Politics* 48:423–32.

Janowitz, Morris
1981 "Mass Media: Institutional Trends and Their Conse-

quences." In Morris Janowitz and Paul Hirsch (eds.), *Reader in Public Opinion and Mass Communication*, 3rd ed. New York: Free Press.

Jefferies, W. E.

1968   "The Orienting Reflex and Attention in Cognitive Development." *Psychological Review* 75:323–34.

Jennings, M. Kent, and Richard G. Niemi

1974   *The Political Character of Adolescence.* Princeton, N.J.: Princeton University Press.

1981   *Generations and Politics: A Panel Study of Young Adults and Their Parents.* Princeton, N.J.: Princeton University Press.

Jensen, Arthur R.

1980   *Bias in Mental Testing.* New York: Free Press.

Johnson, Lyndon Baines

1971   *The Vantage Point: Perspectives of the Presidency, 1963–1969.* New York: Popular Library.

Jones, Edward E., and Richard E. Nisbett

1972   "The Actor and the Observer: Divergent Perceptions of the Causes of Behavior." In Edward E. Jones et al. (eds.), *Attribution: Perceiving the Causes of Behavior.* Morristown, N.J.: General Learning Press.

Jones, Warren H., and William W. Rambo

1973   "Information and the Level of Constraint in a System of Social Attitudes." *Experimental Study of Politics* 2:25–38.

Joreskog, Karl G.

1979   "Statistical Models and Methods for Analysis of Longitudinal Data." In Jay Magidson (ed.), *Advances in Factor Analysis and Structural Equation Models.* Lanham, Md.: University Press of America.

Joreskog, Karl G., and Dag Sorbom

1984   *LISREL VI: Analysis of Linear Structural Relationships by Maximum Likelihood, Instrumental Variables and Least Squares Methods.* Mooresville, Ind.: Scientific Software.

Kagay, Michael R.

1983   "On Two Models of Voter Decision-Making: Stokes' Six-Components and the Kelley-Mirer Rule." Unpublished manuscript.

Kamieniecki, Sheldon

1985   *Party Identification, Political Behavior and the American Electorate.* Westport, Conn.: Greenwood Press.

Kanouse, D. E.

1972   "Language, Labeling and Attribution." In Edward E. Jones et al. (eds.), *Attribution: Perceiving the Causes of Behavior.* Morristown, N.J.: General Learning Press.

Keith, Bruce E., David B. Magleby, Candice J. Nelson, Elizabeth Orr, Mark Westlye, and Raymond E. Wolfinger

1977   "The Myth of the Independent Voter." Paper delivered at the 1977 annual meeting of the American Political Science Association, Washington, D.C.

Kelejian, Harry H., and Wallace E. Oates

1981   *Introduction to Econometrics: Principles and Applications.* New York: Harper and Row.

Kelley, Stanley, Jr.

1983   *Interpreting Elections.* Princeton, N.J.: Princeton University Press.

Kelley, Stanley, Jr., and Thad W. Mirer

1974   "The Simple Act of Voting." *American Political Science Review* 68:572–91.

Kelly, G. A.

1955   *The Psychology of Personal Constructs.* New York: W. W. Norton.

Kessel, John H.

1980   *Presidential Campaign Politics: Coalition Strategies and Citizen Response.* Homewood, Ill.: Dorsey Press.

Key, V. O., with Milton C. Cummings

1966   *The Responsible Electorate: Rationality in Presidential Voting 1936–1960.* New York: Vintage Books.

Kiesler, Charles A., Barry E. Collins, and Norman Miller

1969   *Attitude Change: A Critical Analysis of Theoretical Approaches.* New York: Wiley.

Kinder, Donald R.

1983   "Diversity and Complexity in American Public Opinion." In Ada Finifter (ed.), *The State of the Discipline.* Washington, D.C.: American Political Science Association.

Kirkpatrick, Samuel A.

1970   "Political Attitude Structure and Component Change." *Public Opinion Quarterly* 34:403–407.

1976   "Aging Effects and Generational Differences in Social Welfare Attitude Constraint in the Mass Public." *Western Political Quarterly* 29:43–58.

Klingemann, Hans D.

1973   "Dimensions of Political Belief Systems: 'Levels of Conceptualization' as a Variable. Some Results for USA and FRG 1968/69." *Comparative Political Studies* 5:93–106.

1979a   "Measuring Ideological Conceptualizations." In Samuel H. Barnes and Max Kaase (eds.), *Political Action: Mass Participation in Five Western Democracies*. Beverly Hills, Calif.: Sage Publications.

1979b   "The Background of Ideological Conceptualization." In Samuel H. Barnes and Max Kaase (eds.), *Political Action: Mass Participation in Five Western Democracies*. Beverly Hills, Calif.: Sage Publications.

1979c   "Ideological Conceptualization and Political Action." In Samuel H. Barnes and Max Kaase (eds.), *Political Action: Mass Participation in Five Western Democracies*. Beverly Hills, Calif.: Sage Publications.

Kraus, Sidney, and Dennis Davis

1976   *The Effects of Mass Communication on Political Behavior*. University Park: Pennsylvania State University Press.

Kraus, Sidney, Timothy Meyer, and Maurice Selby, Jr.

1974   "Sixteen Months after Chappaquidick: Effects of the Kennedy Broadcast." *Journalism Quarterly* 51:431–40.

Krech, David, Richard S. Crutchfield, and Norman Livson

1970   *Elements of Psychology*. New York: Knopf.

Kriesberg, Martin

1949   "Dark Areas of Ignorance." In Lester Markel (ed.), *Public Opinion and Foreign Policy*. New York: Harper.

Labovitz, Sanford

1967   "Some Observations on Measurement and Statistics." *Social Forces* 46:151–60.

1971   "The Assignment of Numbers to Rank Categories." *American Sociological Review* 35:515–24.

Lachman, Roy, Janet L. Lachman, and Earl C. Butterfield

1979   *Cognitive Psychology and Information Processing: An Introduction*. Hillsdale, N.J.: Erlbaum.

Ladd, Everett Carll, with Charles D. Hadley

1978   *Transformations of the American Party System*. New York: W. W. Norton.

Lane, Robert

1959   *Political Life*. New York: Free Press.

1962   *Political Ideology*. New York: Free Press.

Lazarsfeld, Paul F.

1935   "The Art of Asking Why: Three Principles Underlying the Formulation of Questionnaires." *National Marketing Review* 1:32–43.

Lazarsfeld, Paul F., Bernard F. Berelson, and Hazel Gaudet
  1944   *The People's Choice.* New York: Duell, Sloan and Pearce.
LeBlanc, Hugh L., and Mary Beth Merrin
  1977   "Mass Belief Systems Revisited." *Journal of Politics* 39: 1082–87.
Lehnert, Wendy G.
  1978   *The Process of Question Answering: A Computer Simulation of Cognition.* Hillsdale, N.J.: Erlbaum.
Lerner, Janet W.
  1976   *Children with Learning Disabilities.* Boston: Houghton Mifflin.
Lipset, Seymour Martin, and William Schneider
  1983   *The Confidence Gap: Business, Labor and Government in the Public Mind.* New York: Free Press.
Lord, Frederick M., and Melvin R. Novick
  1968   *Statistical Theories of Mental Test Scores.* Reading, Mass.: Addison-Wesley.
Luskin, Robert P.
  1987   "Measuring Political Sophistication." *American Journal of Political Science* 31: 856–99.
Luttbeg, Norman R.
  1968   "The Structure of Beliefs Among Leaders." *Public Opinion Quarterly* 32: 398–409.
Luttbeg, Norman R., and Michael M. Gant
  1985   "The Failure of Liberal/Conservative Ideology as a Cognitive Structure." *Public Opinion Quarterly* 49: 80–93.
Luttbeg, Norman R., and Harmon Ziegler
  1966   "Attitude Consensus and Conflict in an Interest Group: An Assessment of Cohesion." *American Political Science Review* 60: 655–65.
MacKuen, Michael B., and Steven L. Coombs
  1981   *More Than News: Media Power in Public Affairs.* Beverly Hills, Calif.: Sage Publications.
Maddox, William S., and Stuart A. Lilie
  1984   *Beyond Liberal and Conservative: Reassessing the Political Spectrum.* Washington, D.C.: Cato Institute.
Mandler, G.
  1975   "Consciousness: Respectable, Useful and Probably Necessary." In Robert Solso (ed.), *Information Processing and Cognition: The Loyola Symposium.* Hillsdale, N.J.: Erlbaum.
Manheim, Jarol B.
  1974   "Urbanization and Differential Press Coverage of the Con-

gressional Campaign." *Journalism Quarterly* 51:648–53, 669.

Mann, Thomas E.

1978   *Unsafe At Any Margin: Interpreting Congressional Elections*. Washington, D.C.: American Enterprise Institute.

Markus, Gregory B., and Philip E. Converse

1979   "A Dynamic Simultaneous Equation Model of Electoral Choice." *American Political Science Review* 73:1055–70.

Markus, Hazel

1977   "Self-Schemata and the Processing of Information About the Self." *Journal of Personality and Social Psychology* 35:63–78.

Mates, Benson

1972   *Elementary Logic*, 2nd ed. New York: Oxford University Press.

Mayhew, David

1974   "Congressional Elections: The Case of the Vanishing Marginals." *Polity* 6:295–317.

McClure, Robert D., and Thomas E. Patterson

1973   "Television News and Voter Behavior in the 1972 Presidential Election." Paper presented at the 1973 annual meeting of the American Political Science Association, New Orleans, La.

McCombs, Maxwell E., and L. E. Mullins

1973   "Consequences of Education: Media Exposure, Interest and Information Seeking Orientations." *Mass Communication Review* 1:27–31.

McCombs, Maxwell E., and Donald L. Shaw

1972   "The Agenda Setting Function of the Mass Media." *Public Opinion Quarterly* 36:176–87.

McGuire, William J.

1960   "A Syllogistic Analysis of Cognitive Relationships." In Milton J. Rosenberg and Carl I. Hovland (eds.), *Attitude Organization and Change*. New Haven, Conn.: Yale University Press.

1966   "The Current Status of Cognitive Consistency Theories." In Shel Feldman (ed.), *Cognitive Consistency: Motivational Antecedents and Behavioral Consequents*. New York: Academic Press.

McPhee, William N., Bo Anderson, and Harry Milholland

1962   "Attitude Consistency." In William N. McPhee and William A. Glaser (eds.), *Public Opinion and Congressional Elections*. New York: Free Press.

Meeker, Mary N.
 1969   *The Structure of Intellect: Its Interpretation and Uses.* Co-
         lumbus, Ohio: Merrill.
Metzner, C. A.
 1949   *Interest, Information and Attitudes in the Field of World
         Affairs.* Ann Arbor: Survey Research Center, University of
         Michigan.
Milbrath, Lester W., and M. L. Goel
 1977   *Political Participation: How and Why Do People Get In-
         volved in Politics,* 2nd ed. Lanham, N.Y.: University Press
         of America.
Miller, Arthur H., and Warren E. Miller
 1976   "Ideology in the 1972 Election: Myth or Reality—A Re-
         joinder." *American Political Science Review* 70:832–49.
Miller, Arthur H., Martin P. Wattenberg, and Oksana Malanchuk
 1982   "Cognitive Representations of Candidate Assessments."
         Paper delivered at the 1982 annual meeting of the Ameri-
         can Political Science Association, Denver, Colo.
 1986   "Schematic Assessments of Presidential Candidates." *Ameri-
         can Political Science Review* 80:521–40.
Miller, George A.
 1962   *Psychology: The Science of Mental Life.* New York: Harper
         and Row.
 1974   "Toward a Third Metaphor for Psycholinguistics." In W. B.
         Weimer and D. S. Palermo (eds.), *Cognition and the Sym-
         bolic Process.* Hillsdale, N.J.: Erlbaum.
Miller, Warren E.
 1987   "Party Identification Re-Examined: The Reagan Era." In
         Thomas E. Edsall (ed.), *Where's the Party: An Assessment
         of Changes in Party Loyalty and Party Coalitions in the
         1980s.* Washington, D.C.: Center for National Policy.
Mueller, John E.
 1973   *War, Presidents and Public Opinion.* New York: Wiley.
Mueller, John H., Karl F. Schuessler, and Herbert L. Costner
 1970   *Statistical Reasoning in Sociology.* Boston: Houghton Mif-
         flin.
Neisser, Ulric
 1967   *Cognitive Psychology.* New York: Appleton-Century-Crofts.
 1976   *Cognition and Reality.* San Francisco: W. H. Freeman.
Neuman, W. Russell
 1976   "Patterns of Recall Among Television News Viewers." *Pub-
         lic Opinion Quarterly* 40:115–23.

1981   "Differentiation and Integration: Two Dimensions of Political Thinking." *American Journal of Sociology* 86:1236–68.

1986   *The Paradox of Mass Politics: Knowledge and Opinion in the American Electorate.* Cambridge, Mass.: Harvard University Press.

Newell, Allen, and Herbert A. Simon

1961   "The Simulation of Human Thought." In Wayne Dennis (ed.), *Current Trends in Psychological Theory.* Pittsburgh: University of Pittsburg Press.

1972   *Human Problem Solving.* Englewood Cliffs, N.J.: Prentice-Hall.

1976   "Computer Science as Empirical Inquiry: Symbols and Search." *Communications of the ACM* 19:113–26.

Nie, Norman H., with Kristi Andersen

1974   "Mass Belief Systems Revisited: Political Change and Attitude Structure." *Journal of Politics* 36:541–91.

Nie, Norman H., and James N. Rabjohn

1979   "Revisiting Mass Belief Systems Revisited: Or, Doing Research Is Like Watching a Tennis Match." *American Journal of Political Science* 23:139–75.

Nie, Norman H., Sidney Verba, and John R. Petrocik

1976   *The Changing American Voter.* Cambridge, Mass.: Harvard University Press.

1979   *The Changing American Voter,* 2nd ed. Cambridge, Mass.: Harvard University Press.

1981   "Reply to Abramson and Smith." *American Political Science Review* 75:149–52.

Nisbett, Richard E., and Lee Ross

1980   *Human Inference: Strategies and Shortcomings of Social Judgment.* Englewood Cliffs, N.J.: Prentice-Hall.

Nisbett, Richard E., and Stuart Valins

1971   "Perceiving the Causes of One's Own Behavior." In E. E. Jones, D. E. Kanouse, H. H. Kelley, Richard S. Nisbett, Stuart Valins, and B. Weiner (eds.), *Attribution: Perceiving the Causes of Behavior.* Morristown, N.J.: General Learning Press.

Nisbett, Richard E., and Timothy DeCamp Wilson

1977   "Telling More Than We Can Know: Verbal Reports on Mental Processes." *Psychological Review* 84:231–59.

Norman, Donald A.

1973   "Memory, Knowledge and the Answering of Questions." In Robert L. Solso (ed.), *Contemporary Issues in Cognitive Psychology.* Washington, D.C.: V. H. Winston & Sons.

Nunnally, Jum C.
  1967   *Psychometric Theory,* 2nd ed. New York: McGraw-Hill.
Ordeshook, Peter C.
  1986   *Game Theory and Political Theory: An Introduction.* Cambridge: Cambridge University Press.
Osgood, Charles E., and Percy H. Tannenbaum
  1955   "The Principle of Congruity in the Prediction of Attitude Change." *Psychological Review* 62:42–55.

Osterlind, Steven J.
  1983   *Test Item Bias.* Beverly Hills, Calif.: Sage Publications.
Page, Benjamin, and Robert Y. Shapiro
  1982   "Changes in Americans' Policy Preferences, 1935–1979." *Public Opinion Quarterly* 46:24–42.
Patchen, Martin
  1964   *The American Public's View of U.S. Policy Toward China.* New York: Council on Foreign Relations.
Patterson, Thomas
  1980   *The Mass Media Election.* New York: Praeger.
Patterson, Thomas, and Robert McClure
  1976   *The Unseeing Eye.* New York: G. P. Putnam.
Peffley, Mark A., and Jon Hurwitz
  1985   "A Hierarchical Model of Attitude Constraint." *American Journal of Political Science* 29:871–90.
Petrocik, John R.
  1978   "Comment: Reconsidering the Reconsiderations of the 1964 Change in Attitude Consistency." *Political Methodology* 5: 361–68.
  1981   *Party Coalitions: Realignment and the Decline of the New Deal Party System.* Chicago: University of Chicago Press.
Piaget, Jean
  1951   *The Child's Conception of the World.* New York: Humanities Press.
Piazza, Thomas
  1980   "The Analysis of Attitude Items." *American Journal of Sociology* 86:584–603.
Pierce, John C.
  1970   "Party Identification and the Changing Role of Ideology in American Politics." *Midwest Journal of Political Science* 14:25–42.
  1975   "The Relationship Between Linkage Salience and Linkage Organization in Mass Belief Systems." *Public Opinion Quarterly* 39:102–10.

Pierce, John C., and Paul R. Hagner
    1980   "Changes in the Public's Political Thinking: The Watershed
             Years, 1956–1968." In John C. Pierce and John L. Sullivan
             (eds.), *The Electorate Reconsidered*. Beverly Hills, Calif.:
             Sage Publications.
    1982   "Conceptualization and Party Identification: 1956–1976."
             American Journal of Political Science 26:377–87.
Piereson, James E.
    1978   "Issue Alignment and the American Party System." *Ameri-
             can Politics Quarterly* 6:275–307.
Pindyck, Robert S., and Daniel L. Rubinfeld
    1981   *Econometric Models and Econometric Forecasts*, 2nd ed.
             New York: McGraw-Hill.
Polsby, Nelson W., and Aaron Wildavsky
    1988   *Presidential Elections: Contemporary Strategies of Ameri-
             can Electoral Politics*. 7th ed. New York: Free Press.
Pomper, Gerald M.
    1972   "From Confusion to Clarity: Issues and American Vot-
             ers, 1956–1968." *American Political Science Review* 66:
             415–28.
Quarles, Rebecca
    1979   "Mass Media Use and Voting Behavior: Accuracy of Politi-
             cal Perceptions Among First Time and Experienced Voters."
             Communications Research 6:407–36.
Reardon, Kathleen Kelley
    1981   *Persuasion: Theory and Context*. Beverly Hills, Calif: Sage
             Publications.
Reisman, S., C. A. Insko, and Stuart Valins
    1970   "Triadic Consistency and False Heart-Rate Feedback."
             Journal of Personality 38:629–40.
Roberts, Donald F., and Nathan Maccoby
    1985   "Effects of Mass Communication." In Gardner Lindzey
             and Elliot Aronson (eds.), *The Handbook of Social Psychol-
             ogy*, vol. 2, 3rd ed. New York: Random House.
Robinson, John P.
    1967   *Public Information About World Affairs*. Ann Arbor: Sur-
             vey Research Center, University of Michigan.
    1972a   "Mass Communication and Information Diffusion." In
             F. Gerald Kline and Phillip J. Tichenor (eds.), *Current Per-
             spectives in Mass Communication Research*. Beverly Hills,
             Calif.: Sage Publications.
    1972b   "Toward Defining the Functions of Television." In E. Ru-
             binstein, G. Comstock, and J. Murray (eds.), *Television and*

Social Behavior, vol. 4: *Television in Day-to-Day Life: Patterns of Use*. Washington, D.C.: Government Printing Office.

Robinson, Michael J.
1975   "American Political Legitimacy in an Era of Electronic Journalism: Reflections on the Evening News." In D. Cater and R. Adler (eds.), *Television as a Social Force: New Approaches to TV Criticism*. New York: Praeger.

Rokeach, Milton
1960   *The Open and Closed Mind*. New York: Basic Books.

Rosenberg, Milton J., and Robert P. Abelson
1960   "An Analysis of Cognitive Balancing." In Milton J. Rosenberg and Carl I. Hovlands (eds.), *Attitude Organization and Change*. New Haven, Conn.: Yale University Press.

Ross, Michael, and Garth J. O. Fletcher
1985   "Attribution and Social Perception." In Gardner Lindzey and Elliot Aronson (eds.), *The Handbook of Social Psychology*, vol. 2, 3rd ed. New York: Random House.

Rumelhart, David E., and Andrew Ortony
1977   "The Representation of Knowledge in Memory." In R. C. Anderson, R. J. Spiro, and W. E. Montague (eds.), *Schooling and the Acquisition of Knowledge*. Hillsdale, N.J.: Erlbaum.

Schramm, Wilbur, and Serena Wade
1967   *Knowledge and the Public Mind*. Stanford, Calif.: Institute for Communication Research.

Schroder, Harold M., Michael J. Driver, and Siegfried Streufert
1967   *Human Information Processing*. New York: Holt, Rinehart and Winston.

Schuman, Howard, and Otis Dudley Duncan
1974   "Questions About Attitude Survey Questions." In Herbert L. Costner (ed.), *Sociological Methodology 1973–1974*. San Francisco: Jossey-Bass.

Schuman, Howard, and Stanley Presser
1981   *Questions and Answers in Attitude Surveys: Experiments on Question Form, Wording, and Context*. New York: Academic Press.

Schweitzer, S., and D. G. Schweitzer
1971   "Comment on the Pearson R in Random Number and Precise Functional Scale Transformations." *American Sociological Review* 36:519–20.

Shaffer, William R.
1972   "Partisan Loyalty and the Perceptions of Party, Candidates and Issues." *Western Political Quarterly* 25:424–33.

1976   "Rejoinder to Fiorina." *Political Methodology* 3:19–26.
Shapiro, Michael J.
1970   "Discovering Interviewer Bias in Open-Ended Survey Responses." *Public Opinion Quarterly* 34:412–15.
Shapiro, Robert Y., and Kelly D. Patterson
1986   "The Dynamics of Public Opinion Toward Social Welfare Policy." Paper delivered at the 1986 annual meeting of the American Political Science Association, Washington, D.C.
Simon, Herbert A., and Allen Newell
1964   "Information Processing in Computer and Man." *American Scientist* 53:281–300.
Simon, Rita James
1974   *Public Opinion in America: 1936–1970.* Chicago: Rand McNally.
Smith, Don D.
1972   "'Dark Areas of Ignorance' Revisited: Current Knowledge About Asian Affairs." In Dan D. Nimmo and Charles M. Bonjean (eds.), *Political Attitudes and Public Opinion.* New York: David McKay.
Smith, Eliot R., and Frederick D. Miller
1978   "Limits on Perception of Cognitive Processes: A Reply to Nisbett and Wilson." *Psychology Review* 85:355–62.
Smith, Eric R. A. N.
1980   "The Levels of Conceptualization: False Measures of Ideological Sophistication." *American Political Science Review* 74:685–96.
1981   "Reply." *American Political Science Review* 75:152–55.
1982   "Attitude Consistency and the American Public." Unpublished Ph.D. dissertation. University of California, Berkeley.
Smith, M. Brewster, Jerome S. Bruner, and Robert W. White
1956   *Opinions and Personality.* New York: Wiley.
Sniderman, Paul
1975   *Personality and Democratic Politics.* Berkeley and Los Angeles: University of California Press.
Squire, Peverill, David P. Glass, and Raymond E. Wolfinger
1987   "Residential Mobility and Voter Turnout." *American Political Science Review* 81:45–65.
Star, Shirley, and Helen Hughes
1950   "Report on an Educational Campaign: The Cincinnati Plan for the United Nations." *American Journal of Sociology* 55:389–400.

Steiner, Gary A.
1963   *The People Look at Television*. New York: Knopf.
Stokes, Donald E.
1966   "Some Dynamic Elements of Contests for the Presidency."
        American Political Science Review 60:19–28.
Stokes, Donald E., Angus Campbell, and Warren E. Miller
1958   "Components of Electoral Decision." *American Political
        Science Review* 52:367–87.
Stokes, Donald E., and Warren E. Miller
1962   "Party Government and the Saliency of Congress." *Public
        Opinion Quarterly* 26:531–46.
Stouffer, Samuel A.
1955   *Communism, Conformity and Civil Liberties*. New York:
        Wiley.
Sudman, Seymour, and Norman M. Bradburn
1974   *Response Effects in Surveys: A Review and Synthesis*. Chi-
        cago: Aldine.
1982   *Asking Questions*. San Francisco: Jossey-Bass.
Sullivan, John L., James E. Piereson, and George E. Marcus
1978   "Ideological Constraint in the Mass Public: A Method-
        ological Critique and Some New Findings." *American Jour-
        nal of Political Science* 22:233–49.
Sullivan, John L., James E. Piereson, George E. Marcus, and Stanley
    Feldman
1979   "The More Things Change, the More They Stay the Same:
        The Stability of Mass Belief Systems." *American Journal of
        Political Science* 23:176–86.
Sundquist, James L.
1983   *Dynamics of the Party System: Alignment and Realignment
        of Political Parties in the United States*, rev. ed. Washing-
        ton, D.C.: Brookings Institution.
Tan, A. S., and P. Vaughn
1976   "Mass Media Exposure, Public Affairs Knowledge, and
        Black Militancy." *Journalism Quarterly* 53:271–79.
Taylor, Shelley E., and Susan T. Fiske
1978   "Salience, Attention and Attribution: Top of the Head Phe-
        nomena." *Advances in Experimental Social Psychology*,
        vol. 11. New York: Academic Press.
Turner, Charles E., and Elizabeth Martin (eds.)
1984   *Surveying Subjective Phenomena*, vol. 1. New York: Rus-
        sell Sage Foundation.

258   *References*

Valins, Stuart
  1966   "Cognitive Effects of False Heart-Rate Feedback." *Journal of Personality and Social Psychology* 4:400–408.
  1967   "Emotionality and Information Concerning Internal Reactions." *Journal of Personality and Social Psychology* 6: 458–63.
  1970   "The Perception and Labeling of Bodily Changes as Determinants of Emotional Behavior." In P. Black (ed.), *Physiological Correlates of Emotion*. New York: Academic Press.
  1974   "Persistent Effects of Information About Internal Reactions: Ineffectiveness of Debriefing." In H. London and Robert E. Nisbett (eds.), *Thought and Feeling: Cognitive Modification of Feeling States*. Chicago: Aldine.
Verba, Sidney, and Norman H. Nie
  1972   *Participation in America: Political Democracy and Social Equality*. New York: Harper and Row.
Wade, Serena, and Wilbur Schramm
  1969   "The Mass Media as Sources of Public Affairs, Science and Health Knowledge." *Public Opinion Quarterly* 33:197–209.
Wamsley, Gary L., and Richard A. Pride
  1974   "Television Network News: Rethinking the Iceberg Problem." *Western Political Quarterly* 25:343–50.
Wassenberg, Pinky S., Kay G. Wolsborn, Paul R. Hagner, and John C. Pierce
  1983   "Gender Differences in Political Conceptualization: 1956–1980." *American Politics Quarterly* 11:181–204.
Wattenberg, Martin P.
  1984   *The Decline of American Political Parties, 1952–1980*. Cambridge, Mass.: Harvard University Press.
Weisberg, Herbert
  1974   "Models of Statistical Relationships." *American Political Science Review* 68:1638–55.
Weissberg, Robert
  1976   "Consensual Attitudes and Attitude Structure." *Public Opinion Quarterly* 40:349–59.
Wheaton, Blair, Bengt Muthen, Duane F. Alwin, and Gene F. Summers
  1977   "Assessing Reliability and Stability in Panel Models." In David Heise (ed.), *Sociological Methodology 1977*. San Francisco: Jossey-Bass.

White, P.
    1980   "Limitations of Verbal Reports on Internal Events: A Refu-
                tation of Nisbett and Wilson and of Bem." *Psychological
                Review* 87:105–12.
Wiley, David A., and James A. Wiley
    1970   "The Estimation of Measurement Error in Panel Data."
                American Sociological Review 35:112–17.
Withey, Stephen B.
    1962   *The U.S. and the U.S.S.R.* Ann Arbor: Survey Research
                Center, University of Michigan.
Wolfinger, Raymond E., and Steven J. Rosenstone
    1980   *Who Votes?* New Haven, Conn.: Yale University Press.
Wolfinger, Raymond E., Steven J. Rosenstone, and Richard A. McIntosh
    1981   "Presidential and Congressional Voters Compared." *Ameri-
                can Politics Quarterly* 9:245–56.
Wray, J. Harry
    1979   "Comment on Interpretations of Early Research into Mass
                Belief Systems." *Journal of Politics* 41:1173–81.
Zajonc, Robert B.
    1960   "The Concepts of Balance, Congruity, and Dissonance."
                Public Opinion Quarterly 24:280–96.
    1980   "Feeling and Thinking: Preferences Need No Inferences."
                American Psychologist 35:151–75.
Zaller, John
    1984   "Toward a Theory of the Survey Response." Paper deliv-
                ered at the 1984 annual meeting of the American Political
                Science Association, Washington, D.C.
    1986   "Pre-Testing Information Items on the 1986 NES Pilot Sur-
                vey." Unpublished paper.

Author Index

Abelson, Robert, 149
Aberbach, Joel, 110
Abramson, Paul, 3n, 187n, 209
Achen, Christopher, 17, 108n
Adorno, T. W., 108n
Andersen, Kristi, 2, 9, 110–11, 113–16, 131–32, 157–58
Anderson, J. R., 226
Anderson, Ronald, 2, 9, 14, 20–22, 29, 31–32, 35, 58
Arseneau, Robert, 166–67
Axelrod, Robert, 82, 110

Balch, George, 187
Bartels, Larry, 210n
Bartlett, F. C., 81
Barton, Allen, 50, 224
Bass, B. M., 119
Beck, Paul Allen, 187
Becker, L. B., 186
Behr, Roy, 90
Bejar, Issac, 162n
Bem, David, 93–95
Bennett, Stephen, 2, 111–14, 116, 157
Benson, Edward, 171
Berelson, Bernard, 1
Berlyne, D., 97n
Bishop, George, 118, 125, 127, 129, 132, 134, 138–39, 145–46, 157n
Blalock, Hubert, 132, 134
Bobrow, D., 81
Bogart, Leo, 184
Bohrnstedt, George, 34
Booth, Alan, 186
Borgatta, Edgar, 34
Bower, Gordan, 226
Bower, Robert, 183, 210n

Bowers, K., 95
Bradburn, Norman, 125
Brown, Roger, 147
Brown, Stephen, 108n, 110
Bruner, J., 82
Brunk, Gregory, 118, 135–37, 142
Burnham, Walter Dean, 3n, 164
Busch, Lawrence, 210n

Campbell, Angus, 1–3, 9–13, 19–22, 35–36, 42, 44–46, 50, 79–84, 96, 108n, 112n, 177–78, 180n, 186, 209, 226
Campbell, Donald, 48
Cantril, Hadley, 124
Carey, J., 186
Carmines, Edward, 16, 45n, 46
Cassel, Carol, 80
Chong, Dennis, 91
Clarke, P., 186
Conover, Pamela, 82, 151n
Converse, Jean, 210n
Converse, Philip, 1–4, 10, 12, 17, 22, 24, 29, 31–33, 50, 53, 56, 81, 96, 105–13, 117, 147, 149–53, 157–58, 160, 171, 177, 180, 186, 191, 209, 216, 224
Coombs, Steven, 90
Costner, Herbert, 36n
Couch, Arthur, 119
Cover, Albert, 165
Craig, Stephen, 187
Cronbach, Leo, 119
Crotty, William, 3n, 165n
Crowder, R., 226
Cummings, Milton, 1

261

Subject Index

Compositor: G&S Typesetters, Inc.
Text: 10/13 Sabon
Display: Sabon